CRAFTING THE MOVEMENT

CRAFTING THE MOVEMENT

Identity Entrepreneurs in the Swedish
Trade Union Movement, 1920–1940

Jenny Jansson

ILR PRESS

AN IMPRINT OF CORNELL UNIVERSITY PRESS   ITHACA AND LONDON

First published 2020 by Cornell University Press

Library of Congress Cataloging-in-Publication Data

Names: Jansson, Jenny, author.
Title: Crafting the movement : identity entrepreneurs in the Swedish trade union movement, 1920–1940 / Jenny Jansson.
Description: Ithaca : Cornell University Press, 2020. | Includes bibliographical references and index.
Identifiers: LCCN 2019046279 (print) | LCCN 2019046280 (ebook) | ISBN 9781501750014 (paperback) | ISBN 9781501750021 (epub) | ISBN 9781501750038 (pdf)
Subjects: LCSH: Landsorganisationen i Sverige—History—20th century. | Labor movement—Sweden—History—20th century. | Working class—Sweden—History—20th century.
Classification: LCC HD8576 .J36 2020 (print) | LCC HD8576 (ebook) | DDC 331.8809485/09042—dc23
LC record available at https://lccn.loc.gov/2019046279
LC ebook record available at https://lccn.loc.gov/2019046280

To Anneli and Mats

Contents

Acknowledgments

I have received many helpful comments from colleagues on early versions of this book. In particular, I thank Jörgen Hermansson, Markus Holdo, Silke Neunsinger, Hilary Orange, Bo Rothstein, Jonas Söderqvist, Johanna Söderström, Katrin Uba, PerOla Öberg, and the two anonymous reviewers for their comments, advice, and support.

I also thank my wonderful colleagues at the Institute for Social Movements at Ruhr-Universität Bochum for offering me a great environment in which to finish the book and Stefan Berger for facilitating my stay in Bochum. A special thanks to the Library of the Ruhr and its helpful staff.

Without the Swedish Labour Movement's Archive and Library in Stockholm and its enthusiastic and knowledgeable staff it would have been difficult to write this book—thank you all.

I am also very grateful for the funding from the Swedish Research Council and the Swedish Foundation for Humanities and Social Sciences that supported the writing of this book.

Finally, to my parents, Anneli and Mats—thank you for your never-ending encouragement.

Abbreviations

ABF	Arbetarnas bildningsförbund (Workers' Educational Association)
FPF	Fackliga propagandaförbundet (Trade Union Propaganda League)
IOGT	International Organization of Good Templars
KF	Kooperativa förbundet (Cooperative Union)
KUF	Kommunistiska Ungdomsförbundet (Communist Youth League)
LO	Landsorganisationen (Trade Union Confederation)
NOV	Nykterhetsorganisationen Verdandi (Temperance Organization Verdandi)
SAC	Sveriges arbetares centralorganisation (Central Organization of the Workers of Sweden)
SAF	Svenska arbetsgivareföreningen (Swedish Employers' Association)
SAP	Socialdemokratiska arbetarpartiet (Social Democratic Party)
SDU	Socialdemokratiska ungdomsförbundet (Social Democratic Youth Organization, 1903–17)
SDUK	Socialdemokratiska ungdomsklubben (Social Democratic Youth Club) This was the most common name of the local associations of SDU. After the party split in 1917, some of the local youth associations kept their original name even though the correct name after 1917 is SSU.
SKP	Sveriges kommunistiska parti (Communist Party of Sweden, 1921–1967)
SSU	Sveriges socialdemokratiska ungdomsförbund (Swedish Social Democratic Youth League, 1917–)
SSV	Socialdemokratiska vänsterpartiet (Social Democratic Left Party, 1917–1921, referred to as the Left Party)
SUF	Socialistiska ungdomsförbundet (Socialist Youth League, also known as the Young Socialists)
SUP	Sveriges ungsocialistiska parti (Swedish Young Socialist Party)

CRAFTING THE MOVEMENT

THE REFORMIST CHOICE

The Swedish reformist labor movement of the twentieth century constitutes a success story. A strong Social Democratic Party—Socialdemokratiska arbetarpartiet (SAP)—and high union density paved the way for an extensive and comprehensive welfare state and diminishing wage inequality. One key component of the dominance of Swedish social democracy was the labor movement's extraordinary ability to mobilize the majority of the working class early on in its mission. In what may have been the most challenging period for social democracy—the interwar period—reformist labor organizations managed to establish reformism and a unique spirit of negotiation on a broad basis, thereby creating a cohesive movement. Why did the reformist branch receive such widespread support when other European labor movements were riven by internal disputes? It is inarguable that in the aftermath of the First World War, Europe was swept by a wave of labor movement radicalization. The war, which itself had mobilized mass protests, particularly by left-wing groups, challenged social democracy, as social democratic parties had accepted democracy and therefore often cooperated with bourgeois governments during the war. Internal disputes arose from ideological splits in the labor movement. The orthodox Marxism advocated by Karl Kautsky and the German Social Democrats (Sozialdemokratische Partei Deutschlands; SPD) was criticized for its passivity, with criticism coming from the revisionists, of whom Eduard Bernstein was the main proponent, and the revolutionary branch, headed by Vladimir I. Lenin. Both argued that Marx and Engels's predictions of the capitalist system's imminent breakdown and the predetermined takeover by the masses were not going to come true. There were no signs of a breakdown of the capitalist system. In that case, they queried, should workers simply wait for history to take its course, or should positive action be taken?

The recession that followed the war and resulted in high unemployment hit most European countries hard and fostered radical proposals for how to bring about socialism. New left-wing factions arose and challenged social democracy, questioning its ability to realize socialism. Other less prudent and more rapid approaches suddenly appealed to the workers. It became harder for the more moderate reformist labor movement to attract the masses because revolution appeared to be a quick fix for achieving socialism.

Amid this situation, in 1917, the radical left wing of the Russian labor movement under the leadership of Lenin transformed revolutionary slogans into reality. The Russian Revolution, which embodied a radical revision of Marxism, changed the labor movement on a global scale and sparked radicalization. This long-awaited revolution acted as a rallying point for radical groups. Shortly afterward, inspired by the events in Russia, Rosa Luxemburg and Karl Liebknecht, following Lenin's lead, attempted to start a revolution in war-torn Germany in 1919. The Spartakusbund was brutally crushed by the army, as sanctioned by the SPD, creating an unbridgeable cleavage between the social democrats and left-wing Germans. The failure of Luxemburg's revolutionary efforts was only one of many such failures to come.

The revolutionary ideas emanating from the Russian Revolution provoked counteractions from right-wing parties and conservatives. In Italy, the labor movement's radicalization after the war resulted in numerous strikes and eventually paved the way for the Fascists and Mussolini to seize power (Bell 1984; Berman 2006, 126–30). In Austria, the radicalization of the labor movement, which had been strong and stable, resulted in a dictatorship when Engelbert Dollfuss took charge in 1933 (Cronin 1980; Wasserman 2014). In Spain, several socialist parties struggled for power. When the socialist coalition Frente Popular came into power in 1936, it pursued a range of reforms, provoking a counter-revolution that brought General Franco to power (Lapuente and Rothstein 2014). Many other examples follow the same pattern. After 1917, the labor movement split between communists, social democrats, and syndicalists. In the worst instances, backlash to radicalization resulted in dictatorships or authoritarian governments, whereas in cases such as France (Bartolini 2000, 107–8) it weakened the labor movement considerably. Instead of fighting together against the Right and the capitalist class, the communists, social democrats, and syndicalists fought with each other, wasting resources and energy, making it difficult to influence politics and in the long run to effectively mobilize the working class.

Like the other European labor movements, the labor movement in Sweden radicalized. The trade union movement in Sweden split in 1910 when a radical faction broke loose and formed a syndicalist organization, the Sveriges Arbetares Centralorganisation (SAC). Support for the syndicalist movement spread in the reformist organizations, and the radical measures advocated by the SAC in labor market conflicts resulted in turbulent industrial relations. In 1903–29, Sweden had the highest rate of strikes among thirteen Western industrial countries (Shorter and Tilly 1974, 333).[1] In 1917, the next setback for the reformist labor movement arrived. The SAP, in which different factions had coexisted, split into two parties when the youth organization decided to go its own way and founded what a few years later would become the Communist Party. These events all pointed in the same direction: Sweden was heading down the same road as the rest of Europe, toward a divided labor movement in which factions would fight each other rather than join forces against employers and right-wing political parties.

History then took another turn. The labor movement in Sweden became strong—in fact, one of the strongest in the world—and cohesive. The left-wing factions fought the reformists for twenty years but were finally defeated and marginalized. The Swedish Trade Union Confederation (Landsorganisationen, LO) concluded a landmark labor market peace agreement, the Saltsjöbaden Agreement (Saltsjöbadsavtalet, also called the Basic Agreement), with the Swedish Employers' Association (Svenska arbetsgivareföreningen, SAF) in Saltsjöbaden in 1938, effectively ending industrial relations conflicts. The primary principle of the parties involved became negotiation, and Swedish labor market practices came to symbolize the ultimate in cross-class cooperation. The outcome of Sweden's strong, cohesive labor movement was the dominance of the Social Democratic Party, which remained in power for forty-four consecutive years, and a trade union movement with the power needed to improve working conditions, reduce the wage gap, and promote the construction of a comprehensive Swedish welfare state. This Swedish developmental path exemplifies a different outcome than that where there was a weak, split labor movement, as in France, or where there was counteraction by right-wing and fascist parties, as in Italy and Spain. The Swedish perspective therefore presents an interesting case for international comparison, not simply because the labor movement chose reformism. All European countries had social democratic organizations and reformist trade unions, so Sweden is not unique in this regard. What made the Swedish reformist labor movement extraordinary was its ability to engage a majority of the workers in its mission. The movement managed to establish reformism and a unique spirit of consensus on a broad basis. Why did the

Swedish reformist branch receive such widespread support when other European labor movements were riven by internal conflict?

Constructing a Reformist Working Class

The radicalization of the European labor movement created unbridgeable gaps in the working class. This was the case in Sweden, where the 1938 labor market peace agreement that was reached in Saltsjöbaden is still referred to as a "class betrayal" by some groups. The fragmentation was particularly acute, in the trade union movement because the unions were open to anyone, regardless of party membership. Workers who supported the Social Democratic Left Party, and later the Communist Party, were welcome as members of the LO. Moreover, the SAC had steadily grown in strength during the 1910s and was becoming a realistic alternative to the reformist unions. The SAC advocated radical measures to fight capitalism, which led to an extraordinary number of industrial conflicts. Many of the conflicts that the SAC started were supported by LO members through sympathy strikes. By the end of the 1930s, LO members were largely devoted to the aims of the reformist labor movement, paving the way for class compromise and the welfare state. In the late 1910s, however, it was certainly not a foregone conclusion which path the Swedish labor movement would take, and a split and consequently weakened labor movement was a very distinct possibility. Ninety years later it is now clear that the reformist branch decisively won the day, but it is far too simplistic to dismiss the influence of the left-wing organizations over the Swedish labor movement. This post hoc perspective causes many to overlook the struggle that took place in the labor movement, particularly the struggle to unite the working class under the reformist ideology in the union movement. The series of events that led to the Swedish working class uniting under this banner should not be overlooked.

This book presents the idea that the missing link in understanding the cohesive and reformist union movement in Sweden is the movement's formation of a coherent self-image. This process was initiated by means of a conscious strategy on the part of the LO leaders. Fighting the left wing and establishing cohesiveness in the movement were done by explaining to the members in particular, and to the working class in general, what kind of organization the LO was. LO leaders constructed a collective identity based on the reformist ideology, and this self-image was disseminated among its members through an educational program arranged by the labor movement—so-called popular education.[2] Identity in class organizations, or in any organization, is not brought about by structures but is constructed by actors. Moreover, the content of self-image in a class organization is not predetermined, and the kind of self-image a labor movement possesses affects its scope of action. Identity is thus the missing link in efforts to fully understand the strength of the Swedish union movement and, in particular, the trait for which the Swedish labor movement is widely renowned: the spirit of consensus. The construction of a cohesive labor organization was a reformation of working-class consciousness. An organizational identity that downplayed class struggle and embraced negotiation was constructed by the LO leaders, and the image of the LO, as defined by that leadership, was impressed on the members through the LO's popular education programs. The importance of identity politics in the Swedish labor movement during the interwar decades is closely examined here through a series of linked arguments; four claims are accordingly developed and investigated in this book.

The first claim is that the LO leadership recognized the problems arising from conflict among left-wing organizations as identity problems. Of course, the emergence of left-wing organizations constituted a threat to the notion of "worker." Suddenly, there were not only workers but *different kinds of workers*, who were promoting communism and syndicalism as well as reformism. The link between class structure and the sense of "we" became blurred. Not only did it become more complicated to distinguish who belonged to the "we" and who were "the others," there were also implications for the enforcement of socialist ideology. From the perspective of social identity theory, a challenge such as the emergence of left-wing organizations constituted a delicate dilemma for the reformist labor movement. The mobilization of workers in unions had been accomplished through struggle against employers, but the struggle was suddenly no longer a joint effort involving all workers. Instead, there were different kinds of workers fighting different battles. The central idea of solidarity became harder to grasp for the working class: With whom did one's loyalties lie? Who are "we," and who are "the others"? The emergence of left-wing organizations and the implications of these organizations (e.g., labor market conflicts) sparked an identity crisis among the reformist organizations. The first claim made in this work is that the LO leadership perceived the left-wing organizations as a threat to the identity of their organization.

The second claim concerns the construction of a cohesive collective identity as the result of strategic action. Identity does not simply come into being, precipitated by social structures; it needs to be produced by actors. In response to the recognized problems associated with the left-wing factions, the LO leadership decided to construct an *organizational* identity using popular education. Through this reformation of its identity, the LO distinguished itself from the left-wing organizations. The second claim accordingly examines whether or not the LO leadership had a plan for how to deal with the disjointed organization, including the use of popular education.

This leads to the third claim: that a particular type of organizational self-image was constructed by LO leaders and presented in the materials used in the popular education programs. This image embodied a reformist ideology in which negotiations as a means of conflict resolution were crucial. Indeed, the phenomenon referred to as the "spirit of consensus" was the LO's way of transforming the theoretical ideas of reformism into actual viable union work. This spirit of consensus was in fact present in the educational material of LO long before the 1938 Basic Agreement was concluded.

The final claim made in this book is that the educational material used by the LO became diffused throughout the labor movement because the approach that the LO leaders chose—popular education—reached the mass

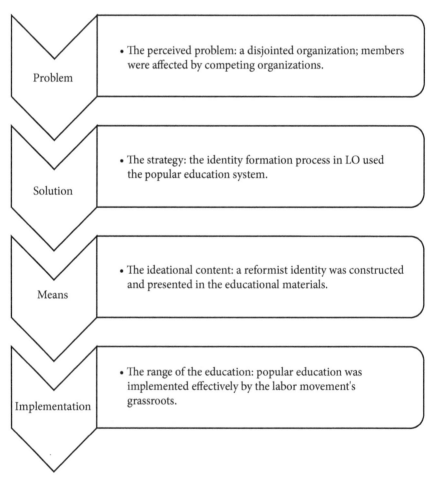

FIGURE 1.1   Sequence of the four claims

of the workers. Education was central to all socialist theorists. Marx, Lenin, and, above all, Gramsci proclaimed the importance of workers controlling their own education: as long as education is controlled and conducted by bourgeois institutions, bourgeois values will be reproduced. The idea of offering education was not new, although the union movement had not hitherto made much use of it. It is in this context that the implementation of popular education in the labor movement is further examined. The available empirical evidence regarding the scope and depth of the LO's popular education provides a substantive indication of its impact. The remainder of this chapter is devoted to clarifying the theoretical point of departure of the proposed thesis and of its four claims (figure 1.1).

Leaders and Identity, and Class Formation

Together the four claims made above underpin this book's argument about identity politics in the Swedish labor movement in the 1920s and 1930s. Examining these claims not only allows a broader understanding of the Swedish case but also has much wider implications. This focus on identity offers a new perspective and merits consideration in two respects.

First, identity is often assumed to exist in class organizations as a matter of course. This is characteristic of the class formation literature, which has been very influenced by Marxism and its determinism. The actor tends to be either ignored or represented as powerless. One possible reason for this is the unclear description of how class consciousness comes into being. According to Marx, class consciousness implies, first, that the workers realize they have common interests and, second, that they identify themselves as members of the working class (Marx 1981, 186). Class formation as the process by which a class *in itself* becomes a class *for itself* puts struggle at the center of the analysis, as struggle triggers class formation. The struggle appears to be an effect of the exploitation of the wage-earning class by the capitalist class. Exploitation is, in turn, an effect of the capitalist system. Marx never elaborated more detailed descriptions of the causes of class consciousness. There is a substantial literature on understanding the formation of class consciousness, but very few studies concentrate on the role of labor leaders in this process. The "structuralist school" treated the class formation process as deterministic, considering that the making of a class in itself inevitably leads to the spontaneous appearance of a class for itself (Balibar 1979, 267; Kuczynski, Österling, and Österling 1967, 52–53, 90–94) or that the consciousness of belonging to a class will automatically appear. The driving force of class formation, however, came from production. Such structural explanations often focus on technical developments and on the process of production (see, for instance, Burawoy 1982) as the independent variable—to put it in methodological terms. The British historian E. P. Thompson launched an important criticism of the Marxist structuralist view, claiming that lived experience was the most crucial variable in the class formation process (Thompson 1979, 9–10, 212–16). Thompson explained class formation by paying attention to the life situation of the working class. The shared life situation of the working class was due to the economic structures in class society; however, political and cultural elements were necessary for the class to be "made." Thompson's explanation did not present an independent variable for understanding class formation that differed from that presented by the structuralists; rather, it presented a mechanism for understanding why the emergence of the working class could lead to collective action (Somers 1992). Further developments along the same lines have been made by Katznelson. Neither Katznelson (Katznelson 1986) nor Somers (Somers 1992) theorizes about or analyzes the role of labor leaders, however.

The so-called linguistic turn criticized structural theorists for endorsing Marxist determinism. Whereas Thompson assumed that structural class came first and was consequently the driving force of class development, scholars of the linguistic turn claimed that language must come before class, experience, or culture, as these phenomena could not possibly exist without a language to express them. According to this school of thought, class was a discursive phenomenon (August 2011, 5; Jones 1984, 7–8; Steinberg 1999, 14–21). Researchers considering language, on the other hand, advocated another kind of structure by empowering language. Discourses empower or constrain actions, so language became the decisive factor determining the actions of workers; however, the actors were given little power over the formulation and articulation of their discourses. In contrast, this study highlights labor leaders' role in constructing identities through building on social identity and organizational theory, thereby bringing a new perspective to the field of class formation.

The second major contribution of this study relates to its focus on organizational identity. Self-perception and self-definitions are constructed by what researchers call social identities. In simple terms, people classify themselves and others in their environment in terms of various categories (Tajfel 1981, 31, 45–49). Social identities are a person's perceived group affiliations—that is, "the perception of oneness with or belongingness to some human aggregate" (Ashforth and Mael 1989, 21). Individuals always have a range of group affiliations, such as gender, being a father, being a member of an association, or simply listening to a certain type of music or wearing a certain style of jeans. "The basic idea is that a social category (for example, nationality, political affiliation or sports team) into which one falls, and to which one feels one belongs, provides a definition of who one is in terms of the defining characteristics of the category—a self-definition that is part of the self-concept" (Hogg, Terry, and White 1995, 259).

Categorization serves two purposes. It creates order for the individual in the social environment by giving him or her tools for systematically defining others, and it allows the individual to locate himself or herself in the social environment. In other words, the self is defined by defining others. Since the processes of defining others also helps to define the self, social identities are relational. The definition of the self depends on the definition of others (those whom one is not), and vice versa (Ashforth and Mael 1989, 21). Tajfel demonstrated the importance of group identities in a series of experiments, in which the participants defined themselves as members of a group that had no significance whatsoever other than its *not* being a certain *other* group (Tajfel 1981). Social identities are therefore crucial to individuals, which is why there is power in identity.

Members who identify strongly with an organization are a force the organization can count on and use, making identity crucial for organizations as well. Organizations easily become the reference point for social identities because they have clear boundaries, making it easy to categorize the self and others (i.e., as members versus nonmembers). If members identify with an organization, they are more likely to work and make sacrifices for it; identity thus constitutes the glue that keeps the organization together (Pichardo 1997; Ravasi and Schultz 2006; Stryker 2000; Tyler and Blader 2001). This is particularly important in social movement organizations since membership is voluntary and seldom confers material benefits. Members are also less likely to stay within a social movement organization when the identification is weak. Identity should therefore be considered a power resource because social identities constitute prerequisites for collective action (Haslam, Reicher, and Platow 2010, chapters 3 and 6). This is also true for class organizations, even though class research has paid little attention to identity as a power resource.

More importantly, the nature of an organization's identity affects how its members and leaders act. Indeed, the content of the identity limits the actions that members and leaders may take. For example, as long as workers' self-perception included being part of a radical class struggle in which employers were viewed as enemies and workers were contentious and unwilling to back down in conflicts with their employers, cooperation with employers was very difficult. The content of an organization's identity—comprising the characteristic features of an organization—is decisive for the scope of actions that can be undertaken, because identity creates a *logic of appropriateness* (March and Olsen 2004), setting limits on what are considered acceptable and unacceptable actions for the organization and its members. Identity can therefore be a means of creating and maintaining discipline in an organization. Class identity has often been assumed to be the given identification of union members, though there are reasons to question this claim. Treating identity as something that "just exists" or "just appears," and that is defined by social structures, tends to assume that there is only one kind of working-class identity. However, each and every class organization has specific traits, and these traits affect the organization's scope of action, its options, and, more importantly, its ability to mobilize the working class. The argument outlined in this book is that class identity may cause trouble for class organizations when *different kinds of class organizations* appear. In such situations, it may be necessary to change the content and to stress traits other than merely structural ones in order to mobilize workers in a particular union; in other words, it may be necessary to construct an *organizational* identity. This is why leaders have an important task in the class formation process. In such processes, when the leaders discern a need to change—to *re-form*—the identity of an organization, they will formulate strategies on how that can be done and will act as *identity entrepreneurs*.

Labor Leaders as Identity Entrepreneurs

It has been claimed that labor leaders play a crucial role in the process of mobilizing workers because they can affect the framing of political issues, articulate grievances, and promote group cohesion (Kelly 1998, 34–38). In his famous book *The New Men of Power*, C. Wright Mills stated that labor leaders need to be "managers of discontent": they need not only be rebels against employers but also to manage rebellions within the labor movement (Mills 1948). In other words, the leaders have the task of creating cohesiveness within their movement. How does this work? Wholly understanding how leaders can be identity entrepreneurs or managers of discontent requires a detailed examination of leaders' role in organizations. What role does the leadership play in organizations? What functions do leaders have? What tasks are they assigned?

In general, the leadership in political organizations is crucial for several reasons. Leaders have executive power in the organization, for one, and they have an important role in solving collective action problems, mobilizing resources, and developing strategies (Morris and Staggenborg 2004; Nepstad and Bob 2006; Rothstein 1998). Because the leadership is assigned to manage the organization and make everyday decisions, it has the power to determine the development of the organization. The organization's executive body also possesses the tools to communicate with the members. It enjoys authority—or at least it should—and therefore has the prerogative to define the organization. Moreover, the leaders' version of the organization's identity is an image that is transmitted to both members and nonmembers. The leaders thus represent the organization both internally and externally, in a sense symbolizing the organization. Because leadership actions are monitored by members and stakeholders, the leaders' image of the organization can be manifested in a range of ways: how they talk about the organization, what logo they choose, how they act, who they choose to cooperate with, and so on. This study claims that leaders are identity entrepreneurs *because their position in the organization gives them the tools needed to define and activate identity*. Leaders seek to construct and promote a particular version of organizational identity that suits their aims, and they do so by using their position in the organization to define who belongs to the in-group, who are the nonmembers, what problems and opportunities the organization is facing, and what characteristic traits are ascribed to the organization—that is, the content of the identity (Haslam, Reicher, and Platow 2010, chapter 6).

Social identity theory emphasizes the importance of the social context for social identities (Tajfel and Turner 2004). Identity is not static; rather, various contextual factors can affect whether or not a certain social identity is perceived as important for a group of individuals. Research has recognized that certain social identities are stronger than others, but there are no definite answers as to why that is so. For example, it has been pointed out that some ethnic groups do not develop a strong ethnic identity even though the structural prerequisites for doing so exist (Huddy 2001, 130–31). This may be because different settings activate different identities, so self-categorization changes between situations (Huddy 2001, 134). If individuals have several group identities, with one being superordinate to the others (e.g., workers in Sweden were not only workers but also artisans, parents, members of the temperance movement, church members, etc.), this implies that the primary one has somehow been activated. Marxist structural theories suggest that class structure activates the social identity of the "worker" (making class structure the most fundamental social structure).

In contrast, this study proposes that organizations can play a crucial role in activating a particular social identity. By their mere existence, organizations create an "us" and a "them" through their membership; if organization leaders are perceived as prototypical of the specific social identity that they share with their followers (the members), and if the leaders manage to put that identity into a context that is understandable to the members, then the leaders can indeed be active identity entrepreneurs (Haslam and Reicher 2007, 126). From this perspective, contextual factors not only include institutions, such as the industrial production process or the language used to express class, but also relationships with other humans. In this way, leaders of organizations can play a crucial role in identity formation processes. Labor leaders are in an advantageous position that empowers them to activate and articulate identity in the organization; they also have a position that allows them to construct *the content of the identity*.

According to this argument, the leaders' way of talking about the organization, and how they carry themselves as leaders, will make an impression on the members. If the leaders realize this, they can then use their position as identity entrepreneurs to promote a certain image of the organization.

The actor's role in identity formation is ultimately a matter of how identities are produced. This inevitably raises a number of important questions. Does this mean that the leadership stands "outside" the organization? Does the leadership possess the ability to look at the organization in a way that is completely detached from the prevailing organizational culture and identity? The answer to these questions is no. The leaders are not unaffected by culture and identity, and they have cultural awareness that constrains what they do, both consciously and unconsciously (i.e., they will sometimes be aware that they are acting in accordance with certain social norms and cultures existing in the organization, and sometimes will be unaware of doing so). Once a "we" has been established, future changes must take that as the point of departure; in other words, leaders are at least partly bound by the sense of "we" already existing in an organization. If the leaders attempt to launch a new image of the organization that differs too much from the old one, members can become alienated. Leaders' maneuvering room is therefore restricted. However, in some situations, they will be able to manage identity strategically. In the case presented in this book, the values and attitudes of the labor movement leadership were reformist (i.e., the Swedish labor movement was reformist), whereas the members had shifted toward radicalized values. The construction of a reformist identity did not lie outside the cultural institutions in which the leadership was located; rather, it was a defense of the movement's identity as the leaders defined it.

The advantageous position of leaders in an organization facilitates their management of identity formation by establishing a certain image. Labor leaders have incentives to re-form the identity of their movement strategically. Once labor organizations are formed, *a logic of organization* guides their actions. A labor organization acts not only based on the logic of the social situation that mobilized the working class but also in accordance with the interests of the organization as such. The overriding interest is assumed to be survival (for similar argument, see Rothstein 1987). The interests of any labor organization will primarily be advocated by its leaders, because they have a different organizational position from that of the members—namely, one with executive powers. The leaders may also have other visions and goals than do the members because of their position. They will doubtless possess more information about the various parts of the organization and about the strategies of other organizations. Last, trade union leaders can be expected to have more frequent contact with employers than does the average trade union member, which probably affects the leaders' perception of the employers. For these reasons, it is reasonable to assume that the labor leadership will often uphold ideas less radical than those of the members. It is not that the leadership elite stands to gain materially from taking a reformist line; rather, an inherited logic of formal organizational development tends to create an elite that acts in accordance with the primary interest of the organization—namely, its survival. Therefore, organizational logic can lead to discrepancies between the radical, ideologically driven members and the leaders. In fact, organizational logic entails a dilemma for labor leaders. As Mills put it, leaders are not only agitators who mobilize resistance; they also need to manage rebellions *within* the movement (Mills 1948, 8–9, my italics) and oversee the survival of the organization. How labor leaders handle such situations is of the utmost importance for the organization's development and is the focus of this book.

Internal Education: Means of Managing Identification

What means of identity formation are available to labor leadership? Identity as a means of organizational control has so far received relatively little attention in contemporary research, and even less research has explored how identity formation processes can be strategically managed (Alvesson and Willmott 2002). However, most research into self-perception and identity formation emphasizes the role of discourse. Discourse plays a crucial role in the formation, maintenance, and transformation of the characteristic traits ascribed to the organization that constitute the core of its identity. Therefore, managing identity should supposedly be done by establishing or changing the discourse. Most of the time, the leadership of an organization "manages continuity," upholding and maintaining the organization's dominant self-perception. Nevertheless, the leadership sometimes alters an organization's identity. Identity management can be done in a number of ways: by defining members in terms of their names and the attributes of their positions in the organization, by defining others, by defining the context in which the organization works, or by establishing a specific framework for interpreting the work of the organization and, through that lens, making sense of the organization's actions. Other ways of managing identity include explicating morals and values, and establishing a distinct set of rules through which "norms about the 'natural' way of doing things" are established (Alvesson and Willmott 2002, 14). In institutional terms, this last way of controlling members through identity management is what March and Olsen (2004) called the "logic of appropriateness." In other words, identification with an organization implies that some actions are sanctioned and compatible with the role of the member, whereas other actions are unsuitable: "Actors seek to fulfill the obligations encapsulated in a role, an identity, a membership in a political community or group, and the ethos, practices and expectations of its institutions" (March and Olsen 2004, 3). Members can therefore be controlled by establishing a web of norms serving as guidance for decision-making. According to the thesis presented in this book, such a web of norms is what the LO leaders wanted to create.

What are the best ways of managing identity formation in an organization? In what institutional settings is top-down identity construction most likely to work? This study suggests that internal educational programs constitute a forum in which identity formation takes place. There are several reasons to believe that education programs had an impact on workers in Sweden. First, trade union education offered a perfect opportunity for the leaders of the labor movement organization to communicate their definitions and views of social problems, class struggle, and the aims of the labor movement to members. In other words, internal education constituted a suitable setting for managing the organizational self-image. This was not only true for the labor leaders in the 1920s but is also true for organizational leaders in general. By privileging some themes over others in workers' education, leaders could influence what was taught, thereby producing and reproducing certain ideological ideas. The popular education system, moreover, constituted an excellent means of disseminating ideas to the rank and file. Study activities intended to educate and enlighten the rank and file provided a forum where labor leaders, because they could control and design the study activities, could reach a wide range of the membership. The means of communicating with members were fewer in the 1920s than they are today, and workers' education was one of the few channels of direct communication. This approach was not unique to 1920s labor leaders in Sweden. Education as a means of inculcating specific ideologies and perceptions of society has been noted by most socialist theorists.

Whoever controlled what was taught in the education programs could influence the ideology of the movement. In particular, courses on "trade union studies" or "the history of the labor movement" constituted good opportunities to plant ideas about "who we are" among members at the grassroots level, since these courses concentrated on what trade unions are and do. A coherent image of the aim and ideology of the movement also functioned as a glue or binding agent among workers around the country. By transmitting the same image of what it meant to be a worker through education programs across the country, the Swedish working class could be encouraged to think along the same lines, which is a precondition for cohesiveness in a movement. Content could thus breed solidarity, and controlling the content of education affected the kind of working-class consciousness that developed. Moreover, since workers' education challenges members to contemplate such issues as class, the labor movement, and the position of workers in society, identity formation in these settings was clearly connected to class identity.

A second reason for the success of this popular education was the broader education system in Sweden, both formal (i.e., compulsory schooling) and popular. Although the level of education in the 1920s was rather low compared with that of today, Sweden had a longer tradition of compulsory schooling than did other countries in the 1920s. The compulsory *folkskola* was established in the mid-nineteenth century and offered a six-year education. The effect of the school reform of 1842 was a high literacy rate. The *folkskola* also cut its bond with the church, which had been the major educational institution in the past. Literacy was a prerequisite for the education programs of the labor movement, simply because the workers had to be able to read the materials produced by the LO. Parallel to the formal education system, Sweden's major social movements of the nineteenth century—the temperance movement and the Free Church movement—established a system of popular education, an approach later adopted by the labor movement. When the LO implemented its educational strategy in the 1920s, study activities were already an accepted and established element of working-class culture, and they had been so since the late nineteenth century. Moreover, libraries founded and run by the temperance movement already existed all over Sweden. Because higher formal education entailed fees, few workers could extend their education beyond the six years of free compulsory school. As a result, the popular education programs offered by the trade unions and the temperance movement were the only chances of further education for most members of the working class. It is therefore reasonable to assume that the participants took such education seriously. It was seen as an opportunity and an honor for adults to obtain further education.

Third, education programs encouraged identity formation as much by their form as by their content. The popular education system in Sweden, which was inspired by Grundtvig, featured informal learning (Eraut 2004; Eshach 2007).[3] Popular education was a process of learning and teaching (B. Andersson 1980, 19); it was "free and voluntary," and its prime teaching method was the study circle. The study circle, possibly the most important legacy of the temperance movement, constituted small reading groups. The ideal circles of temperance movement activist Oscar Olsson did not have teachers, and the chair of the meetings rotated among the participants. According to Olsson, assuming the role of the chair was a learning experience in itself, and this was supposed to maintain the nonhierarchical and democratic characteristics of the circles (Törnqvist 1996, 26–30). "Free and voluntary" meant that no one could force study circle participants to study a particular subject. Although they were encouraged to study certain subjects, participants were free to choose subjects on their own.

Study circles were also voluntary in that participation was based solely on the participant's desire to learn (Gustavsson and Wiklund 2013, 7–11). There are reasons to believe that small educational settings focusing on discussions and deliberation are more likely to promote the development of a sense of "we" than, for example, are teaching methods such as lectures or teacher-led seminars (Jansson 2016). Research into the impact of study circle activities on participants in recent times suggests that the participants perceive the circles as helping deepen their interest in the subject of study, and as building fellowship among participants, bolstering self-esteem, and improving social skills. The circles also helped to develop and embrace "citizens' values," which include forming and expressing personal opinions and arguing for them in the group, taking responsibility, and making decisions collectively (E. Andersson et al. 1996, 65–66). There are reasons to assume that these various forms of workers' education attended by workers from the local community created a sense of belonging. In such educational settings, the participants often worked together or belonged to the same union section or political organization, and the intimate study situation ought to have created group identity at a very local level of the labor movement. Moreover, the identification process that occurred during study activities should have been transferable into solidarity in other arenas. Compared with lectures, in which the participants only sat and listened, nonhierarchical and interactive study activities such as the study circle ought to have had a more profound impact on identity formation.

The thesis of the identity entrepreneur—and its theoretical underpinnings as presented here—guides this book's empirical analysis of the leadership of the Swedish trade union movement during the challenging interwar decades. The remainder of this book is an empirical analysis of the thesis and of the four claims made above, with each claim discussed in its own chapter. Chapter 2 presents the background to the development of the Swedish labor movement in the 1910s and defines the problems perceived by the LO leadership—that is, the Secretariat. The chapter demonstrates that the vigorous left-wing organizations constituted a real problem for the reformist labor movement. More importantly, these left-wing organizations were *perceived* as a problem for the leadership of the LO. Both how the executive body of LO (the Secretariat) talked about other organizations and how it acted indicate that syndicalists and communists were perceived to be a major problem or even threat. Chapter 3 examines solutions to this problem, to determine whether there is reason to believe that the LO leadership strategically attempted to construct an organizational identity, and whether popular education was used to change the self-perception of the organization among its members. Next, the organizational self-image conveyed by LO's educational materials is analyzed. The theory presented here states not only that identity in organizations can be formed from above but also that the identity constructed in this case had certain characteristics. What kind of image this was and the content of this constructed identity are therefore crucial questions for the argument presented here. Chapter 4 analyzes the identity of LO. Chapter 5 examines the fourth claim—namely, that implementation of the popular educational strategy succeeded in reaching most of the workers. Popular education at the national and local levels is analyzed, with the town of Skutskär serving as a specific case. Finally, causality is discussed by considering what conclusions can be drawn from analyzing the union activities and the education provided in Skutskär. Conclusions are then presented and discussed in chapter 6.

PROBLEMS IDENTIFIED BY THE LO LEADERSHIP

The 1910s were turbulent years for the Swedish labor movement, as for most labor movements in Europe. Established in the late nineteenth century, the labor movement in Sweden, as in most countries, consisted of a political branch—the Social Democratic Party (Socialdemokratiska arbetarpartiet, SAP)—and a trade union branch. The SAP, founded in 1889, was the first formal labor organization at the national level. Nine years later the unions (directed by the party) formed an umbrella organization, the Swedish Trade Union Confederation (Landsorganisationen, LO). The founding of the LO was an attempt to bring together the unions in one organization, creating a powerful actor that could challenge employers (Lindbom 1938, 9–13; Westerståhl 1945, 9–33). The social democratic movement had been doing reasonably well considering the slow pace of industrialization in Sweden, but with the emergence of new, more radical organizations, both the party and, perhaps even more so, the LO faced problems. This chapter is devoted to a detailed analysis of these problems.

Social Democrats, Left Socialists, and Communists

The SAP had its first real foothold in the southern region of Skåne, where August Palm, the first socialist agitator in Sweden, started his mobilization tour in the city of Malmö in the 1880s. Some of the most influential social democratic newspapers were based there; naturally, some of the most influential social democratic politicians started their careers in Skåne, including the main actors considered in this book: Per Albin Hansson and his brother Sigfrid Hansson (Gidlund 1992, 100). Soon after its founding, the SAP identified itself ideologically with the German revisionists and declared its support for Eduard Bernstein's revisionism rather than for Marxism (Hadenius 1976, 17; Lindbom 1938, 27–31). Ideology was often trumped by pragmatism, however, which often and particularly during the interwar period became a strength of the SAP (Berman 1998).

Although formally separate, the party and the unions were, as in most countries at that time, interconnected through overlapping membership as well as activists (Allern and Bale 2017). Most leaders of the SAP and the LO had a background in one of the social democratic youth organizations, which, because there were several of them (see figure 2.1), came to play a crucial role in the development of the Swedish labor movement.

In 1892 the predecessor of the first social democratic youth organization was founded in Stockholm. This group, intended to organize young adults and nicknamed Young Socialists (Fernström 1950, 11–15), took the name the Socialist Youth League (Socialistiska ungdomsförbundet, SUF) in 1897 (Lindbom 1945, 8). Among the SUF activists was Albert Jensen, who later became a founding father of the syndicalist union, the Central Organization of the Workers of Sweden (Sveriges arbetares centralorganisation, SAC), in 1910 and one of SAC's leaders in the 1920s. Not long after the SUF's founding, it became clear that it was attracting radical elements. This caused the first split of the youth organization, and in 1903 a new youth organization was founded, the Social Democratic Youth Organization (Socialdemokratiska ungdomsförbundet, SDU) (Lindbom 1945, 71–75; Peterson 1970, 11). SUF, on the other hand, became the backbone of the Young Socialists' Party (Sveriges ungsocialistiska parti, SUP), formed in 1908 (Gunnarson 1965, 182–83; Lindbom 1945, 116). Although some of these organizations, such as the SUP and the SUF, were small and initially not particularly influential, they nevertheless illustrate the early split of the labor movement and the variety of labor organizations that developed in Sweden.

It was in this environment that the brothers Hansson, Per Albin (who eventually became SAP leader and prime minister of Sweden) and Sigfrid (who came to play an important role in the LO), started their political careers in an SDU club in the southern Swedish city of Malmö. They were both part of the inner circle of the newly founded youth organization (Hansson 1927b; Lindbom 1945, 80–81). Per Albin was appointed an SDU official in 1905, and as a full-time employee of the youth organization he also became the editor of the SDU's monthly magazine *Fram* (Lindbom 1945, 72; Lindström 1960, 159). *Fram* published working-class literature as well as articles on current political issues. Many of the party activists who went on to play a crucial role in the development and split of the party wrote articles for this magazine, including Zeth Höglund and Fredrik Ström. Other central actors in the SDU from the start were Gustav Möller and Fabian Månsson (Bäckström 1963a, 41–45; Hansson 1927b; Lindbom 1945, 71, 76–80).

Rickard Sandler joined the SDU a few years later. He was the son of a people's high school teacher and had studied at Uppsala as well as Göteborg universities.[1] Sandler worked for some time as a teacher at the people's high school in Brunnsvik in the Dalarna region, which in the late 1920s became the center of the LO's educational strategy. Sandler was a prominent activist in the SDU and had a particular passion for educating the working class (Ohlsson 2010, 24–33). In a booklet published by *Fram* in 1908, he described his ideal working-class high school (Sandler 1908). Five years later, the first step toward education for the workers was taken by Sandler when he founded the Workers' Educational Association (Arbetarnas bildningsförbund, ABF) in 1912.

It did not take long for the SAP's new youth organization, the SDU, to split into new factions. Shortly after the SDU founding, a radical and a reformist faction emerged in the organization, and the 1905–1917 period was characterized by the faction's struggle to control the SDU. Disagreement existed almost from the SDU's founding, but the radical faction's influence over the youth organization became clearer after 1905 when the SDU articulated criticism of the SAP and simultaneously suggested using radical methods to improve working-class conditions. The reformist faction that was faithful to the SAP, led by Per Albin Hansson, lost most of its influence over the SDU after the 1909 congress when a majority of the youth organization's members supported Zeth Höglund's more radical approach and vision for the organization (Lindbom 1945, 137–49; Lindgren 1950, 166–78).

The SAP maintained its distance from the youth organizations throughout this period. Both youth organizations, the SDU and SUF, were welcome to agitate and mobilize workers, but they were to do so on their own. A formalized relationship between the SAP and the youth organizations was not established until the party split in 1917, possibly because the party concluded that it needed better control and influence over its youth organizations.

In the early 1910s two issues in particular were on the labor movement agenda: universal suffrage and anti-militarism. The latter issue had become salient for several reasons. The introduction of universal conscription in 1901 made military service compulsory, causing problems especially for farmers during the summer months. Furthermore, the universal suffrage movement connected military service to universal suffrage, saying that no one should be forced to go to war for a country in which one was not entitled to vote. Another anti-militarist argument especially advocated by the left wing of the SDU was that Sweden could never defend itself in the event of war, so resources spent on the army were wasted (Bäckström 1963b, 50–54; Lindbom 1945, 182–83). The left-wing factions of SDU were particularly successful in mobilizing support for anti-militarism and, in so doing, it became obvious that, with the appropriate arguments, the left-wing faction had the power to mobilize the grassroots. Unsurprisingly, anti-militarism became a recurrent issue of debate between the SDU and the SAP (Bäckström 1963b, 92–93; Möller and Hansson 1916).

Anti-militarism was not confined to the Swedish labor movement; in fact, anti-militarist tendencies could be found throughout the international labor movement, fueled by fears of a major European war. However, in Sweden a reaction to increased military buildup in Europe before the First World War mobilized a major rearmament movement among conservatives. The Liberal Party, which came to office after the 1911 election, faced massive resistance to its disarmament policy from the Right Party. A humiliating public demonstration in favor of rearmament in February 1914 forced the Liberal prime minister, Karl Staaff, to resign. Later that year the First World War broke out, which was used as a reason for reinforcing the army (Kihlberg 1963).

The rearmament debates caused a reaction within the labor movement. The anti-militarist movement in Sweden, based in the SDU, culminated in 1916 when the SDU organized a workers' peace conference in Stockholm. In 1916 the defense question was strongly prioritized, as the war posed a threat and there were no guarantees that Sweden would be able to maintain neutrality. The peace conference was therefore perceived by the political Right as very provocative. Even the SAP and LO had urged local party organizations and unions not to support the conference by sending representatives (Björlin 2012; Höglund 1939, 369–73; Landsorganisationen 1916, 61). Despite the labor leaders' condemnation of the conference, 265 representatives from different local associations participated. The conference agreed on a manifesto for peace. The manifesto prompted the Right to take action, and those responsible for the conference, Zeth Höglund, Ivan Oljelund, and Erik Hedén, were charged with treason, Höglund and Oljelund both being sentenced to prison (Höglund 1939, 373–81; Lindbom 1945, 219–23; Ljunggren 2015, 78). The peace conference not only resulted in tensions between the labor movement and the Right Party but also fueled antagonism between the SAP and the SDU. The left-wing faction of the party gradually formalized its work, and at the 1917 party congress, the SAP leadership, led by Hjalmar Branting, proclaimed that the battles within the party had to end: either the youth organization should subordinate itself to the party or another solution should be found. This resulted in a split into two parties, the Social Democratic Left Party (hereafter referred to as the Left Party) and the Social Democratic Party. The former, not surprisingly, had its core in the SDU (Lindbom 1945, 226–30), which joined the new Left Party (Bolin 2004, 68–70; Lindbom 1945, 226–30). The Left Party was democratic and anti-militaristic and at first did not support the Moscow branch of the international labor movement. However, that changed quickly, and the Left Party became the Communist Party of Sweden (Sveriges kommunistiska parti, SKP) in 1921 (Hermansson 1984, 11–12). The Communist Party split again in 1924 because of disagreements regarding relations with the Comintern and Moscow. A revolutionary branch faithful to Moscow and led by Karl Kilbom remained in the party, whereas a less revolutionary faction led by Zeth Höglund left the Communist Party to form another communist party (Sverges kommunistiska parti). Many of those who broke off later rejoined the

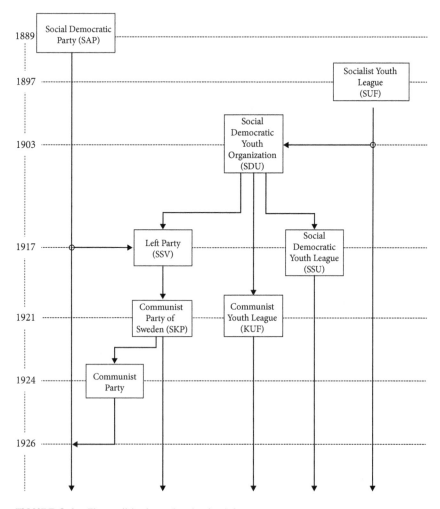

FIGURE 2.1   The political parties in the labor movement

SAP; Höglund returned in 1926 after having led the new communist party for two years (Gröning 1988, 159–61; Hermansson 1984, 11–12).

Because of the protracted battle between the leftist SDU and the SAP, the relationship between the reformist branch of the labor movement and the left-wing organizations was tense. It is also not difficult to imagine that the emergence of different types of workers must have caused some confusion regarding solidarity issues. The LO leaders remained faithful to the SAP—in fact, the LO president is still traditionally a member of the party's executive committee (*verkställande utskottet*, VU). However, as the overall development of the party's youth organization illustrates, not all workers agreed with the SAP's reformist path. Although the LO repeatedly asked local sections to refrain from cooperating with the left-wing organizations—the Left Party, the SDU, and later the Communist Party—the left-wing parties retained influence over parts of the LO cadres.

LO and the Syndicalists

Due to late industrialization, the Swedish trade union movement developed comparatively late; the LO was founded nine years after the SAP, in 1898, though trade unions had existed since the 1870s. Despite the union movement's late formation, the pattern of development resembles that of most other European countries in that the first unions arose from the traditional guilds of artisans and craftsmen (Bell 1978; Hadenius 1976, 17; Lundkvist 1977, 52–56). The unions' predecessors were small self-help associations that provided health insurance and other benefits for their members (Lindbom 1938, 11–15), a tradition that continued in the unions.

The SAP and the LO were close, with links such as joint committees and overlapping personnel, and collective affiliation was practiced for most of the twentieth century. The organizations were nevertheless distinct (Casparsson 1947, 37–41, 49–53, 137–55; Jansson 2017). The leadership of the LO, the Secretariat (Landssekretariatet), had executive power in the organization and initially comprised a group of five to ten people. This leadership group continually grew over time as the organization became bigger. The LO's Representantskapet (Representatives) consisted of chairs of the affiliated unions and constituted the governing body between congresses, meeting two or three times a year. The LO congress was the superior governing body and assembled every fifth year for a conference lasting three to four days. The congress, which was intended to mirror LO membership as a whole, consisted of members of the various affiliated unions. Besides electing the LO president, the task of the congress was to make policy decisions. Since the reformist union movement was and still is democratic, decisions made by the congress had to be (and must still be) respected by the Secretariat. At the beginning of the twentieth century, the confederation was loosely structured, and the affiliates were relatively independent of the central organization (Hadenius 1976, 18–22).

The individual trade union members were organized in local trade union associations called sections (*avdelningar*), which were tied to the affiliates. A section often consisted of workers from a single workplace. The affiliates were, like the LO, democratic organizations holding their own congresses, to which all sections sent representatives. How much power was possessed by the sections differed between the affiliates, but before the 1940s decisions were generally made in the local sections. Given the complex nature of the LO, the leadership had weaker connections to individual members than did the affiliates. Its connections to the members existed via the affiliated unions, and there were no direct channels of communication before the 1920s. This poor and sporadic access to the local sections limited the LO's influence over identity formation in the organization.

The trade unions' first decades were filled with conflicts between workers and employers. The initial battle for the union movement was for recognition of its existence. Many employers refused to accept unions at their workplaces and fought the workers' right to organize by making it difficult for trade union members to obtain employment. Despite these attempts to thwart the union movement, unions grew in number, making it harder for employers to ignore them. The growth of the union movement eventually forced the employers to organize themselves as well and, after a short general strike for universal suffrage in May 1902, a number of prominent business owners and managers founded the Swedish Employers' Association (Svenska arbetsgivareföreningen, SAF). It was simply easier to confront the workers via a unified organization of their own (Lundh 2009, 15–16). A few years later, in 1906 the SAF and the LO managed to reach a crucial agreement, the so-called December Compromise, in which the employers recognized the workers' right to organize trade unions (and freedom of association) and the workers recognized the employers' right to hire and fire workers (Bengtsson 2006, 16–17; Casparsson 1947, 224–28), resolving some of the issues that had led to severe conflicts.

However, the relationship between the employers and the workers did not improve significantly after the 1906 agreement, and the number of work stoppages did not decrease (see figure 2.3). On the contrary, labor market conflicts remained very common and the tension between the trade union movement and the employers' organization escalated into a general strike in 1909. In an attempt to lower wages in some of the main export industries in Sweden, a comprehensive lockout was proclaimed by the employers in the summer of 1909. Encouraged by the left-wing faction of the SAP, the youth organization SDU, and the young socialists' organizations SUF and SUP, the LO responded to the lockout by declaring a general strike. Assuming the government would quickly step in and put an end to the conflict, the LO mobilized as many as three hundred thousand workers. The conservative government led by the Right Party did not intervene, however, and the conflict quickly drained the unions' strike funds. After one month the LO had to surrender (Casparsson 1966, 128–29; Hirdman 1990, 74–80; Schiller 1967).

The effects of the general strike were devastating for the LO. It lost half its members overnight and required almost ten years to recover from that loss. Another direct effect of the general strike was the weakening of the LO's central organization. The confederation's role and status had been debated within the LO even before the general strike, and afterward the critics could more easily push through reforms that shifted the power resources from the central organization to the affiliates. The general strike was cited by some of the affiliates as an example of the LO's incapacity to govern the trade union movement, and the LO saw itself stripped of its newly gained powers (Hadenius 1976; Swenson 1989, 44).

The general strike was a miscalculation, and memory of this trauma changed the Swedish trade union movement. Roughly speaking, two contrasting experiences can be identified among the men and women involved in the strike. First, there were those who chose to interpret the strike as "learning a valuable lesson" and abandoned the general strike as an instrument of industrial conflict. Indirectly, proponents of this view recognized that capitalism could not be fought on the basis of conflict alone, as the employers simply had too many resources at their disposal.

The other interpretation was that of disappointed union members who chose to interpret the strike as a failure of the leadership of the unions and the labor movement. These men and women, devoted to the struggle against capital, concluded that if the labor movement had dared to be more radical, labor would have won. The LO leaders should have held out for a few more weeks and involved even more occupational groups. Instead, according to this interpretation, because of the weakness of the LO and its leadership, what should have been a victory turned into a failure (Jensen 1910). In contrast to the first interpretation, this interpretation held that capital could be defeated through strikes. The groups advocating such an interpretation of the strike became fertile ground for the emergence of left-wing organizations, and it was in this environment that the syndicalist Central Organization of the Workers of Sweden (Sveriges arbetares centralorganisation, SAC) was founded in 1910.

The SAC originated in the Young Socialists organization, the SUF, and the radical wing of the SDU (Bergkvist and Arvidsson 1960, 8–12; Blomberg and Blomberg 1993, 14–15). From the beginning, the SAC was a class-struggle organization in a far more radical sense than the reformist labor movement had ever been. At the center of syndicalist ideology was action. Passivity would never win any battles, so the workers had to act in order for the struggle against capital to succeed. The idea of binding agreements was rejected, since that would constrain the actions of the working class (Karlsson and Warlenius 2012, 20–22; Persson 1975, 239–46). Strike funds were also met with skepticism in the new organization.

During the first years of the SAC's existence, the union focused on mobilizing support among the workers, and syndicalist local associations (*lokal samorganisation*, LSs) were founded all over Sweden. The LSs were not based on sectors or occupations, as were the reformist unions, but rather were geographical units that brought different sectors together. The class struggle was the concern of all workers, so why divide them into different organizations? The existence of multiple organizations would only lead to struggle between the workers, which could never lead to socialism. The main organizing principle of the SAC was strong local associations (one criticism of the reformist unions was the authoritarianism that the centralized system allegedly created), so the SAC was decentralized, and the local associations had powers to act in the interest of their members

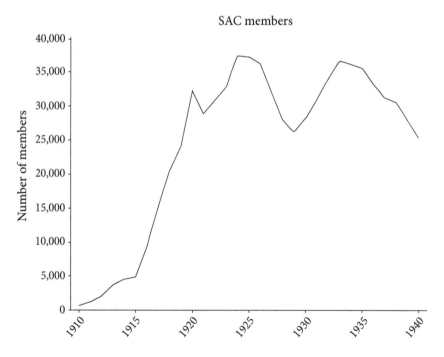

FIGURE 2.2   SAC membership, 1910–1940. *Source:* SAC annual reports, 1910–1940.

(Bergkvist and Arvidsson 1960, 7–11). The SAC had to revise some of its ideals quite soon after its founding, and the central idea that workers should never conclude binding agreements of any kind was abolished almost immediately. In addition, strike funds were quickly established even though they were considered unnecessary (Blomberg and Blomberg 1993, 14–23; Jerlström). Nevertheless, the SAC grew continuously in the 1910s.

For the LO, the first few years after 1909 were recuperative, as the LO re-recruited and reorganized its members after its defeat in the general strike. This reconstruction was hard because disappointment was widespread in the working class in the aftermath of the strike and because many employers would not hire trade union members.

The labor market was comparatively peaceful during the First World War (Hadenius 1976, 31). By the end of the war this changed, however, and unemployment rose rapidly in Sweden, as in the rest of Europe. The Swedish export sector had benefited greatly from the war because of the demand for raw materials; at the same time, the import of goods had decreased markedly, causing food shortages. These processes together led to high inflation in Sweden (Schön 2007, 274–82), though wages had not increased in proportion to prices (Schön 2007, 275), making the situation dire for the working class. Moreover, once the war was over, the demand for export goods fell, fueling unemployment.

It was quite common for employers to seek wage reductions, which triggered strikes. The workers' struggle against wage cuts sometimes paid off, but usually it merely drained the strike funds while resulting in comparatively small gains. Another problem affecting both strike effectiveness and worker morale was strikebreakers (Åmark 1986, 114–18). The employers' organization even attempted to organize strikebreakers into organizations as alternatives to unions, intended to provide the employers with a workforce during labor market conflicts (Flink 1978, chapter 2). The employers used lockouts quite frequently in response to strikes, which was costly for the unions. The situation during the first decades of the twentieth century—characterized by highly confrontational labor market relations—was not very promising for the Swedish labor movement.

Problems for the LO Leadership

The LO leaders appear to have faced a number of interrelated difficulties around 1920. The main problems emanated from two sources: the high conflict level, which drained strike funds, and competing left-wing organizations. The SAC's emergence as a viable actor on the labor market and its steadily growing membership seem to have worried the LO Secretariat. These main problems can be broken down into four more specific difficulties, which are analyzed in this section.

Problem 1: The Conflict Level

After the general strike, labor market conflicts decreased for some years, and during the first part of the First World War the labor market was calm if not peaceful. The situation changed around 1916–17 for several reasons. The left-wing organizations were active, and the peace conference of 1916 had mobilized resistance against the war and the military in general. This was combined with the universal suffrage movement. The war also caused inflation and a recession, and the food shortages that followed in 1917 caused demonstrations, riots, and the formation of comprehensive protest movements (Blomqvist 2017; Bosdotter et al. 2017). On top of that, the Bolsheviks seized power in Russia, inspiring left-wing organizations all over the world. For example, the increase in SAC members surged around this time, as shown in figure 2.2.

The recession in the wake of the First World War was characterized by an extraordinarily high level of labor conflict. The economic crisis had hit industry hard. The prevailing economic analysis in Sweden and most of Europe at that time consistently claimed that unemployment was caused by excessive wages, and, as a result, employers tried to push wages down. These attempts, and the layoffs due to falling demand for industrial products, were met with strong resistance from workers. Compared with other countries, Sweden experienced a high number of strikes, and these were also longer than in France, for example, where the labor movement tended to mobilize larger numbers of strikers but for shorter periods (Korpi 1980, 116–17; Shorter and Tilly 1974, 333). Many strikes in Sweden in the 1920s and 1930s lasted for months. The LO Secretariat must have been deeply concerned by strike prevalence and duration. Strikes were costly, and the strike funds were insufficient to provide for members who were constantly involved in labor conflicts. It was important to maintain strike funds because, in their absence, a coordinated general lockout could easily crush the union movement or at least considerably weaken labor's negotiating position with employers.

Decisions to go on strike were out of LO jurisdiction, however, and the various affiliates had different policies on how to handle work stoppages. One factor that probably increased the number of labor conflicts was the voting procedures in some affiliates. The decision to go on strike was made at the local level by referendum. In other words, those directly affected by a conflict were the ones who decided whether or not to escalate it into a strike. For example, Paper Mill Workers' Union members held referendums on extending wage agreements,

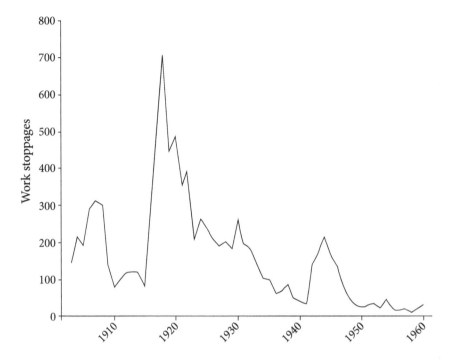

FIGURE 2.3   Number of work stoppages in Sweden, 1903–1940. *Sources:* SCB 1925; SCB 1940; SCB 1942b; Socialstyrelsen 1921; Socialstyrelsen 1940.

accepting agreements, and entering into conflicts in which *all* members partici-pated. The Metal Industry Workers' Union had a similar system (Beckholmen 1984), as did the Forest Workers' Union (Karlbom 1968, 169–70). This system was susceptible to actors' emotions, and personal conflicts on the shop floor between workers and employers could escalate into work stoppages. Removing the deci-sion on how to react to conflicts from the individuals directly affected by them would likely have prevented decisions from being made purely on impulse. (This is one reason why the labor market peace agreement reached in Saltsjöbaden was so successful: all negotiations and decisions regarding conflicts were lifted from the local to the top organizational level of LO.) Coordinated conflicts in differ-ent sectors were pursued through voting. The local sections voted, and if most sections voted in favor, a strike would be called by the affiliate in question. These stoppages met with similar lack of success, but LO could do little more than urge the affiliates and sections to be careful and pick their fights wisely. The main effect of these work stoppages was the so-called bloodletting of the strike funds.

Work stoppages became a frequently discussed issue within the LO. In a meeting with the Representatives in 1921, a proposal was discussed regarding intensifying conflicts and coordinating them between the affiliates in response to ongoing wage cuts, along with the economic implications of such a strategy (Hansson 1921, 10 October; Representantskapet 1921, 10–11 October). Edvard Johansson, secretary of the Secretariat and later LO president, argued that increasing the number of strikes would have only negative effects on the trade unions. The economic crisis could not easily be resolved, and the unions needed to act cautiously and wait for the crisis to end (Representantskapet 1921, 10–11 October). Sigfrid Hansson, the editor of the LO's magazine *Fackföreningsrörelsen*, made the following note in his diary regarding the debate at the meeting: "It became clear in the debate that the situation was perceived as hopeless. The unions have been bleeding in economic terms during the period of unemployment; this bloodletting, as well as the general economic situation, has of course very much weakened the organization's power to act" (Hansson 1921, 10 October).[2]

The risks associated with such conflicts caused the LO leaders to call for cautious and "coordinated behavior" (Landsorganisationen 1925d). Fear of losing financial resources was obvious among the LO leaders, probably because the memory of the general strike of 1909 was still vivid. It also seems that "bleeding" the unions' strike funds was a conscious strategy of employers (Swenson 2002, 100–101). Nevertheless, the arguments regarding cautious behavior did not stop some unions from intensifying the conflicts (Landsorganisationen 1921; Landsorganisationen 1922a). The unions' leaders were unconvinced that the risk of bloodletting was a sufficient reason to stop fighting, or they assumed that the workers' fighting spirit would be unaffected by the fate of the strike funds and that conflicts would go on regardless of financial means. There were obviously diverging opinions at various levels in the LO regarding this problem. The level of labor conflict was an explicitly defined problem for the entire organization, but for large parts of it—particularly among left-wing supporters—the problem emanated from *the employers*, and the solution was to fight conflicts caused by attempted wage cutting with more conflicts. The Secretariat, on the other hand, seems to have worried about what more conflicts would do to the labor movement as a whole.[3]

Problem 2: Competing Organizations

Another problem associated with the growth of the syndicalist movement and to some degree the communists was that the LO for the first time had to face competition for members. Before 1910 some unions (e.g., the railroad workers' union) were unaffiliated with the LO, and a small syndicalist movement had existed for some time, but these were unions either based on a single occupation or representing very marginalized cohorts of workers. There was no umbrella organization that competed with the LO for members and influence on the Swedish labor market. The LO had to face real competition for the first time when the SAC was founded. By definition, the SAC came to pose a threat to the LO because it constituted an alternative for Swedish workers.

The SAC grew rapidly: From 1910 to 1917 it had gone from 21 local associations (LSs) with seven hundred members to 202 local associations with fifteen thousand members, and by 1920 those figures had doubled (SAC 1910a; SAC 1917; SAC 1920). It must have been worrying for the LO president, Herman Lindqvist, and the Secretariat to observe the rapid growth of the SAC—there was no telling when or even whether the expansion would end.

How serious was the threat to the LO? The SAC had expanded quickly but still had nowhere near the number of members the LO had in 1917. As figure 2.4 shows, the LO did lose members around 1920–22, but the size of the membership gap between the LO and the SAC was still profound.

SAC recruited members not only from the LO but also from the large mass of unorganized workers. In particular, unskilled workers in the mining industry

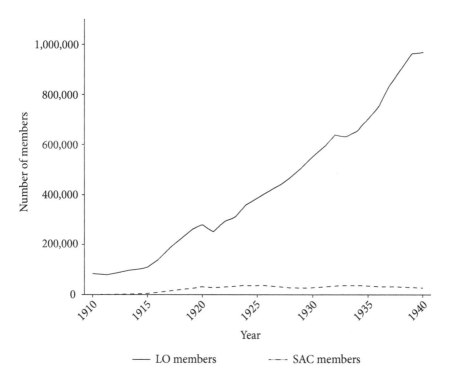

FIGURE 2.4   Number of members of LO and SAC, 1910–1940. *Sources*: LO and SAC annual reports, 1910–1940.

in northern Sweden and forest workers in northern and central Sweden were enticed by the syndicalists' messages. The risk was not only that the LO would lose members to the SAC but also that the SAC would recruit members in sectors and regions where the trade union movement was weak, possibly giving the SAC dominance in certain geographical regions. The industrial sectors involved were also the most important export sectors in Sweden, so mobilizing workers in them was important for the union movement's overall impact on the labor market (Horgby 1997, 121–26; Horgby 2012, 42, 466n6; Karlbom 1968, 216).

Records from the SAC document its diligent efforts to organize and to recruit new members all over the country. In contrast to the LO's sparse records on organizing activities, the SAC provided detailed accounts in their annual reports. The number of speeches, participants, involved regions, and new members recruited after meetings were all noted and published (SAC 1914; SAC 1915, 19–23; SAC 1917). It was obviously important to the SAC that it publicize its work and efforts. Around 1920 the SAC seems to have been agitating all around the country, but they were particularly successful in northern Sweden (Landsorganisationen 1924a; Landsorganisationen 1924b; Sätterberg 1928b).

Another dimension of the problem of competing organizations was the damage such splits in the trade union movement would cause in the long run. Even if the LO managed to stop its membership losses to the SAC, a fairly strong syndicalist movement would inevitably split the trade union movement in Sweden. The LO Secretariat was well aware of the development of union movements in other countries where different branches of the labor movement fought each other rather than the employers. A strong syndicalist movement would considerably weaken the labor movement, especially since Swedish employers were well organized.[4]

Competition for members was indeed a problem for the LO, but the SAC's size was hardly the most difficult challenge. Even if the SAC grew further, the LO leaders must have felt fairly confident about maintaining their membership lead. However, the syndicalist organization caused other problems for the rank and file besides being an alternative to the LO.

Problem 3: Radical Conflict Methods

Another problem, much more pressing than the size of the competing organization, entailed methods. The SAC advocated direct action using all available means to challenge the current order of society (SAC 1910b). The SAC praised the general strike as a means for fighting bourgeois society, but other methods, such as obstruction, boycotts, and even sabotage, were also in the SAC toolbox (Jensen 1912; Jensen 1920). Such methods were also advocated by the communist movement (Bolin 2004, 239–47). These radical means of conflict enjoyed some support among LO members. In particular, the general strike was intensely debated at the beginning of the 1920s.

The notion of the general strike as an instrument of conflict had more or less died within the LO leadership after 1909. The LO leaders interpreted the failure of the general strike as indicating that such strikes simply do not work. They were resigned to the belief that capital would always have the upper hand economically and that it would be very hard for workers to compete against the resources available to their opponents.

Despite the earlier negative experience, some parts of LO kept returning to the concept of the general strike as a possible and even favorable tactic for the workers in their struggle against the employers. One could argue that at least the leaders of the affiliates should have drawn other conclusions from the experiences of 1909, but in some sectors that was not the case. Several affiliates, especially the Metal Workers' Union, advocated the general strike. At a meeting with the LO Representatives in 1920, the Metal Workers' Union proposed a new general strike that, according to the proposal, was to be coordinated with the SAC. The background to this proposal was a labor market conflict in which the employers had tried to reduce wages in the metal sector. The Metal Workers' Union had responded by calling a strike, which was met with a lockout. The Employers' Organization, the SAF, had also informed the LO that they intended to extend the lockout to other sectors (Representantskapet 1920, 29–31 January).

The debate among the LO Representatives dealt in particular with two issues regarding the proposed general strike: when the strike should be initiated in order to obtain the best results and whether the SAC should be invited to join the LO in the strike (Representantskapet 1920, 29–31 January). One of the Representatives even suggested that no extra funding should be granted to the Metal Workers' Union's strike fund, on the grounds that if the workers who were locked out were miserable enough, the chances of success of the new general strike would be much better. Other participants in the meeting condemned this idea, which, though not a majority position, does signal the variety of views among the Representatives regarding the proposed general strike (Representantskapet 1920, 29–31 January).

The attitude toward the general strike was surprisingly receptive. The LO Representatives—who were, after all, the leaders of the affiliates—ultimately decided to postpone voting on the issue, but the argument against calling a new strike was not that it would drain the union's strike funds. Rather, the problem was that some member groups of the LO would be unable to join the strike, especially the important municipal workers, who had a collective agreement and whose right to strike was limited by legislation. Only a few contributions to the debate, all of which came from the LO leaders and the Municipal Workers' Union, argued that a general strike would exhaust the strike funds and damage the union movement for a long time to come. Most meeting attendees were disposed to inviting the SAC to join the strike, so friendliness toward the syndicalists was clearly not limited to the local level (Representantskapet 1920, 29–31 January). The meeting ended by assigning the Secretariat the task of ascertaining the best time to hold the general strike, postponing the proposed strike until that had been established. At that time a new meeting would be called, to which the SAC should be invited (Representantskapet 1920, 29–31 January).

The dream of a general strike remained alive in the left-wing organizations, and since some of the LO affiliates sympathized with the Left Party and the SAC, it was still a matter of debate in the 1920s. The general strike was debated again by the Representatives in 1921 and 1923 and at the LO congress in 1922 (Landsorganisationen 1922b, 183–87; Westerståhl 1945, 152–53). In 1925, in response to a wave of lockouts initiated by the SAF, eighteen of thirty-four affiliates suggested holding a new general strike (Casparsson 1951, 35), but once again the decision was postponed, and the proposal was never realized.

The LO leaders were not pleased by the talk of a new general strike, and the same arguments made in debates on the level of conflict in general were eminently applicable to the general strike. Such action would simply drain the unions' strike funds, weakening the labor movement in the long run.

When the Swedish Employers' Association, SAF, instigated a major lockout in 1925, the LO Secretariat sent a letter to all local sections in an attempt to rally the troops and prepare members for an upcoming battle. The Secretariat urged the members to keep calm and not act impulsively and exacerbate the conflict:

> In these circles [i.e., the employers], it is believed that the workers would lose their composure and let themselves be deceived into extending the conflict to areas that are beyond the reach of the Employers' Association's lock-outs [i.e., the public sector], thereby turning the mood against them and evoking such countermeasures that they would be defeated, thus shattering the trade union movement. It [i.e., the Employers' Association] has even openly expressed a desire that the workers launch a new general strike. Thus, in this case the irrational desires of the employers coincide with the propaganda for a general strike being produced by the Moscow-affiliated Communist Party. The extreme right-wing and extreme left-wing lines and views of the matter coincide.
>
> The current conflict situation is not so bad that the Swedish trade union movement would be unable to obtain victory through united and purposeful behavior. It only requires the patience and calm of the

workers directly affected by the battle, their sacrifice and solidarity. (Landsorganisationen 1925d, 18 March)

The message was clear: the workers should not let themselves be deceived and provoked into intensifying the conflict. Moreover, the Secretariat warned the workers about the communists who were trying to lead LO members astray with their propaganda.

The other tactics advocated by the syndicalists in labor market conflicts—obstruction and sabotage—were also problematic for the LO. These methods might have appealed to many workers, but the outcome would certainly have been to poison their relationship with the employers. This relationship was already tense at the beginning of the 1920s, as the attempts to cut wages and the lockouts (the great lockout in 1925 and the paper industry lockout in 1928) intensified the conflict between workers and employers. Concluding collective agreements, however, an important objective for the LO, required the establishment of trust between the parties, which syndicalist methods undermined.

Problem 4: The Enemy Within

The left-wing organizations indeed caused problems for the LO by initiating conflicts and competing over members. Nevertheless, the biggest problem lay within the organization itself. Many LO members joined the SAC in its conflicts in acts of solidarity with fellow workers, which of course increased the number of conflicts for the LO. This internal support from LO members for the left-wing organizations also explained the support for the general strike, as the left-wing organizations managed to drag LO members into conflicts by appealing to solidarity between workers. A closer look at the labor market conflicts lets us estimate how problematic the SAC was in this regard.

Figure 2.5 shows the labor market conflicts in which the SAC was involved during 1916–21. Despite its short span of years, the graph covers the most important period of labor unrest and illustrates quite well the problem facing the LO. Many of the conflicts the SAC started were sanctioned by LO members. In other words, the SAC started conflicts and the local LO affiliates' sections would join them, sometimes using the strike funds to finance them. As figure 2.6 illustrates, 65 percent of the SAC's conflicts in 1919 had support from LO members, a very large proportion and easily sufficient to worry the LO leaders.

Although these figures indicate cooperation in industrial conflicts, the LO and the SAC rarely cooperated at the central level. These graphs indicate a discrepancy between the central and grassroots levels in the LO. At the local level, LO members tended to join and support the syndicalists, whereas such cooperation had weak support at the top.[5] The SAC was also very doubtful concerning joint actions with

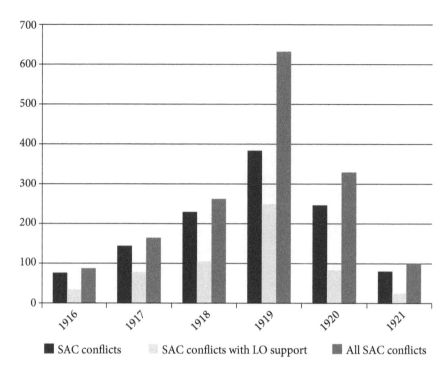

FIGURE 2.5 Number of SAC labor market conflicts, 1916–1921. *Note:* SAC conflicts are labor market conflicts started and administered by SAC; SAC conflicts with LO Support are SAC conflicts in which LO members participated; mixed conflicts are labor market conflicts that the SAC and LO jointly started and administered. *Source:* SAC annual reports, 1916–1921.

the LO, especially before 1920. The general opinion among SAC leaders was that the social democratic unions gave in far too easily and that the conflicts the SAC lost were usually mixed conflicts or conflicts in which LO members had acted as strikebreakers; the LO was blamed for these losses (SAC 1913, 17).

The SAC indeed troubled the LO, and its increased influence, combined with the founding of the Left Party in February 1917, eventually led the LO Secretariat to take action against the left-wing organizations. Six months after the Social Democratic Party split, the LO held its seventh congress in Stockholm in August 1917. In an attempt to settle the "syndicalist issue" once and for all and to bind the affiliates to a promise not to cooperate with the SAC, the Secretariat, obviously shaken by the developments in the party, proposed a prohibition against cooperation with any part of the SAC and also condemned syndicalist methods. LO members were not to join the syndicalists in conflicts on a sympathy basis (Landsorganisationen 1917, 40–42).

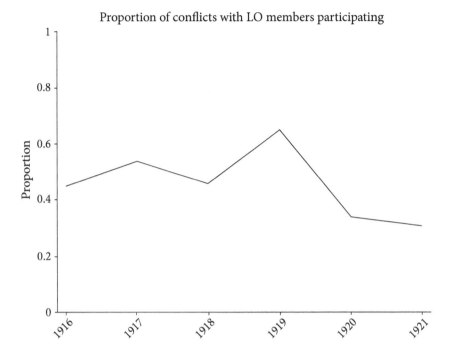

FIGURE 2.6   Proportion of SAC labor market conflicts in which LO members participated. *Source*: SAC annual reports, 1916–1921.

The proposal met resistance at the congress, and a long debate followed. The arguments against the proposal originated in the idea that all workers should eventually unite against capital, so the proposal was seen as obstructing the workers' struggle. In the end, a cohesive and united labor movement had to be the primary goal. The proposal was interpreted as a violation of the principle of solidarity: "Each strike and blockade decided on by the majority of the workers concerned, intended to protect workers' vital interests and directed against capitalism, is part of the working class's liberation struggle and must be maintained by unswerving solidaristic cohesion" (Landsorganisationen 1917, 42).

Moreover, several speakers at the congress emphasized that although the syndicalists had started many conflicts, such action was sometimes necessary to fight the employers. They were not, as the LO Secretariat claimed in its proposal, a complete waste of resources (Landsorganisationen 1917, 42–44). As the debate continued, it was obvious that not even all seven members of the Secretariat stood behind the proposal (see Anders Sjöstedt's commentary, Landsorganisationen 1917, 42). The Secretariat saw itself defeated, and there was no condemnation of the SAC at the congress (Landsorganisationen 1917, 147–54).

The proposal demonstrated either desperation or the naïveté of the president, Herman Lindqvist, to think that such a proposal would win support at that point. In contrast, the action echoed for many years in the organization and was cited by the SAC to gain ground among workers. The debate at the congress clearly demonstrated that the SAC had more support among LO members than was comfortable for the LO leaders.

The LO Secretariat was more careful when making public statements about the SAC after 1917, but it at least tried to minimize contacts. For example, in 1921 when the SAC sent a letter to the LO Secretariat suggesting cooperation in mobilizing all workers in Sweden to "take their rightful share of production during the economic crisis," the Secretariat simply turned down the proposal, arguing that the Representatives had already decided how to handle the economic crisis (Landssekretariatet 1921b). Categorizing the proposal in terms of the economic crisis rather than in terms of uniting all Swedish workers in a single organization was important because it allowed the Secretariat to dismiss the proposal without consulting the rest of the organization. If they had defined it as an organizational issue they would have been forced to bring in the LO Representatives and perhaps also the congress. After all, the idea of a merger between the organizations did have some support among the Representatives and the congress (Landsorganisationen 1926b; Representantskapet 1920, 29–31 January, 376–80).[6] The Secretariat had learned something from the 1917 attempt to end all cooperation with the SAC.

The other left-wing organizations, associations, and parties also enjoyed support among LO members. It was never the Communist Party's intention to start new communist unions; instead, they wanted to take over the LO (Andersson 1921; Kennerström 1974, 8–9; Nycander 2002, 36–37; Åmark 1986, 138–42). The LO already had a functioning organizational structure, presence in most of the country, and resources that made its affiliates attractive to workers. The LO administered a modest unemployment insurance scheme and compensation for sickness and accidents, not to mention the strike funds, which made it easier to start and support labor market conflicts. It is not surprising that the Communists considered it more expedient to take over the LO affiliates than to start from scratch. The LO leaders were well aware of this.

The Left Party and later the Communist Party realized that unions were a good way to communicate with the workers, but since the LO had declared itself faithful to the SAP, other ways of gaining influence over the unions were needed. Since there was support among the grassroots for radical approaches, the strategy instead became one of infiltrating the LO unions at the local level and transforming the union movement from within. Accordingly, the Left Party started the Trade Union Propaganda League (Fackliga propagandaförbundet,

FPF) in 1919, in an attempt to radicalize the trade union movement (Bolin 2004, 244). The FPF was intended to establish a "struggle center" whose main task was to direct actions against the diluted and bourgeoisified reformist trade unions (Andersson 1921, 3); moreover, it was linked to the Comintern, the Third International established in Moscow in 1919 (Casparsson 1947, 364–68). All trade union members were encouraged to join FPF, as active union members would be the best means of spreading its ideas and thus changing the reformist unions from within (Andersson 1921, 3).

The establishment of the FPF gave rise to considerable discussion among the Representatives in 1921 (Representantskapet 1921). It was hard, maybe impossible, to forbid LO members or even sections to join the FPF. There are no reliable data as to the number of FPF members, but Casparsson estimated it as a maximum of five thousand (Casparsson 1947, 365). Representing an ambitious attempt of the Communists to exercise influence over the unions, the FPF nevertheless failed to have any noteworthy impact, and the organization was dissolved in 1922.

Instead, the Communist Party changed its strategy and, starting in 1925, tried to initiate a forum for left-wing trade union members. In an attempt to gather the left-wing sympathizers in the trade union movement, the Communists supported a conference organized by the Metal Industry Workers' Union in Göteborg in 1926. The conference, presented as an open-minded dialogue between supporters of a somewhat more radical policy toward employers, resulted in the founding of the Unity Committee (Enhetskommittén, 1926–29). The LO had condemned cooperation with the Communists, but even though the affiliates had agreed not to cooperate at official meetings, the local organizations still sent representatives to the Unity Committee. The Secretariat repeatedly sent memos and letters to the local sections, demanding compliance (Casparsson 1951, 71–72; Landsorganisationen 1925b; Landsorganisationen 1934).

Finally, the problems posed by the left-wing organizations were revealed when Herman Lindqvist resigned as the president of the LO in 1920. In early 1920, rumors about Lindqvist had circulated in both the left-wing and conservative press, alleging that he owned shares in a company named AB Arbetarbränsle and in a piano factory. These rumors, which turned out to be true, spotlighted the important question of what constituted ethical behavior for labor leaders. Needless to say, the left-wing organizations condemned such ownership as bourgeois. On the other hand, as the LO Representatives also admitted, although owning shares was problematic for a labor leader, property rights could not be taken lightly—broadly speaking, if Lindqvist had the money it was his private affair how he spent it (Casparsson 1947, 472–82; Representantskapet 1920, 29–31 January).

Nevertheless, AB Arbetarbränsle was just the start. The conservative press found out that Lindqvist had also bought a plot in a graveyard in Stockholm, not to mention a gravestone designed by an architect. The conservative press portrayed Lindqvist's acquisition as if he was building a mausoleum, which in turn stirred up the left-wing press. The rumors resulted in innumerable written complaints to the LO Secretariat from sections all over the country. Since the issue had stirred up the grassroots membership, the Representatives could not ignore it. Consequently, Lindqvist's personal affairs were thoroughly discussed at the Representatives' meeting in January 1920. Though the Representatives had originally assembled to discuss a labor market crisis (the employers' organization had threatened to lock out several sectors in the coming week), they instead held a long debate concerning whether Lindqvist could remain in office. Most of the Representatives supported Lindqvist because he had been president since 1900 and had managed to bring the LO out of its deepest crisis following the general strike of 1909. Though he was still popular among the Representatives, many questioned whether he would have any credibility among the workers after the "Arbetarbränsle affair." Some advocated for his resignation. Lindqvist prepared himself for this debate and wrote a resignation letter, which he handed to the Representatives. Several of the speakers at the meeting accused the left-wing organizations (mainly the Communists) of deliberately fanning this controversy among the grassroots. The rancorous tone among the grassroots and in the media could only be interpreted as political persecution, according to some Representatives. The conservative press, of course, reveled in the controversy (Casparsson 1947, 472–82; Representantskapet 1920, 29–31 January). The ensuing "scandal" that led to the resignation of the leader of the reformist union movement, a man who had been in charge for twenty years and had helped build the LO, was the result of media pressure, particularly from the left-wing press—at least, that was the interpretation of the Representatives and the Secretariat. The Secretariat worried about the influence of the left-wing organizations: even though they were relatively small they could apparently cause harm to the LO (Landssekretariatet 1920a; Landssekretariatet 1920b).

Problems Facing the LO in 1920

The situation the LO found itself in around 1920 can be described as dire in many ways, and it seems that the key problems, principally entailing cohesion, were all connected. Labor market conflicts had caused serious economic problems for the LO and had to be addressed. Problems were also caused partly by internal support for the new left-wing organizations and the radical ideas they promoted.

The number of conflicts increased because of communists' and syndicalists' confrontational stance toward employers. The founding of the SAC and later the Left Party forced the LO to position itself against these new organizations, which were either competing with it for members or introducing radical ideas into the movement. This competition threatened to weaken not only the LO but also the labor movement as a whole. The LO Secretariat was well aware of the developments in other European countries, where divided union movements had little prospect of challenging employers. The LO had to distance itself from the left-wing organizations to keep its members and to appear attractive enough to mobilize the unorganized masses. However, although the LO leaders had a distinct ideological awareness, there was an obvious discrepancy between the leaders and the grassroots. Willingness to support the left-wing organizations, lack of discipline, and an eagerness to escalate labor market conflicts into work stoppages all threatened the LO. The problem of internal support in the LO for the left wing was a matter of weak organizational identity. A disjointed organization in which members and member organizations were only loosely tied to the umbrella organization made it easier to be unfaithful to the LO and reformism by supporting syndicalists and communists.

The confusion among members of the trade union movement regarding the party split was obvious. One example can be found in the local section of the Swedish Paper Mill Workers' Union in the town of Skutskär. This section was for a time aligned with both the Social Democratic Party and the Left Party (Sågverksindustriarbetareförbundet avd. 54 1938). Why was there such a discrepancy between the grassroots and the leadership? One explanation could be that the ideological differences between the organizations made less sense on the shop floor. People working side by side in a factory, mine, or sawmill obviously knew each other—indeed, they were often relatives—and to refuse to help out in a labor conflict was probably unthinkable. This in turn indicates different perceptions of potential threats on the part of the members and the Secretariat. As one participant at the LO congress in 1917 put it, "workers around the country do not share the view of syndicalism that is held by some gentlemen here" (Landsorganisationen 1917, 43), referring to the leadership's view of the SAC.

The interpretation of the problems I have presented here stresses the lack of a cohesive organizational identity. The new left-wing organizations had formulated new and different meanings of being a worker, blurring the tie between the class structure and the sense of "we." Not only did this make it more complicated to distinguish between "we" and "others," it also had implications for implementing socialist ideology. Once the labor movement had split, the central idea of solidarity would become harder for the working class to grasp. To whom should one be loyal and show solidarity? Why should distinctions be made between syndicalists, reformists, and communists? In the end a worker is a worker. In identity terms, this meant that class identity was stronger than the more exclusive organizational identity of the LO.

The labor leaders in both the reformist unions and the left-wing organizations were assigned the task of explaining these changes to the workers. For the left-wing organizations, the task was probably less of a challenge, as they had simply continued along the path laid out by Marx or Lenin. Such radical theories were the very reason their organizations had been founded. From their point of view, the reformists were the ones departing from the true path—namely, the path toward revolution. For the reformist labor leaders, however, the situation was delicate. Their explanation that there were different kinds of workers had little support in the theories of socialism, nor did their belief that the class struggle could and should be conducted by more restrained methods. Furthermore, it seemed that the left-wing organizations, with their far more radical methods, were making more progress in the fight against capital.

Of course, the difference between the LO leadership and members in their views of the left-wing organizations made it hard for the leadership to know which branch the members would support in the event of a conflict between the left-wing factions and the reformist organizations. The developments in 1920 spurred the LO Secretariat to take action. Before 1920 there were no signs that the Secretariat understood that it had to work actively at identity formation, which seems to have been taken for granted. After the appointment of Arvid Thorberg to succeed Lindqvist as the new president of the LO, however, things started to change.

A PLAN FOR IDENTITY MANAGEMENT

The resignation of Herman Lindqvist in January 1920 is best described as a critical juncture for the Swedish Trade Union Confederation (LO). It was no longer possible to ignore the severity of the problems caused by the different ideological factions of the labor movement. Developing a strategy for handling the left-wing organizations thus became necessary for the LO Secretariat. Returning to the thesis outlined here, a few methodological remarks regarding the analysis are in order. Analyzing strategic action entails establishing whether the LO leaders *intended* to create cohesiveness in the organization using popular education as a means of identity formation. Tracing the motives of actors requires the examination of both their stated intentions and their actions, the latter generally being congruent with the motives. Exploring the strategic actions of the Secretariat includes analyzing its explicit interpretations of the situation. Did the Secretariat consciously make a connection between left-wing organizations, identity, and popular education? Since problem definitions and solutions recorded in meeting minutes may be purely rhetorical, it is also necessary to scrutinize how the Secretariat *acted* against the left-wing organizations as well as toward the LO members and affiliated unions that sympathized with them.

The Leaders' Definition of the Problem

Strategic action requires that actors be aware of their preferences and options. In the case of an organization, it also requires an awareness of the problems one faces. Thus, it is first necessary to establish whether the LO's problems were recognized by the LO leadership as identity problems, and then to determine whether popular education was perceived as the solution. The Secretariat was well aware of the problems caused by the left-wing organizations, but it was careful not to discuss these issues openly. Being in a precarious situation in the 1920s, the LO leadership could not know who would be in the line of fire of the left-wing faction the next time. However, a clear definition of the problems was discreetly published in the annual report of 1921:

> In 1921, organizing and awareness-raising have been directed toward internal stabilization. The Secretariat took the view that the strength now attained by the trade union movement requires a focus on educating and disciplining members to manage the tasks they encounter in trade union work. This is important, as the Secretariat by no means lacks ambition with regard to expanding the superficial perception of the membership that it is enough merely to possess a membership book and duly pay their membership fees. If the organization is to fulfill its role successfully as the means whereby the workers can defend the benefits they have already obtained and to prepare for and attain further improvements of an economic and social nature, it is necessary that the number of "supernumerary members" be reduced by awakening personal interest in and responsibility for the movement's work. The more the movement's scope increases, the greater the necessity of this deepening of understanding. (Landsorganisationen 1921, 38)

According to the LO Secretariat, the movement was unstable. The main cause of the stabilization problem at that time was the left-wing organizations. Moreover, the leadership stated that it was necessary to make the members more aware of what the LO stood for. LO members were to be educated in the functions of the trade union movement in order to awaken their personal interest. As the Secretariat put it, personal interest was the only way to escape the problem of "supernumerary" members—trade union members who assumed that their only duty to the union movement was to pay their membership dues. According to the Secretariat, a good trade union member should be involved in the everyday work of the union. The labor movement could not be successful with passive members.

Awakening personal interest among the members of an organization is important in developing loyalty and commitment to that organization; personal interest itself can be awakened through identification with the organization, according to organizational theory (Ashforth and Mael 1989; van Knippenberg and Ellemers 2003, 30–34). This important effect of awakening personal interest through organizational identification was clearly understood by the LO

Secretariat. Although the LO would continue to recruit new members, its leadership was aware that high membership numbers were no guarantee that the organization would be able to fulfill its mission. To do that, loyal and devoted members who were aware of the organization's aims were crucial, and loyalty would come through identification.

The personal engagement in the movement desired by the LO Secretariat was also intended to promote internalization—that is, the adoption of the organization's values by the members. In theory, this kind of engagement is a process that, much like loyalty, is likely to happen through identification with the organization (Ashforth and Mael 1989). The leaders' analysis suggests that the members did not understand what the trade union movement was aiming at—that is, the members did not understand what LO stood for. This can only be defined as an identity problem. Getting the individual members to understand who they were as LO members and what part they played in the organization were crucial in constructing a cohesive identity. The Secretariat's aim of realizing some of the potential of a strong organizational identity, including the internalization of values, would be achieved by consolidating the movement through teaching the members what the trade union movement stood for, by constructing a strong organizational identity.

At some level, the LO Secretariat clearly understood the importance of building a collective identity and what the logic of appropriateness entailed for the members. If the members could be brought to realize what the LO stood for, this would constrain their scope of action. If the organization was understood to be reformist, the members would be unable to join syndicalists in strikes because such action would not be compatible with LO membership.

With respect to the connection between identity formation and education, in their annual report of 1921 the LO leadership explicitly stated that the solution to the identity problem was to foster and educate the members. It would be difficult to control the identity formation process, a fact that the LO leaders certainly realized. Although an organization's leaders' actions can affect members' impressions and definitions of reality, the process of identity formation is never completely top-down because "organizational members are not reducible to passive consumers of managerially designed and designated identities" (Alvesson and Willmott 2002, 621). The LO leaders did the only thing they could do, which was to establish various institutions or structures that would encourage the members to view the organization in a certain way. In more concrete terms, the leaders could not control what happened on the local level in trade union education but could only launch an education system and hope for the best.

In the 1921 annual report, the leadership wrote that the LO's mobilization activities had switched that year from recruiting new members to "stabilizing the organization." The means of creating a cohesive—and *stable*—organization were also specified. The Secretariat wrote that the first measure taken to stabilize the movement was founding the magazine *Fackföreningsrörelsen* (The Trade Union Movement). Launching an in-house magazine had been discussed at LO congresses for over ten years, but nothing occurred until 1920, when a motion to start a magazine was finally adopted. The second means of accomplishing the "internal consolidation process" (Landsorganisationen 1921, 38) was to foster deeper engagement in the Workers' Educational Association (ABF). Finally, the Secretariat wrote that it had started a publication series, Landsorganisationens skriftserie (LO's Booklet Series), to spread ideas and information that would be useful to the members. In these ways, the LO leadership clearly linked the identity problems of the organization with education.

Solving the Problem: Leaders' Actions

On a discursive level, the LO Secretariat acknowledged the identity problem that threatened to tear the organization apart. Stabilizing this situation was to be achieved through education. The Secretariat's statement in the annual report 1921 provides some support for the thesis that the leaders of LO consciously attempted to manage identity formation in the organization. However, are there other pieces of evidence or indications that point in the same direction? To find out, it is necessary to examine the actions of the LO leadership to see how the Secretariat carried out its strategy.

Seizing Control of the Workers' Educational Association

The most important institution for popular education of the working class in the 1920s was the ABF. This association, founded in 1912 by the social democrat Rickard Sandler, was a "meta-organization" that organizations could join but individuals could not (this differs from the Workers' Educational Association in Britain, which individuals could join). The ABF was open to all social movements mobilizing the working class, including political parties, unions, the temperance movement, and the cooperative movement. The Cooperative Union (Kooperativa Förbundet, KF) was the ABF's biggest member organization (ABF 1920b) until 1921, when it was surpassed by the LO. Initially, the ABF had six member organizations: the KF, LO, SAP, SDU, Railroad Workers' Union, and Typographical Workers' Union (ABF 1912, 3). In 1913, the workers' temperance organization Nykterhetsorden Verdandi (NOV) joined (ABF 1913, 7). The ABF was funded through membership fees paid by member organizations in accordance with the number of individual members. In addition to being supported by the fees, ABF libraries were allocated funding by the state (Arvidson 1985, 116–17; Berg and Edquist 2017, 90; Heffler 1962, 25–35).

Local ABF associations, called "local education committees," had other local associations as members. However, a local association could not join the local ABF unless it was part of a national organization that was an ABF member. For example, local syndicalist associations were unable to join local ABF education committees until 1922, when the central organization of the SAC joined the ABF. The local ABF associations had far-reaching autonomy, and local activities differed from town to town, depending on the constitution of the local education committee.

The ABF offered various forms of education, including study circles, lectures, lecture courses, and correspondence courses. Any organization could arrange study circles, but the facilities provided by the ABF (including funding for books and access to the local ABF library) were accessible only to ABF members.

The ABF's main aim was to make information and literature accessible to workers by establishing libraries all over Sweden, with fiction being the most common genre in ABF libraries in the first few years. Popular education was not a new phenomenon; it had existed for some time in Sweden, in the form of people's high schools or folk colleges (Mustel 2018) and other study activities. The temperance movement, which also established libraries, often located on temperance movement premises, played an important role in these early popular education settings (Nerman 1952, 9–20). However, the temperance movement's educational provisions were quite unfocused compared with Sandler's vision, in which all forms of working-class education were gathered under a single umbrella organization.

Sandler introduced the study circle as the main tool of education in the ABF. The study circle was a democratic nonhierarchical vehicle of study. The posts of chair and secretary rotated among the members, since the idea was that everyone should learn the relevant skills, including how minutes should be taken. Participation in a democratic forum was an important skill for workers in its own right. The most common form of study circle was the reading circle, in which participants read and discussed particular books. The ABF provided syllabuses for such study circle courses. The local ABF organization would obtain financial support for the purchase of books, as the local ABF library would buy the required books and lend them to the circle. Once a particular circle stopped meeting, the books it used were available to other circles studying the same subject. The financial support that the ABF gave to local associations was usually calculated on the basis of financial circumstances. The study circle would collect money to buy books, and the ABF would usually match the amount the study circle participants had managed to raise. This procedure matched that of the government funding of the ABF in that funding covered half of a study circle's book costs (Heffler 1962, 48–49). Many circles were founded in the first years of the ABF; however, by the end of the 1910s, many of these circles had ceased to exist, prompting internal debate in the ABF about "circle death" and attempts being made to revive them (ABF 1915). The ABF was obviously interested in increasing the number of study circles, so the missing factor may have been the commitment of the member organizations. The LO remained fairly passive during the first ten years of the ABF's educational and awareness-raising efforts, paying the membership fees but not actively engaging in the work of educating the working class. This attitude on the part of the LO changed in the late 1910s.

Despite the LO's passivity, the ABF expanded quickly, generally due to the SDU and the SAP. By 1920, the ABF had local associations all over Sweden, along with libraries that could be used for study circles, correspondence courses, and individual reading. Because of this network of local education committees, taking control of the ABF would be a helpful step for the LO in using popular education to construct an organizational identity. Launching a new competing organization would have been much more difficult. Moreover, the government funding of such libraries, and indirectly the study circle activities, could only be obtained by nationwide "study associations" organizing popular education (Andersson 1980, 107), and organizing such an association would have been very costly.

When the ABF was founded in 1912, Sweden had only one labor party and one labor youth organization, so the inclusive policy of organizing education for *all* workers' organizations was uncontroversial. After the SAP and the SDU split in 1917, the situation became far more complex.

In 1918, the Left Party and the SAP's new youth organization, the Social Democratic Youth League (SSU), were granted membership in the ABF by its governing body, the ABF Representatives (ABF Representantskap 1918b, 10 May)—thus, two organizations had become four. Admitting these two new members met with no resistance in the ABF Representatives, possibly because the SAP-loyal SSU and the Left Party had applied for membership at the same time and the ABF had a well-established inclusive tradition.

At the first meeting at which the new organizations were represented, in 1919, Nils Flyg, the representative of SDU (which by then had become the Left Party's youth organization), proposed that the central bureau of the ABF should move from Brunnsvik in the Dalarna region to Stockholm. More importantly, Flyg also proposed changes in the ABF leadership. It was certainly true, he declared, that the ABF leader at the time, Rickard Sandler, had been the best person for the job in 1912, especially after he left Parliament and could focus solely on his job at the ABF. However, since Sandler had become editor of the newspaper *Ny Tid* in

Göteborg shortly after leaving Parliament, he had, according to Flyg, neglected the ABF. Moreover, Flyg continued, the ABF had grown considerably during the previous few years, making the workload for the ABF leader noticeably heavier than it had been in 1912. In particular, Flyg stated that the ABF's educational programs were not being developed (which was the main task of the ABF leader). For socialism to be realized, it was necessary for the ABF leader to focus on education, not administration. Flyg concluded his critique by stressing that Sandler indeed possessed the intellectual qualities required to be such a leader, as long as he focused on education (ABF Representantskap 1918a, 8 August).

These criticisms of Sandler were harsh. After all, the ABF was Sandler's project, and he had built it from the ground up. The fact that Sandler was also a prominent actor within the SAP and, despite loyalties to the left-wing's ideological position, had remained loyal to the party leader, Hjalmar Branting, during the party split, may have been one reason for this criticism.

Flyg's proposal to move the location of the central bureau of the ABF was rejected by the ABF Representatives. The votes of the various delegates were not recorded, but the president of the Railroad Workers' Union, Carl Vinberg, while agreeing with Flyg at the start of the discussion, seems to have rejected the proposal in the end (ABF Representantskap 1918a). Vinberg was also a member of the Left Party (even being a member of the party board from 1917 to 1918), so it is hardly surprising that he initially supported Flyg (Hansson 1936b, 1133).

Although moving the central bureau from Brunnsvik may have had logistical advantages, they were certainly not the only reason Flyg proposed this. Brunnsvik was already a stronghold of the reformist labor movement in 1918, and it may have been difficult for other organizations to gain full access to the ABF central bureau. Flyg's proposal could be interpreted as an attempt to break Sandler's and the SAP's grip on the ABF. Sandler himself responded to the proposal by declaring that he and his wife, Maja, wanted to take a one-year leave of absence from the ABF (ABF Representantskap 1918a).

It is difficult to know exactly how the social democratic representative, Gustav Möller, and the LO representative, Ernst Söderberg, interpreted Flyg's proposal; no records of internal discussions have been found in SAP or LO documents. Nevertheless, the facts speak for themselves. At their very first meeting with the ABF Representatives after obtaining membership in the ABF, the left-wing organizations attacked the reformist branch's organization of the popular education system, probably sending a warning signal to the reformist organizations.

In July 1919, Sandler returned to the ABF Representatives, this time as the SAP representative, replacing Möller, who had left the position that year. One of the last things Möller did as the SAP representative to the ABF was to propose a change in the organizational structure of the ABF Representatives.

In his proposal, Möller stated that the three biggest organizations—the SAP, LO, and KF—which provided 85 percent of the ABF's membership fees, ought to be guaranteed better representation in the ABF Representatives. At that time, the ABF had nine member organizations, and more wanted to join. Because the "big three" organizations contributed such a large proportion of the budget, Möller argued that they should have more influence over its use. Under the old voting rules governing the ABF Representatives, each member organization had one vote, giving the smaller organizations as much influence as the big ones. Möller suggested that the member organizations should be allocated votes in proportion to their size (ABF Representantskap 1919b, 13 July).

At that time, the voting procedures would have given the left-wing organizations a majority over the reformist organizations, if the left-wing organizations had managed to unite. In 1919, the Left Party, the SDU, and the SUP (the Young Socialist Party), were all members of the ABF. The SUP had been granted membership earlier that year (ABF Representantskap 1919c, 23 May). In addition to these organizations, the Railroad Workers' Union representative, Vinberg, was a member of the Left Party. Meanwhile, the SAC had grown and was putting considerable effort into organizing and education on its own account. Therefore, it was only a matter of time before the SAC applied for membership in the ABF (which it did in 1922). Such an event would give the left-wing organizations the majority if the three reformists—the LO, SAP, and SSU—were unable to rally support from the KF and the temperance movement (ABF Representantskap 1919b, 13 July).

The ABF Representatives failed to come to a decision, as the proposal was too important to be rushed through. Accordingly, the participants in the meeting agreed to adjourn (ABF Representantskap 1919b, 13 July). Another meeting was held in October 1919. Sandler, the appointed chair, started by presenting an economic report concluding that the membership fee for ABF was too low to cover expenses. Either ABF would have to change its activities and make cutbacks, or the membership fee would have to be increased. Sandler suggested a fee of 5 öre per member per organization, instead of the then-current 3 öre. The ABF Representatives all agreed that the fee should be raised, but several hesitated to give firm approval because the decision needed to be ratified by their organizations. The LO representative, Arvid Thorberg, was one of those who hesitated (ABF Representantskap 1919a, 9 October). Of course, starting the meeting with a discussion of the financial future of ABF reminded everyone who paid the greatest share of the study activities.

The next issue on the agenda was Möller's proposal to change the representation structure. Even though the debate on representation that followed did not refer back to the discussion of membership fees, it was probably very clear to everyone what the financial conditions were. Both the KF's representative, Emil Öhrne, and Eduard Viberg of the Typographical Workers' Union supported restructuring the ABF Representatives. However, Viberg also suggested that the number of members in the ABF Representatives should stay the same and that only the numbers of votes should vary depending on the size of their respective organizations. Fredrik Ström, the representative of the Left Party, was then given the floor. Ström claimed that the suggested change could undermine the cohesiveness of the ABF. He emphasized that the small organizations would never try to push through reforms that the large organizations did not support. Ström even went so far as to say that he could not guarantee that the Left Party would remain a member of the ABF under the new rules (ABF Representantskap 1919a, 9 October). Sandler explained that when he had written the then-current rules, the organization had three large and three small member organizations. However, several additional small organizations had since joined the ABF, justifying the suggested restructuring. Sandler also stressed that ABF unity was important and that a solution that everyone could accept was therefore preferable. Sandler proposed that the ABF Representatives appoint a subcommittee to come up with a proposal. He also suggested that Ström himself be part of the committee, along with Öhrne (KF) and Vinberg (Railroad Workers' Union). Ström replied that although he did not oppose changes in the provisions, he believed that every member organization should have due influence. He declined to take part in the committee and suggested that Flyg, the SDU representative, participate instead. For his part, Flyg regretted that this issue had been put on the agenda—in his view, it opened the door to political conflicts. Flyg also stressed the importance of keeping the organization united. Issues that could not be resolved with the then-current ABF voting procedures should instead be resolved by the leaders of the member organizations, not the ABF Representatives. Thorberg, the LO representative, said little at the meeting and was not involved in the debate. Unsurprisingly, Thorberg supported Sandler's proposal and declared that the LO would not accept anything less than a change in the voting procedure (ABF Representantskap 1919a, 9 October).

This debate revealed a number of fault lines among the ABF Representatives. The small left-wing organizations, the Left Party, and the SDU were obviously opposed to any change. In contrast, the other small member organizations, such as the Railroad Workers' Union and the Typographical Workers' Union, supported the large organizations on principle. Representatives of both organizations expressed their understanding that it was unfair for the "big three" to make the biggest financial contribution but not have proportionate influence. Although the reformist parties—the LO, SSU, and SAP—wanted change, Sandler was clear that change should not compromise ABF unity. All the representatives expressed concern about the ABF's future if the organization were to become a battlefield for the different branches of the labor movement. This concern may have indicated genuine concern about popular education and the labor movement, but it could also be interpreted as a mere debating point used to discredit other factions.

A subcommittee was appointed consisting of Flyg, Öhrne, Vinberg, and Thorberg; they were given a few hours to prepare a proposal that would be discussed in the evening of the same day. The subcommittee's proposal in its original form unfortunately has not survived, and the debate that followed was very short. The ABF Representatives approved the subcommittee's proposal (ABF Representantskap 1919a, 9 October). The adopted proposal followed Möller's original suggestion that votes in the ABF Representatives be proportionate to the number of members. Furthermore, any organization with fewer than five thousand members would not be entitled to a representative in the governing body (ABF Representantskap 1920a, 23 September).

These changes in the provisions changed the composition of the ABF Representatives, shifting the power relations within the ABF. The timing of these changes prevented the left-wing organizations from gaining any notable influence over the ABF. The reformist labor movement likely perceived the left-wing organizations' presence on the ABF Representatives as a threat and took action. Seizing control of the Representatives was important because it determined the content of the popular education disseminated by the ABF. This would be particularly important, from the LO's point of view, if they were to use popular education as a means of identity formation. With several left-wing organizations already in the ABF, and with the SAC applying for membership, the reformist organizations would no longer be guaranteed a majority. A few years later, the Left Party split into two parts: the Communist Party, which was loyal to Moscow and joined the Comintern, and another Left Party. This split resulted in even more labor movement organizations in Sweden. Notably, the Communist Party also joined the ABF. Thanks to Möller's proposal, however, the reformist organizations had a majority in the ABF Representatives (ABF Representantskap 1919a, 9 October; ABF Representantskap 1919b, 13 July; ABF 1920b).

Establishing *Fackföreningsrörelsen*

Another tool that could be used to stabilize the LO, as pointed out in the annual report of 1921, and that had an obvious connection to popular education was the magazine *Fackföreningsrörelsen*. Herman Lindqvist's unexpected departure from the LO opened the door to a new leadership. The man appointed Lindqvist's successor was the secretary of the LO, Arvid Thorberg, who had been secretary since 1908 and had therefore witnessed the failed general strike from the inside

(Hansson 1930b). During his time as LO secretary, Thorberg had traveled around Sweden as an organizer, giving him experience of debating with the grassroots and acquainting him with the ideological tendencies of LO members throughout the country (Hansson 1930b).

After taking office in February 1920, one of Thorberg's first actions was to revive an idea that had been repeatedly debated over the past ten years: publishing a magazine for the organization. Although the affiliated unions had their own magazines focusing on internal matters, the LO did not and thus lacked a good communication channel to the trade union members. Given the growing support for the Left Party and the syndicalist movement in some LO affiliates, this lack had proven troublesome for the LO. A weekly magazine could make good that shortcoming and, moreover, promote the LO's organizational identity.

The LO congress had several times discussed starting an LO magazine. In 1909, a congress decision empowered the Secretariat to start a weekly magazine at any time it deemed appropriate (Landsorganisationen 1909, 125–29). Interestingly, the question of a magazine did not originate from the Secretariat. Because of major membership losses in the aftermath of the general strike and a resulting decrease in financial resources, the magazine was not prioritized in 1909. At the congress in 1912, the Secretariat was again asked to reconsider the idea of a magazine, but it responded that it was not the time (Landsorganisationen 1912, 141). In the 1917 congress, the idea of starting a weekly magazine was once again proposed. This time, the Secretariat acknowledged the advantages of a magazine: "In the course of the fragmentation of the Swedish labor movement, several magazines have emerged that have shown a strong tendency to exacerbate these divisions, even within the trade union movement. A real need has therefore emerged for Landsorganisationen to have a magazine of its own" (Landsorganisationen 1917, 94). The congress decided to start a magazine, but once again the LO Secretariat was empowered to judge when the time was right; for example, the Secretariat considered that 1917 was not a good time because of the war and its economic implications, including inflation (Landsorganisationen 1917, 88–96).

When Thorberg came to office, however, he decided to launch the magazine that had been debated for so long. It is unclear why the magazine had been postponed during the presidency of Herman Lindqvist, as the affiliates supported the idea (the proposals at congresses came from various affiliates, not the Secretariat) and would probably also have provided financial support. Furthermore, the Secretariat acknowledged in 1917 that other organizations' magazines were causing the LO problems, even though this assessment was not enough to persuade the Secretariat to start a magazine of its own. One can question Lindqvist's judgment in this case; it is entirely possible that Lindqvist underestimated the usefulness of such a magazine, and perhaps he underestimated the whole fragmentation problem. Thorberg's assumption of the presidency cer-tainly meant a change of course in this regard.

If Thorberg and the LO Secretariat wanted to use *Fackföreningsrörelsen* for identity formation, they would have been very careful in appointing its editor. Sigfrid Hansson (Landssekretariatet 1920c) was an excellent choice for this role, although Thorberg could hardly have foreseen how useful Hansson was going to be to the LO.

Hansson began his career in the SDU in Malmö, along with his brother Per Albin and Gustav Möller. Originally a mason, Hansson quickly became involved in politics and was one of the founders of the SDU in 1903. His first assignment as a journalist was in 1905, when he started to work for the magazine *Ny Tid*. In 1908, Hansson began to write for *Social-demokraten*; he also published articles in the SDU's magazine *Fram*, which his brother was editing. Like his brother, Hansson had been part of the "conservative" wing in the youth organization, and he continued as a conservative voice in the LO Secretariat. During the First World War, he worked as a correspondent in Åland; after the war, he returned to Sweden and resumed work for *Social-demokraten*, until Thorberg recruited him (Dahl 1946).

Hansson's first assignment for the LO that can be traced in the Secretariat's minutes was to report Lindqvist's resignation, some months before Hansson started to work for *Fackföreningsrörelsen*. On Monday, 2 February 1920, the day after Lindqvist resigned as LO president, the Secretariat assembled, and the members were surprised to note that the turn of events on the weekend had gone unnoticed by the press. After a short debate, the remainder of the Secretariat decided to write a press release that included Lindqvist's official explanation for his decision: that he had been in office for a long time and wanted to let a younger trade unionist take over. The Secretariat decided that this press release should be written by a skilled writer, to avoid any more negative publicity on the subject, and assigned the task to Sigfrid Hansson (Landssekretariatet 1920a, 2 February).

The inaugural issue of *Fackföreningsrörelsen* was published in December 1920; the magazine was then published weekly starting from the beginning of 1921. The magazine's primary aim was to convey debate on current issues such as working hours, collective bargaining, and social policy to local sections, while its secondary aim was to improve the level of education of Swedish workers. Hansson gave the magazine an international character typical of the era, as the labor movement in the 1920s was international. Keeping up to date with labor movements in other countries showed solidarity and helped members learn how other union move-ments solved problems and organized themselves. Approximately one article in each issue dealt with a foreign labor movement, and there was also a column with press items from abroad. Hansson often published articles written by foreign labor movement activists or theorists (Landsorganisationen 1920–1926). Because of his international ambitions, Hansson was well connected to the European and US union movements.[1] The magazine also dealt with theoretical subjects such as the foundations of Marxism, industrial democracy, and social democracy (see, e.g., Lindström 1924; Wigforss 1921). Nevertheless, Hansson was apparently cautious about publishing articles written by outside authors, sometimes even sending articles for prepublication review by specialists (Hansson 12 April 1926). By the time Hansson started editing *Fackföreningsrörelsen* in 1920, he had accumulated considerable journalistic experience in the labor movement's various newspapers, although he was still fairly inexperienced as an author. He quickly established himself as the most prominent contemporary historian of the Swedish trade union movement of the 1920s. Hansson published several books, most of which presented the history of different affiliates, and he also wrote about various social movements in Sweden.[2] With his very distinctive writing style, characterized by an objective, scientific tone, Hansson's writings proved very useful when the LO needed course material for study activities.

The reason for appointing Sigfrid Hansson as editor is not clearly expressed in the minutes of either the LO Secretariat or Representatives, but he was a good choice because of his connections to the SAP, his experience as an editor and writer, and his working-class background. Because of his relationship to Per Albin Hansson, he had a strong connection to the SAP; in fact, shortly after he started working for *Fackföreningsrörelsen*, he became a member of Parliament representing the SAP. Choosing the right editor was also obviously important for the LO's education strategy, and Hansson was a good match for that too. He was devoted to popular education and unafraid of being controversial, to the extent that he sometimes even advocated conservative positions.

The magazine was meant to be read by the local sections, and chapter 5 presents a discussion of just how widely read the magazine actually was. The LO Secretariat tried to induce as many LO local sections and members as possible to subscribe. Every year, sometimes several times, the Secretariat sent messages to the local sections urging them to subscribe. The LO even subsidized subscriptions in certain cases (Landsorganisationen 1923a; Landsorganisationen 1924d; Landsorganisationen 1925c; Landsorganisationen 1927a; Landsorganisationen 1928a). Clearly, the magazine was considered so important for the LO's educational mission that the Secretariat was willing to put extra resources into it. Hansson's hostility toward syndicalists and communists meant that he was criticized for publishing disparaging articles about the left-wing organizations aligned with them (Landsorganisationen 1922b, 208–15). As the editor of *Fackföreningsrörelsen*, Hansson wrote weekly analyses of recent events, which may have been the most important arena for disseminating ideas in the movement. Many of the articles published in *Fackföreningsrörelsen* were, moreover, used as literature in the study circle courses on "trade union studies" and "organizational studies." Hansson was undoubtedly in a favorable position to spread his personal interpretations of developments, as will be analyzed in chapter 4.

Changing the Organizing Strategy

The statement in the 1921 annual report proclaimed that organizing was to be directed internally instead of toward unorganized workers and SAC members. Recruiting new members was to be subordinated to nurturing the LO's existing members. Until the 1920s in the LO, "organizing" had referred only to recruiting new members through political speeches. Of course, popular education could also be a way of recruiting new members, although that was never the aim. Both the lectures and study circles were intended to enlighten the workers. Instead, in the annual report, the LO Secretariat suggested integrating the organizing and enlightening activities, which would obscure the difference between organizing and education. If the LO was to use trade union education as a means of forming identity in the organization, it was seen that the organizing activities ought to mirror this effort and, for example, focus on lectures for the members on the trade union movement.

What is known today about the LO's organizing efforts? The main methods used to disseminate the ideas of the labor movement in the late nineteenth century were organizers and newspapers. Research into early social democracy in Sweden reveals that the spread of the SAP in Sweden occurred through meso-level networks of organizers in the last decades of the nineteenth century (Gröning 1988, 72–80; Hedström, Sandell, and Stern 2000). Thus, outreach by traveling activists was important in mobilizing the working class.

A full-time "organizing ombudsman" (*agitationsombudsman*) was hired in 1907 and assigned the task of leading, coordinating, and administering the LO's organizing and recruiting activities. Claes Emil Tholin was a member of the SAP board and worked in close cooperation with Herman Lindqvist. During Tholin's time as the organizing ombudsman, organizing and recruiting took the form of organizing tours; that is, Tholin himself spent most of his time traveling around Sweden to agitate at mass meetings (Landsorganisationen 1919, 45–49). Tholin resigned from his post at the end of 1919 when the government made him a representative on the Work Council (Arbetsrådet), tasked with overseeing the implementation of the eight-hour day (Landsorganisationen 1919, 47). At the annual meeting of the LO Representatives in May 1920, a new ombudsman was appointed, Per Bergman (Landsorganisationen 1919, 129). Unfortunately, little information is available about Bergman. He was a carpenter who began his career in the SDU before becoming active in the union movement (Fackföreningsrörelsen 1938; Hansson 1909). Bergman had been black-listed by the Swedish Employers' Association after the general strike in 1909 (Fackföreningsrörelsen 1938; Hansson 1936b, 229; Koch 1912) but was eventually appointed ombudsman of the Wood Industry Workers' Union. Three years later, Bergman was appointed to the LO post. In 1930, he advanced to become the secretary of the LO Secretariat (Fackföreningsrörelsen 1938). Along with Hansson and Thorberg, Bergman seems to have played a central role in implementing the LO's identity formation strategy.

With Bergman's appointment, the LO's approach to organizing changed. The LO Representatives decided that constant traveling was inefficient and that organizing would improve if the ombudsman remained in Stockholm and gave fewer speeches but ones that conveyed more carefully crafted messages. The Representatives also decided that the organizing ombudsman should write promotional material for the newly established booklet series (Bergman 1920; Landsorganisationen 1920, 75, 126).

Nevertheless, organizing tours continued in the 1920s, albeit with some changes. The members of the LO Secretariat were very involved in education and organizing, and trips around the country for talks and speeches were undertaken by Bergman and the whole Secretariat. The Secretariat even held its own ABF lecture courses in Stockholm (ABF 1928; Landssekretariatet 1921a; Bergman's reports). That the members of the Secretariat personally gave so many lectures indicates the importance the LO attached to education and organizing. Of course, this commitment also enabled the Secretariat to control what was said at such meetings. No complete figures remain on how many lectures were held every year, but data are available on individual years. For example, Bergman himself gave 108 lectures at meetings with the rank and file in 1922 and 185 in 1925 (Landsorganisationen 1922a, 58; Landsorganisationen 1925a). In 1934, members of the Secretariat gave approximately 180 lectures all over Sweden, most of which were given by the president and the secretary (Landssekretariatet 1934a). Having the leaders give talks in person not only demonstrated that the highest level of the LO took an interest in engaging with the grassroots. It also showed an important part of practicing identity entrepreneurship—namely, that how leaders act, talk, and behave shapes how members perceive an organization. Charismatic leadership can come to personify the organization through the routinization of charisma (Ashforth and Mael 1989, 22). However, for such a process to take place, the leaders must be visible to the rank and file.

The most profound change in organizing strategies was the hiring of more organizing ombudsmen (*agitationsombudsmän*). These were posted in regions where the Secretariat considered extra support for the local sections to be necessary. Norrland was prioritized because the Left Party and later the Communist Party and the SAC enjoyed strong support there, with the SAC being particularly successful in the mining industry. In the 1910s, the SAC and the Mining Industry Workers' Union—an LO affiliate—were equally significant in the most important mining district, Kiruna; in the 1920s, the local section of the Mining Industry Workers' Union regularly cooperated with the SAC (Eriksson 1991, 338–42; Horgby 2012, 42n6). The Left Party had supporters in Norrbotten, Västerbotten, Gävleborg, Kopparberg, Värmland, Stockholm, and Göteborg (Dalin 2007, 39–40; Horgby 2012, 43), and the Communist Party was successful in the mining, metal, paper, and construction industries (Horgby 2012, 48)—all important industries largely located in Norrland.

In 1924, the LO Secretariat accordingly informed the LO's affiliates that it had hired two organizing ombudsmen to agitate and educate in Norrland, particularly in the regions north of Sundsvall. The Secretariat encouraged the affiliates to mail the names and addresses of local section activists to the Secretariat so that the ombudsmen could contact them (Landsorganisationen 1924a; Thorberg 1925). The ombudsmen provided a new channel for direct contact between the grassroots and the LO, which must have been exactly what the Secretariat wanted. Direct contact could provide the leaders with better information about the grassroots in regions where the LO was threatened by left-wing organizations, and could also act as a channel for spreading the image of the organization approved by the LO leadership.

The first organizing ombudsman, David Berg, was hired to agitate in the region of Norrbotten. Berg had a background as an ombudsman in the Metal Industry Workers' Union and was therefore familiar with the situation facing the reformist unions in Norrbotten, a county in which the metal sector was very important and communists and syndicalists enjoyed alarmingly strong support among LO members (Casparsson 1951, 568; Landsorganisationen 1922a, 58; Landsorganisationen 1924c). The second organizing ombudsman, Fridolf Widén, worked for the Wood Industry Workers' Union and came from Östersund, where he also was stationed as ombudsman (Landsorganisationen 1922b, 13; Landsorganisationen 1924a).

The ombudsmen regularly sent reports to the Secretariat about their work and the developments in the region. Particular attention was paid to the left-wing organizations' activities. Parts of the reports from the late 1920s and early 1930s are preserved. These documents clarify the LO Secretariat's intentions regarding the organizing ombudsmen. First, the ombudsmen were obviously tasked with preventing communists from infiltrating the LO unions and with stopping local sections from supporting the communists and syndicalists, thus dealing with "the enemy within the movement" problem. Second, the ombudsmen were tasked with preventing, as far as possible, the syndicalists from forming local sections. In villages or towns where no left-wing organizations had yet founded local organizations, the ombudsmen were required to strengthen the reformist unions, preventing communists and syndicalists from forming competing organizations (Sätterberg 1928b; Sätterberg 1932a; Sätterberg 1932b; Thorberg 1924). The reports from the organizers testify to a race between the SAC and the LO to organize the workers in Norrland.[3] Recruiting unorganized workers—of whom there were plenty in Norrland—could strengthen the SAC considerably, so the LO needed to preempt the SAC and recruit these workers first.

Similar reports have been preserved from Bergman's organizing tours. The surviving reports written by Bergman reveal that the LO Secretariat was worried about the left-wing organizations. Bergman reported in detail on communist and syndicalist attendance at meetings, whether there were left-wing organizations in local towns and villages, and whether there was a risk of these organizations becoming more influential (Bergman 1929a; Bergman 1929b).

No reports from Widén survived, so little is known about his work. Widén was stationed in Jämtland, where it had been difficult to organize the workers in the 1920s. The region was marginally industrialized, and the main industry was forestry. The forest workers had no history of organizing (unlike skilled workers, whose unions emerged from the guild system), so they were difficult to organize and were more open to the novelty of the syndicalists. The SAC was very successful in the forest industry (Karlbom 1968, 213–34; Persson 1991, 37–45), and of the forty-one hundred trade union members in Jämtland in 1920, 34 percent were members of the SAC (Rolén and Thomasson 1990, 259).

In 1925, the LO Secretariat hired an additional organizing ombudsman, Ernst Sätterberg, who was stationed in Skellefteå in the county of Västerbotten (Casparsson 1951, 568). In Västerbotten, forestry was the most prominent sector, and the main occupational groups were forestry workers (*skogs- och flottning*) and sawmill workers. In these occupational groups, the syndicalists had fairly strong support.

Sätterberg's activities are not described in much detail in the materials, though some things are clear from the reports sent to the LO Secretariat. Sätterberg traversed the region regularly and visited approximately ten to fifteen different local sections every month. His mission was to facilitate negotiations, recruit new members, establish new sections, and hold "instructional meetings." Sätterberg occasionally reported that he had helped to establish new sections for LO affiliates in particular workplaces before the SAC managed to do so (Sätterberg 1928b). The "instructional meetings" were by far the most common kind of meeting in 1928. What exactly they involved is not described in the reports, but they were directed toward LO members (Sätterberg 1928a; Sätterberg 1928b).

Sätterberg always commented on whether or not the section had managed to get its members to attend the meeting; if not, he would demand that the section arrange a new meeting. What "instruction" was given to the sections is also difficult to ascertain, but these meetings may have been forums in which Sätterberg talked about the trade union movement and instructed local sections on organizational work (in other words, the content of the study circle course on "organizational studies"). However, it is known from the reports that Sätterberg's main activity was to organize meetings with LO members; in other words, the organizing activities were "directed inward" as the Secretariat claimed they would be in the annual report of 1921.

Sätterberg revisited the same sections and held instructional meetings there repeatedly. In this way, his approach to organize differed from that of Tholin when he was organizing ombudsman. Since Tholin had been working on his own, he had been unable to spend much time in individual sections. His aim had been to cover a large part of Sweden; however, because of the large area involved, his organizing tours was more superficial and fragmented than were the targeted organizing activities in the 1920s, which strengthened the local trade union movement and probably contributed to more active grassroots. The efforts of Sätterberg as organizing ombudsman were mainly directed toward ensuring that the sections remained active. If Sätterberg visited a section that was "dying," as he sometimes put it in his reports, he would talk to the section's board and demand that they act to revive the grassroots (Sätterberg 1928a; Sätterberg 1928b).

This organizing effort was exclusive to the "troublesome regions" in the north. The LO district in the southern region of Skåne—where, in addition to the LO, the SAP had strong support early on—asked for an organizing ombudsman, arguing that the party's district organization was too busy to handle all the organizing activities. However, the LO Secretariat rejected the request, arguing that northern Sweden needed these ombudsmen more (Landsorganisationen 1936, 526–30). The organizing ombudsmen were not intended to support member organizations that were already reformist in orientation.

The Secretariat appears to have allotted more resources to organizing activities in the 1920s than in the decades before. Although little is known about the LO's organizing activities before 1920 (there are no reports archived), it is clear that things changed. Recruiting new members was no longer the sole goal of the LO's organizing activities, and educational elements became discernible.

Establishing the LO School

The trade union school in Brunnsvik, in the Dalarna region, opened for the first groups of trade unionists in the summer of 1929. The school had its origins in a proposal tabled at the LO congress in 1926 (Landsorganisationen 1926b). The idea of a high school for workers had been proposed from the very start of the labor movement. Unsurprisingly, Rickard Sandler was the main proponent of the school, writing a booklet on the subject as early as 1908 (Sandler 1908). The idea of a workers' high school was characteristic of the reformist socialist tradition. The youth organizations were particularly devoted to the idea of "raising" the workers intellectually through education, and popular education—study circles and, above all, the establishment of libraries—was promoted by socialist youth organizations of all types.

A workers' high school was also discussed in the ABF. In 1913, Fredrik Ström, the SAP's representative to the ABF at that time (although he became the representative for the Left Party after 1917), initiated an ABF feasibility study of starting a workers' high school (ABF Representantskap 1913). The ABF's involvement in such a school is unsurprising, since Sandler was the executive leader of the ABF in the 1910s. The ABF Representatives launched a thorough investigation into the costs, goals, and practicalities of starting such a school (ABF Representantskap 1915). However, although the issue was revisited several times, no progress was made (ABF Representantskap 1920b). The ABF instead arranged summer courses at the people's high school in Brunnsvik thanks to an agreement between it and the school's board, but that was as far as the idea went (ABF Representantskap 1918a). One reason why the idea of an ABF school was not implemented may have been a certain reluctance on the part of the LO and the SAP to pursue such a major project jointly with the other organizations. As the largest members of the ABF, the reformist organizations would certainly have had to contribute the most financially, and they were probably unwilling to pay for education for their competitors. Moreover, the reformist organizations eventually became big enough, and were motivated enough, to create a system of their own. The LO had shown interest in starting a school for internal education for quite some time and had dispatched people, including Hansson, to study similar schools in Germany, Britain, and Austria. One alternative to starting an LO school was cooperation between the union movement and a university. Such cooperation existed in Great Britain between the trade union movement and Ruskin College in Oxford (Landsorganisationen 1924e; Landsorganisationen 1926a; Landsorganisationen 1929). The LO decided against such a system in Sweden.

The proposal to start a workers' high school was suggested by a section of the Brewery Industry Workers' Union in Stockholm (Landsorganisationen 1926b, 400–401). The numerous debates at LO congresses regarding opening a workers' high school had never resulted in action (much like the debates about an LO magazine). By 1926, however, things had changed, and the LO Secretariat apparently came to value workers' education more than previously. The congress decided to investigate the costs and practicalities of starting the school. This investigation, which also considered possible cooperation with the ABF and the people's high school in Brunnsvik (Landsorganisationen 1926b, 401–2), led to the establishment of a school. The main idea behind the LO's school was to offer courses on trade unionism to members, and Sigfrid Hansson was given the task of designing it (Hansson 1928c; Nordin 1981, 439–40).

Founded in June 1906 by Karl-Erik Forsslund, Uno Stadius, and Gustaf Ancarcrona, Brunnsvik People's High School quickly became a people's high school with strong connections to the labor movement (Furuland 1968, 311–14; Söderqvist 2019, 59–63). Because of Forsslund's positive and cooperative attitude toward the labor movement (although he was not a party member), the school lost its funding from the municipality, leading to crowdfunding of the school for a few years, during which various organizations, including labor organizations, were the main funders (Heffler 1962; Johansson 2002; Nordin 1981; Söderqvist 2019). Forsslund was reluctant to have formal attachments to political parties, however, so the school remained independent of the labor movement organizations (Heffler 1962).

The people's high school in Brunnsvik had been used before by the LO and the ABF for courses, particularly summer courses, in trade union studies (Hansson 14 June 1923); thus, it was a natural choice for the LO to locate its own school nearby. The LO acquired land connected to the people's high school and built new buildings there, including residences for the students. The affiliates had access to the buildings and could organize courses of their own (Brunnsvik 1930, 6). The LO school required a manager and a study leader, the latter being responsible for supervising education and imposing a logical framework on the various subjects. This important task was assigned to Hansson himself (Landsorganisationen 1928b, 7). Once the LO school began, summer and winter courses were prioritized.

In 1929, the very first summer course was offered at the LO school (Brunnsvik 1930, 6). This twelve-week course comprised five blocks of subjects. It had been established in Hansson's preparatory reports that "trade union studies" were to be given a prominent place in the instruction (Hansson 1928c), and the biggest block of subjects covered the labor movement's history, trade union studies, and social policy. The second block covered macroeconomics, statistics, and economic geography (Landsorganisationen 1928b). These were all subjects that were important to the labor movement. In addition to these ideological subjects, general subjects were included in the summer course, although fewer hours were spent on them. These subjects were Swedish, English, German, mathematics, and book-keeping (Landsorganisationen 1928b). Hansson recruited an impressive list of teachers for the summer course. The future minister of finance and one

of the designers of the Swedish welfare state, Ernst Wigforss, taught macroeconomics, Rickard Sandler taught statistics, Hansson himself taught trade union
studies, and lecturer Gunnar Hirdman taught the history of the labor movement (Landsorganisationen 1928b). The LO school at Brunnsvik quickly became
a school for the labor movement elite and a gathering place for leading social
democrats and trade union officers.

The establishment of the LO school at Brunnsvik showed how highly the
LO Secretariat valued education. The school's elite character revealed its participants to be devoted labor movement activists. The teachers and students at
Brunnsvik were convinced reformists who were crucial for union work in Sweden; their commitment to the movement and to LO was important in constructing an organizational identity. The school at Brunnsvik is examined further
in chapter 4.

Controlling the Study Leader Courses

Given that education was a means of constructing an organizational identity, it is
likely that the LO's leaders wished to control education at the local level as much
as they could. Such control was fairly difficult to exercise because the grassroots
had considerable freedom in organizing study activities. The central organization
of the ABF provided individual study circles with syllabi, but the individual study
circles made the final decisions on what to study. Even though the LO made sure
that the material used in the circles had the right content, there were no guarantees that the circles would use the material provided, as the study circles were free
and voluntary. Moreover, since the circles lacked teachers, it was very difficult to
control the circles' activities.

One way of controlling the circles was through the study leader courses introduced by the ABF. Study leaders were officers appointed to help local education committees and trade union sections get started with and run study circles.
Rather than being teachers, these leaders were instructors who provided local
support for study circles. Different subjects had different study leader courses.
The subject of trade union studies, the most important course for the LO (thoroughly analyzed in chapters 4 and 5), was managed by Hansson from 1923
onward (Heffler 1962, 44–45, 71–75, 111). Workers who wanted to become study
leaders and instruct local associations in how to run study circles in trade union
studies were required to read the course material for trade union studies, the
book *Den svenska fackföreningsrörelsen* (The Swedish Trade Union Movement)
by Hansson; they also had to complete a questionnaire. The completed forms
were sent to Hansson personally for marking; if he was not satisfied with the
answers, he would return the form, marked up in red ink, to the study leader

aspirant. The questions asked on the form covered some of the most important aspects of the book and helped determine whether the would-be study leaders had actually read the course material. However, in particular, the questions covered what Hansson considered crucial issues, mainly concerning the characteristics of reformist trade unions. One question dealing with the origins of trade unions in Sweden is particularly interesting. In his answer template, Hansson stated that the Swedish trade unions did not originate from socialism, nor had they supported socialism in the past. Rather, the Swedish trade unions originated from liberalism (also see chapter 4) (Hansson 1929).

In this historical account, Hansson was clearly distancing himself from class identity. Denying any affinity with socialism, as discussed in the next chapter, was a way of distancing LO members from the left-wing organizations. Asking about this concept within the framework of study leader education was a way of finding out whether those trying to become study leaders were social democrats or whether they believed in revolution. After all, if successful, study leaders would come into contact with many members, so it was important to ensure that the ideas they disseminated were reformist. The questionnaire was also a way for Hansson to learn who these people were and where they lived. The surviving material for the study leader education comprises no more than an outline of the content, so it is unknown what the information on the participants in the study leader courses was used for. However, it is clear that Hansson possessed considerable information about the grassroots. Furthermore, in his capacity as editor of *Fackföreningsrörelsen*, Hansson had access to the LO Secretariat, was engaged in organizing, and traveled around the country lecturing on trade unionism. It is reasonable to assume that Hansson had frequent contact with Bergman, LO's chief organizing ombudsman. It would have been easy for Hansson to pass on whatever information he collected through the study leader course to the organizing ombudsmen.

Education as Means of Identity Formation

An analysis of minutes, reports, and other documentation reveals how much effort the LO put into popular education. To what extent was this effort part of a deliberate strategy? The LO Secretariat did explicitly define the organization's problems as identity problems and did choose popular education as the solution to these problems. Moreover, how the Secretariat referred to agitation and education coherently linked the perceived problems with their causes and proposed solutions.

However, the LO Secretariat's intentions regarding education are expressed only in one statement in the annual report from 1921. Could there have been other reasons why the Secretariat put such an emphasis on popular education? The simultaneous efforts to control the ABF, launch the magazine, and apply a new approach to organizing, all of which focused on education, could not have been merely coincidental, considering how much time and how many resources were devoted to these activities.

Another explanation of the changes in the LO's approach in the early 1920s could be the introduction of the eight-hour workday in 1919—an important victory for the workers. The matter had been under examination for years, not only in Sweden but in the international labor movement. In Sweden, the working day had been ten hours, six days a week, so the eight-hour day shortened the working day by two hours, giving workers more leisure time (Wallander 1982, 37–41). However, opponents of the eight-hour day argued that the extra two hours of leisure each day were an important negative effect of the reform, aside from losses in productivity and lowered incomes. The critics, mainly from the Employers' Association and the Right Party, were concerned about what the workers would do with this spare time. According to them, the extra leisure time presented a risk of increasing alcoholism and related problems, such as gambling and "sinful living" in general. Ensuring that the workers did something worthwhile with their time was therefore important for the labor movement. One way of handling the spare time problem was popular education, under the supervision of the ABF (ABF 1919; ABF 1924a).

However, the eight-hour day is not mentioned in existing documentation from the LO Secretariat as a reason for particular action regarding popular education. Moreover, the potential problems associated with a shorter working day do not appear to have been perceived by the LO as more serious than the threat posed by the left-wing organizations. Although the greater free time afforded by the eight-hour workday made it easier for the LO to convince workers to join study circles, it was hardly the main reason for the LO's engagement in popular education. If the main reason for emphasizing the importance of education was to rescue the workers from their spare time, there would have been no need to take control of the ABF. Moreover, the type of education the workers engaged in would not have made a difference. Any education, whether about fiction or gardening, would have been sufficient to keep the workers occupied. However, as revealed in chapter 5, the "hobby" circles covering such innocuous topics constituted only a small share of the study circle courses; the most common study courses were those on trade union studies.

Another possibility is that the LO Secretariat was coming to accept the ideas on education of socialist theorists. The LO's increased efforts to persuade workers to participate in education could simply have been an implementation of these ideas. In that case, however, why were such efforts not made before the split of the labor movement? The efforts to promote workers' education were made *after* the split of the labor movement had created challenges for the Secretariat. Stressing the importance of education and encouraging members to participate would not necessarily have involved exerting control over the ABF Representatives. If enlightenment was the overall aim of the LO, it could have been done through the old organizational structure. Moreover, control of the study leader courses would have been unnecessary. The only plausible conclusion is that the Secretariat wanted to control what was taught in the study circles.

A reasonable interpretation of the actions of the LO Secretariat assigns great importance to Thorberg, Hansson, and Bergman. Thorberg perceptively realized the seriousness of the growth of the left-wing organizations and recruited Hansson and Bergman. Thorberg redirected the LO's contacts with the grassroots toward identity-building. Instead of organizing tours, whose only aim was to recruit new members, organizing activities were redirected toward teaching members about reformism. The LO controlled popular education as much as it could. As discussed in chapter 5, popular education was free and voluntary; indeed, these were the conditions of state funding. As a result, the LO could not force members to attend popular education but could only encourage participation and control the administrative infrastructure. It did so by organizing study leader education and creating syllabi for study circle courses. Thorberg's takeover constituted a critical juncture at which the reformist union movement changed its strategy toward the left-wing organizations.

Looking at all the various actions taken by the LO Secretariat regarding education and agitation, a fuller picture emerges of the Secretariat's position on the problems posed by the left-wing organizations and on the role of popular education. Although incomplete, the picture we have does lend support to the thesis presented here. The next step is to focus on the materials used in that popular education.

4

CONSTRUCTING IDENTITY

In 1921, the LO Secretariat declared that "the magnitude now attained by the trade union movement requires a focus on educating and disciplining members to manage the tasks they encounter in trade union work" (Landsorganisationen 1921). The subsequent actions of the Secretariat indicate that the LO attempted to actively construct and enforce a collective identity in the face of the threat from the left-wing organizations. However, the thesis of this book—namely, that the LO used popular education to construct an organizational identity—also suggests that the identity under construction was not that of "workers in general" but rather of a *particular kind* of worker, the LO member, who embraced reformism and a spirit of consensus. The subject of this chapter is therefore the image of the LO that emerged in the educational materials used in the most popular study format: the study circle.

Defining Identity: The Organizational Identity Approach

Determining the characteristics of the identity formation process and ascertaining the nature of the message communicated to the grassroots both require a theoretical definition of identity. The classic definition of organizational identity offered by Stuart Albert and David Whetten is simple but captures the core of social identity in organizations: organizational identity is the collective understanding of what is central, distinctive, and durable in an organization (Albert and Whetten 1985). My main interest here is not in organizational identity as the interaction between members and leaders (which is what the theory originally sought to capture) but rather in the *content* of the identity imposed by leaders on members. This content is best measured through a focus on the broad concepts of centrality and distinctiveness. "Centrality" refers to the essential features of the self-image that the organization constructs, while "distinctiveness" relates to what separates the group from other groups. Group identity is built on a sense of who belongs to the group and who does not: "one of us" versus "one of them." Hence, if we analyze how "the others" are described, elements of what "we" refers to begin to emerge. Research has even demonstrated that some individuals join an organization simply because they wish to distinguish themselves from a particular group (Elsbach and Bhattacharya 2001). Finally, the concept of "durability" refers to persistent traits in the

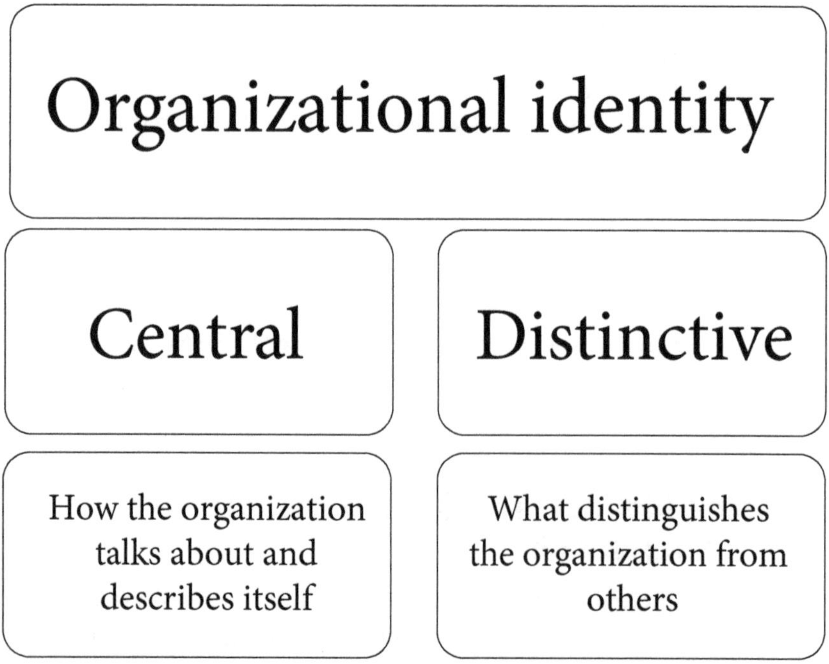

FIGURE 4.1   Indicators of organizational identity

organization's self-perception; as the time dimension is not particularly germane in this study, the durability concept has been omitted from the analysis.

Measuring Central and Distinctive Features

How are centrality and distinctiveness best measured? For a distinct and transparent analysis of this matter, an operationalization is needed. My analysis is based on the concepts of "history," "properties," and "action"; in other words, the central and distinctive features of an organization can be captured if we focus on where "we" come from, what "we" are, and how "we" act. These concepts should be interpreted as arenas in which we may find the organization's central and distinctive features.

History

The first category, history, is an important component of identity formation. It has been claimed that historiography plays an important role in the construction of national identities (Berger 2005; Berger, Donovan, and Passmore 2002). According to narrative theory, social identities are constructed through stories about the past, present, and future (Somers and Gibson 1994, 38), the past being part of the contextualization of the present. Similarly, the description of an organization's history defines its origins, which can explain the present. Historiography bridges the past and present in the organization, thereby contextualizing the present (Friedman 1992, 837). Within narrative theory, coordinated stories about the individual and about the collective and its history produce class identity (Steinmetz 1992).

In situations of identity reformation, the organization's history can preserve continuity. Reformulations of identity should be undertaken within the realm of the existing self-image. If not, there is a risk that members will be alienated and not recognize the organization. Leaders naturally want to prevent that from happening, even if they wish to reformulate the organizational identity. History can be used to frame new traits in such a way that they appear to have existed for a long time, thus tying the "old" identity to the new one. Inevitably, writing history is a selective process: the entire history of the organization can never be written, only parts of it can. The prioritization of certain historical elements can lead members to perceive their organization in a certain way (Linderborg 2001, 1–2, 31–35). Ultimately, those with the power to write the history of the organization can influence how it is perceived by the members.

Properties

While historiography emphasizes the development of the organization, analyzing the organization's properties or characteristics is intended to uncover something about the organization's nature. The core of identity formation is to define and describe oneself or an organization in a certain way. How the organization describes itself—its "identity claims"—is very important (Whetten and Mackey 2002). Ascribing various properties to the self constructs depictions of "ideal selves." These ideal selves can serve as verbal symbols of the organization. Research has demonstrated that verbal and nonverbal symbols are important in an organization's identification process (Cardador and Pratt 2006, 177–78). Moreover, Ashforth and Mael (1989) noted that "organizations often seek to generalize identification with an individual to identification with the organization through *the routinization of charisma*" (p. 22, my italics). In other words, identification with a group can be similar to identification with an individual. Identifying with an individual often implies that the individual wishes to be like that other person and thus adopts properties of the other. Ashforth and Mael suggested that such identification processes can also be applied to identification with the organization through charismatic leadership (exercised by leaders with qualities that individuals wish to adopt) or through the construction of the "ideal member." The image of the ideal member can attract the attention of members and generate an identification process in an organization. An organization's leadership can symbolize the ideal member, thereby enhancing members' identification with the organization. Describing an ideal and assigning it certain properties can therefore contribute to the members' identification with the organization.

In the identification process, the description of the properties or characteristics ascribed to others is as important as the identity claims. Such a description delineates what the self is *not* and what traits and features are not assigned to the organization.

Action

The properties ascribed to the organization also guide its actions. The description of the organization's and its members' actions contains a crucial disciplining element, so it is useful to study actions in more detail. Discipline can be created in the organization through reality claims or by explicit exhortations concerning how trade unions, and trade union members in particular, should be and should act. Such claims set out the "objectively" right ways for members to act. Research also suggests that organizations that can provide their members with "behavioral

TABLE 4.1   Operationalization of organizational identity

	CENTRAL FEATURES	DISTINCTIVE FEATURES
History	How does the organization portray its own development and history?	How does the development of the organization compare to that of others?
Properties	How does the organization describe itself?	What properties are ascribed to the "others"?
	What properties are ascribed to the organization?	What properties distinguish the organization from these other organizations?
Action	How does the organization act?	How do the "others" act?
	How should its members act?	How does that differ from how the organization itself acts?

consistency"—that is, mechanisms that encourage a certain kind of behavior for all members—can more easily construct organizational identities (Cardador and Pratt 2006, 177). I propose to examine how the actions of LO and of the "others" are described in LO's educational materials, as well as how "correct" behavior on the part of unions and their members is portrayed there.

The Educational Material

A variety of educational formats were arranged by the Workers' Educational Association (Arbetarnas bildningsförbund, ABF), but the main activities were lectures and study circles, with the latter becoming very popular among LO members in the 1920s. To meet the demand, the ABF-produced syllabi for the various study circle subjects included reading suggestions and educational materials. Consequently, there is a wide range of materials (mainly booklets) from which to choose when analyzing the projected image of an LO member.

The most important study circle courses were trade union studies and organizational studies (a detailed study of the study circles is presented in chapter 5). Sigfrid Hansson's trade union studies course was not the only study circle course on organizational issues, as a range of courses treated similar themes. Many study circle subjects had more than one syllabus, and different ABF member organizations could have different syllabi for a study circle course in the same subject. For instance, the SSU, LO, and Left Party produced organizational studies syllabi with slightly different contents.

Most of these syllabi were published in one of the two popular education magazines, *Studiekamraten* (The Study Comrade) and *Bokstugan* (The Book Cottage). *Studiekamraten* was originally started and run by the Social Democratic

Youth League (Sveriges Socialdemokratiska ungdomsförbund, SSU) in 1919 but shortly afterward was transferred to the ABF. *Bokstugan*, founded and published by the ABF and the IOGT in 1917, was a magazine specifically for study circles. These magazines appear to have been widely distributed among the study circle libraries throughout the country.[1] It seems that most of the ABF local libraries subscribed to at least one of the magazines, as it was a good way to keep up to date and to gain access to the syllabi and the literature. Subscribing was even recommended by the organizational studies syllabus (Socialdemokratiska-Ungdomsförbundets-studieråd 1930). Access to and familiarity with the syllabi were necessary to ensure that the workers followed the education plans laid down by the leadership, so the availability of *Studiekamraten* and *Bokstugan* among the local associations and libraries was very important.

Trade Union Studies and Association Studies

Between 1920 and 1940, trade union studies (*fackföreningskunskap*) had at least three syllabi, written by Rudolv Holme, Sigfrid Hansson, and Hugo Heffler respectively. The third was an abbreviated version of Hansson's syllabus, covering the same literature as did Hansson's course but containing fewer assignments and questions for discussion.

Holme's syllabus focused on the development of the Swedish labor movement. The first version was published in 1924 and was entitled "Syllabus for the Trade Union Movement and Syndicalism" (Holme 1924). Holme was an activist in the syndicalist movement, which is evident from the first version of the syllabus, in which much of the literature was about syndicalism. Nevertheless, Hansson's book *Den svenska fackföreningsrörelsen* was part of the recommended literature, indicating that the book was respected throughout the labor movement, probably because it dealt with the whole history of the union movement in Sweden (Holme 1924; Holme 1928). Shortly afterward, Holme left the SAC (Bäckström 1963a, 383). His move to the reformist union movement is reflected in his updated syllabus of 1926, renamed "Syllabus for General Association Studies," which included both Hansson's book *Den svenska fackföreningsrörelsen* and the social democratic theorist Nils Karleby's book *Socialismen inför verkligheten* in the recommended reading. The syllabus also contained questions and exercises about the labor movement and its various branches. This study circle course had the same features as did courses on organizational and association studies, stressing procedures for holding meetings, and because of its general characteristics the syllabus could be used by associations from different movements. However, the political message was clearer in Holme's syllabus than in the courses on organizational studies (Holme 1926).

Finally, what appears to be the most influential syllabus in trade union studies was designed by Sigfrid Hansson. Hansson wrote one syllabus for a course in trade union studies in 1923. As noted in chapter 3, Hansson was in charge of study leader education at Brunnsvik, and his first syllabus in trade union studies was designed for this summer course, offered at the people's high school in Brunnsvik each summer from 1923 onwards. However, the syllabus spread to the study circles, and within a year it was being used all over the country (ABF 1926). In 1927, a complete syllabus was published in the LO's booklet series (Hansson 1927c). The literature recommended in the syllabus consisted of articles from the magazine *Fackföreningsrörelsen*, booklets, and a few books. Booklets were popular as educational materials because they were cheap to produce and could be offered at a low price. However, the main reading for the course on trade union studies was Sigfrid Hansson's *Den svenska fackföreningsrörelsen*. This textbook was originally published in the booklet series, so the LO Secretariat sent letters to the sections encouraging them to buy it (Landsorganisationen 1923a). The book became very popular because at that time it was the only complete description of the Swedish trade union movement and its historical development. This also explains why it was published in several different editions, the first in 1923 and the last in 1943.

Organizational and Association Studies

David Berg, the organizer ombudsman, stationed in Norrland, designed a syllabus for courses in association studies. Berg's syllabus was published in 1924 in *Studiekamraten* (Berg 1924). The syllabus did not contain any literature on the labor movement per se but was aimed primarily at establishing procedural norms for meetings, the main goal being to teach the participants how to conduct themselves. The best way to study meeting procedures, according to the syllabus, was to discuss a topic or even take a course in a specific subject and apply the norms and rules on meeting procedures when studying this topic, preferably trade union studies (Berg 1924).

In 1930, the SSU published a new syllabus on organizational studies. The syllabus resembles Berg's in that the main focus of the course was meeting procedures. However, the literature list was somewhat longer, and the very first book on the list—recommended to every course participant—was Sigfrid Hansson's *Arbetarrörelsen* (The Labor Movement). It was very similar to the main book in trade union studies but shorter and much cheaper (Hansson 1930a).

Both association studies and organization studies were intended to teach the rank and file practical organizational skills and how to run the movement properly. It is difficult to determine which syllabus was used most frequently because the study circles were very lax in reporting to the ABF which syllabus they had used. In addition, the ABF seems to have regarded the courses as interchangeable, periodically alternating the course names "Association Studies" and "Organizational Studies." A rough estimate indicates that Berg's syllabus was more common in the 1920s, whereas the SSU's syllabus was more common in the 1930s.[2]

Selected Educational Material

The educational material analyzed here is taken from the syllabus for the study circle course in trade union studies and from the magazine *Fackföreningsrörelsen*. This selection was made for three reasons. First, trade union studies and organizational studies were the most common subjects studied by study circles during the 1920s and 1930s (see chapter 5), so the messages conveyed in these courses reached many workers. Second, the contents of trade union studies and organizational or association studies courses would in theory suit strategic identity formation, because they dealt with the foundations of the trade union movement and offered a good opportunity to define the LO.

The third reason for the selection is that the trade union studies course was intended to teach members how to run local trade union sections, so it can be assumed that at least the activists in the local associations attended these study circles. The activists among the grassroots were crucial for the leadership because of their central position and influence over the local sections, which had far-reaching authority in some of the LO affiliates. Local section activists were a group whose loyalty the LO desperately needed.

Central Features of the LO's Self-Image

The first part of the analysis of the educational material focuses on what was central for the organization—in other words, how the LO depicted itself in the educational material.

The History of the LO

Three themes above all were emphasized in Hansson's account of the LO's history and development: first, that trade unionism had a long tradition in Sweden; second, that the LO had strengthened over time; and third, that the LO had never been a socialist organization—not even at the start.

The very first trade unions in Sweden had emerged from the guild system, which originated in medieval times.[3] Skilled craftsmen had long organized guilds, which eventually were transformed into the new form of organization, the trade union (Hansson 1923, 27–28, 35–36; Hansson 1924). Hansson put considerable stress on the legacy of the guilds, especially in the early editions of his book (Hansson 1923, 18–19, 37–41). In later editions, however, he highlighted negative aspects of the guild system and emphasized the superiority of trade unions (Hansson 1923, 37–41; Hansson 1938b, 18–19).[4] Clearly, the LO wished to be regarded as an organization with long traditions. This was, among other things, a way of distancing itself from the syndicalists, which, as we will see, were framed as a very new organization.

Another characteristic of the history of the LO was its stress on the organization's constant growth. The LO had grown increasingly strong over time (Hansson 1923, 206; Hansson 1926a, 3; Hansson 1930d), transforming itself from a small and rather ineffectual organization into a powerful body enjoying widespread respect (and inspiring fear in the Right). The mobilization of workers had paid off: after several decades of struggle, the LO was an organization that could not be ignored regarding labor market issues (Fackföreningsrörelsen 1930; Hansson 1923, 206–16, 224–25; Hansson 1926a, 3; Hansson 1935d, 13–14; Hansson 1938b, 252–56, 261–69). Regardless of what the left-wing organizations claimed, the LO was the organization that had accomplished the difficult task of mobilizing the workers, so the successes of the labor movement were ultimately the result of the LO's work. Early trade unions were portrayed in the materials as humble actors with much less power than the employers. Due to the increasing number of their members and the work of previous generations of LO members, however, trade unions had become an important force in society (Hansson 1923, 148; Hansson 1926a, 3).

Ideologically, Hansson described the Swedish trade union movement's development as a journey from liberalism to social democracy, with a short stop in socialism (Hansson 1926b, 408–19). The LO had never been a socialist organization, not even early in the labor movement's history (Hansson 1923, 276–77; Hansson 1926b; Hansson 1935f, 40–44; Hansson 1938b, 293–97). In Hansson's portrayal, the process of building a coherent trade union movement during the nineteenth century was a struggle between liberal ideas, on one hand, and the socialist ideas championed by the Social Democratic Party (Socialdemokratiska arbetarpartiet, SAP), on the other. It was the SAP that had emerged victorious (Hansson 1923, 23–27; Hansson 1932, 8–12; Hansson 1938b, 18, 25–29), so the unions moved from liberalism to social democracy without difficulty. Hansson (Hansson 1926b, 419) explained the development in the SAP magazine *Tiden* as follows: "With these observations, I think I have shown that the trade union movement in our country was far from being socialist in origin; on the contrary, it took quite some time and required considerable effort before socialist ideas really took root in the labor movement. . . . After the breakthrough actually occurred, it did not take long until social democracy captured one union after another, and the unions also became the foundation on which the Social Democratic Party was built during the following decades."[5] Clearly, Hansson wanted to avoid giving the labor movement a "socialist" history, which can be interpreted as a way for the LO to distance itself from the syndicalists and communists. By choosing the reformist path, the LO had moved away from the path leading toward a socialist society and instead embraced the capitalist system, making it easy for the syndicalists to criticize it for betraying its origins. If the LO had had no socialist origins, however, this argument would lose its force. Moreover, if the goal was to improve relationships with capital, this was probably the best way for the LO to go. The deprecation of socialism also assigned the LO a status as a particular kind of organization *within* the labor movement. The liberal origins of the LO were acknowledged by other members of the LO Secretariat but not emphasized to the same degree as by Hansson (Johansson 1924a).

Finally, the events of the LO's history were described very objectively and "scientifically" in the book. Hansson presented all the statistics available in describing how the different affiliates and the LO had developed over time. Hansson's description of the history of the union movement seemed to have been inspired by the idea of three stages of union movement development, originally developed by Richard Calwer in an article in *Fackföreningsrörelsen* in 1921. According to the article, the union movement's first stage was conflictual and was marked by a substantial number of strikes. In their first stumbling steps, it was natural for the unions to test their strength relative to that of the employers. It was also necessary, Hansson explained, *so that the workers would realize that spontaneous strikes do not enhance the workers' struggle.* In other words, wildcat strikes were very immature and beneath the dignity of the reformist unions, which, at that time, were on the verge of step three. The second stage was characterized by a centralist organization and the realization that the labor movement could influence the government through political activity. The third step was to use this political leverage to seize power over the state and to use the state to democratize production (Hansson 1921a). How the democratization of production was to happen is not well developed in the article, but Hansson seems to have shared Wigforss's vision of industrial democracy.[6]

The general strike of 1909 was a key event in the LO's past, so it is interesting to know how it was portrayed. Though the main book *Den svenska fackföreningsrörelsen* briefly describes general strikes in very general terms, assuming that the reader was already familiar with the concept, the strike of 1909 is surprisingly not described in detail. Hansson stated that the strike was caused by the radicalization that preceded the conflict: "The general strike of 1909 must therefore be considered to have been evoked by powerful psychological factors, generated by a highly developed class consciousness, created by external compulsion from ruthless employer policies. The experiences of this strike did not create much faith in this means of exerting pressure" (Hansson 1923, 185). In an article in *Fackföreningsrörelsen* in 1934, Hansson developed his account of the strike and described the general strike as the result of syndicalist agitation and the rhetoric used by the reformist unions in 1909. The rhetoric was unfortunately the same type of agitation that was common when the union movement was young (and immature). The rhetoric had a strong impact on the union members, many of whom were relatively young; as a result, a battle between employers and workers was more or less bound to happen. Hansson also stressed that in comparison with general strikes in other countries, the Swedish one stands out because the disciplined and responsible workers refused to cause any disorder (Hansson 1934c). Two remarks can be made regarding this description: first, the syndicalist rhetoric is first cited as a reason for the failure in the 1930s; second, Hansson stressed responsibility even when describing a major catastrophe for the union movement. The immaturity of the movement appears to have caused the fatal decision to start the strike in 1909 and, as we shall see, was also a property attributed to the syndicalists. In other words, emulating the syndicalists could lead to a new general strike.

Properties

Hansson described the LO as a "democratic-centralist" organization. Democracy was the most important principle of trade unionism (Hansson 1921a; Hansson 1923, 78; Hansson 1934b) and the means of empowering the working class. An unquestionable devotion to democracy was of course one of the main characteristics separating the reformists from the revolutionary Left. Accepting democracy and rejecting revolution also meant accepting the bourgeois state, however, which was controversial in the reformist labor movement. The SAP had been criticized for cooperating with the enemy. Democracy within the union movement, on the other hand, meant that union leaders had to be elected. Legitimizing democracy was hardly a problem.

It was harder to find support for centralism among the LO members. The central organization became the scapegoat for the failed general strike in 1909, and subsequently the affiliates had restrained the central organization's powers. Hansson's solution to this dilemma was to establish a clear connection between democracy and centralization. First, Hansson proposed *representative* democracy as the superior system. Consequently, the election of leaders sufficed for democracy to be realized. Second, because of the growing membership, Hansson explained, more and more affiliates were being founded, eventually making it necessary to centralize the umbrella organization, which was the only way to make democracy work in the LO. Such centralization as had taken place did not, in Hansson's estimation, undermine democracy within the organization but, if anything, had made it work better (Hansson 1922e, 313–14; Hansson 1923, 77; Hansson 1938b, 110, 115–19). As centralism had arisen through the democratic system in the trade unions, it represented a development of democracy (Hansson 1923, 83–84). In this way, democracy was used as an argument for centralizing powers in the LO. Of course, democracy was a very appealing trait to lay claim to—who could object to democracy?—while centralism was highly controversial. Since centralism was desirable for the leadership, however, it somehow had to be positively linked to democracy. "It must therefore be established," Hansson wrote, "that the centralist system has in no way curtailed democracy. It may rather be regarded as a development of democracy, in that it has established guarantees that rights and obligations are distributed equally between all members" (Hansson 1923, 84).[7]

Opponents of centralism were portrayed in the educational materials as young firebrands who lacked appreciation of the importance of centralism and who entertained a "primitive notion of what democracy was" (Hansson 1923, 83; Hansson 1927a, 180–81). These uneducated members and nonmembers had not understood that centralism was a natural development in both the workers' and the employers' organizations. Once these members matured, however, they would come to realize the superiority of centralist arrangements (Hansson 1923, 83–84; Hansson 1934a, 112–13). Such centralism was, moreover, a significant aspect of the "old trade unions," as opposed to the new ones (in other words, the syndicalist unions) (Hansson 1938b, 96). Both the 1923 and 1938 editions of Hansson's work assure LO members that democracy and centralism are compatible, even mutually beneficial.

The materials also characterized the LO as a responsible organization. It was important to emphasize that the LO did nothing to threaten the social order: when it entered into a labor market conflict, for example, it took pains to ensure that other parties were not thereby put at risk. It took responsibility for maintaining all necessary societal functions during strikes (Hansson 1923, 232–33). In the 1923 version, in fact, it was asserted that the LO would ensure that so-called third parties were not affected by labor market conflicts; it was prepared to guarantee that society would not suffer from such conflicts.

Another sign of responsibility was the description of collective agreements: the parties on the labor market, Hansson stressed, were responsible agents who took responsibility for labor market peace during periods when collective agreements were in force (Hansson 1938b, 254–55). As we shall see, the LO's claim to be a responsible actor was a way for it to distance itself from the syndicalists. Moreover, the new organizations, the SAC and the Communist Party, had criticized the LO—and apparently recruited new members using the argument—claiming that the discipline it advocated greatly restricted workers' freedom to act (Johansson 1924a). Of course, discipline was important to the LO, which inevitably curtailed its members' freedom to act in relation to their employers, but "discipline" was not a good word to use to retain old or attract new members. "Responsibility," on the other hand, sounded much more attractive.

Not only did the materials describe the workers as responsible, they also portrayed the employers that way. In addition, they stressed the importance of leaving labor market issues in the hands of the labor market organizations: the state should *not* interfere, since it had neither the knowledge nor the capacity to do so (Fackföreningsrörelsen 1936a; Fackföreningsrörelsen 1936b; Fackföreningsrörelsen 1936c; Hansson 1938b, 265). This brings us back to the responsibility discussion: labor market parties are able and willing to take responsibility for labor market issues. The LO was framed as an organization that could and should take such responsibility. Regarding legislation as a means to create labor market peace, Hansson proclaimed:

> Such a law must mean that the state assumes the obligation to guarantee, at all times, that the workers obtain the highest standard of living that the general state of the economy permits, and that the employers obtain assurances that wages are not to be set higher than the current economic situation allows. . . . Such a guarantee, however, cannot be given by the state . . . because macroeconomic science cannot yet provide adequate guidance in these issues. Practical statistics are also too incomplete to serve as a basis for a general assessment of these issues. The state cannot guarantee the workers that the employers will carry on in business with the wages that have been determined by arbitration, any more than it can guarantee employers that workers should be available for wages set in this way.
>
> The state thus appears to lack the prerequisites to decide what wages ought to be suitable at any particular time and to ensure that companies stick to these fixed wages, or that workers accept them. Employers' and workers' organizations are also in agreement in their opposition to any legislation on compulsory arbitration of disputes relating to these interest conflicts. (Hansson 1938b, 265)[8]

This interpretation of how the labor market should be organized is at the heart of the Basic Agreement, as both employers and workers realized that they had a common interest in keeping the state away from the labor market. The emphasis on the existence of common interests between employers and workers, as well as the highlighted opportunities for negotiated solutions, served to downplay class conflict and facilitate the emergence of a culture of negotiation. The state was unable, according to the materials, to guarantee workers the highest possible standard of living or employers the lowest possible wages. Accordingly, legislation to create labor market peace was inappropriate, indeed probably impossible (Hansson 1938b, 265). Such legislative proposals only showed the ignorance of the Right. The same formulations appear in the editions of 1927, 1934, and 1938.

How Trade Union Members Should Act

A good trade union member is responsible, loyal to the organization, and proud of being part of the movement, according to the study materials. Moreover, a good member pays membership dues on time and contributes to the union through volunteer work on its behalf (Hansson 1926a, 3–7). A member should also have a certain level of education, so that one understands how unions work. A deficient education could lead, for example, to the delusion that centralism has a negative effect on workers' influence on the labor market (Hansson 1923, 83). Immature behavior, such as blockades—a fairly common means of conflict in the syndicalist movement—could hurt not only the workers involved but also the reputation of the entire union movement, and, with its credibility damaged among the public, the union movement would suffer tremendously. Therefore, LO members needed to act responsibly, and mature members realized this (Hansson 1933d).

The connection with the organization's properties is clear: the LO was a democratic and centralized organization, so members ought to act accordingly. Hansson wrote in 1926 that "the minority is always obliged to subordinate itself to the majority" (Hansson 1926a, 33–34). Decisions ought to be made on a majority basis, and once made they ought to be followed in accordance with the rule of law. If the charter of the organization and the rules adopted by the congress are not respected, the entire democratic system within LO might fall apart (and bring down the organization with it) (Hansson 1923, 83; Hansson 1926a, 6; Hansson 1935b, 24). Consequently, for internal democracy to be realized and respected, a good union member never acts on one's own initiative but instead lets the union decide what measures are best in a given situation (Hansson 1926a, 6). This requires a certain amount of loyalty. Disloyal behavior did not belong in the LO: it was not a proper way for LO members to act and benefited only communists and syndicalists (Hansson 1933c). Again, this was a way of stressing the organization's difference from the syndicalists, who called for more power to be given to the grassroots (with frequent labor market conflicts as a result). It also involved a disciplining message: "You should do as you are told."

The very basis of the "social organization," according to Hansson, was solidarity, together with a willingness to make sacrifices for the collective (Hansson 1928a; Hansson 1938a). This in turn meant that, while the union member would give up some autonomy, one would gain equality on the labor market, something that liberalism had failed to deliver (Hansson 1935e, 55–59). The worker's personality would develop too (Hansson 1922d).

Turning to the actions of the *organization*, conflicts should be resolved through negotiations, according to Hansson. The materials claim that Swedish trade unions had always primarily sought to negotiate voluntary agreements with employers concerning working conditions; the strike was the weapon of last resort, to be used only after all attempts at negotiation had proved fruitless (Hansson 1923, 148–49; Hansson 1927a, 186–87). It was never in the LO's best interest to go on strike, because it preferred to negotiate (Hansson 1923, 149–50; Hansson 1935b, 29–33). On this particular point, we can see a minor change in the materials over time. The 1923 edition blames employers for the high number of strikes; the 1938 edition states that both sides had always tried negotiations as the first step to resolving a conflict but that such a strategy had not always worked—hence the high number of work stoppages during the earlier period (Hansson 1938b, 165). Both workers and employers had come to realize that work stoppages were damaging for both parties and that the solution lay in negotiations.

One way of reducing the number of conflicts, according to Hansson, was to reach collective agreements for the entire workforce—in other words, national agreements were very desirable (Fackföreningsrörelsen 1936a; Hansson 1938b, 257). While the push for national agreements originally emanated from the employers' side, both employers and workers agreed, according to Hansson, that a lot of time and effort could be saved if general issues were settled in national agreements, especially since the system would then be more predictable (Hansson 1923, 248; Hansson 1938b; Hansson 1942, 257). Hansson stressed the importance of labor market peace during a collective agreement: once an

TABLE 4.2   Summary of central features of LO's self-depiction

	LO'S SELF-DEPICTION
History	Strong, growing organization; long tradition; never a socialist organization but had evolved from liberal to social democratic; organization had matured
Properties	Centralist, democratic, responsible, and mature; feared by the Right
Actions	Important to follow adopted rules and to act responsibly (e.g., pay membership dues on time); members must be willing to make sacrifices for the organization (i.e., devote time to it and be actively engaged); negotiations preferred over strikes

agreement had been concluded, work stoppages were not to take place. Nor was this injunction restricted to members: the entire organization and all its affiliates had to adhere to adopted rules and agreements (Hansson 1942, 252–56).

Distinctive Features: Description of Others

Having analyzed the LO's self-depiction, we next examine how the LO framed others. The LO's positioning relative to other groups is another indicator of its self-perception. There were several others. First, the LO had to distance itself from other trade unions and from left-wing factions, such as the syndicalists. Second, it needed to position itself relative to capital, in other words, the employers and the political Right.

Demonizing the Syndicalists

The materials describe the SAC unions as "new trade union[s]," as opposed to the old ones united in the LO (Hansson 1923, 74, 84–85; Hansson 1938b, 96). The LO was an old organization with traditions that could inspire members with trust, while the syndicalists were "the new ones." This depiction mirrors the LO's attempt to distance itself from the syndicalists, making the latter look young, inexperienced, and unorganized.

The SAC was portrayed as an irrational body, with a strange and complicated organizational structure. The syndicalists' aim was to build a decentralized organization that would reinforce the local level, and Hansson saw this as indicative of a lack of maturity, for two reasons. The first line of argument emphasized the SAC's illogical behavior: since the syndicalists were, compared with the LO, a new organization (Hansson 1923, 74, 84–85; Hansson 1938b, 96), they might be expected to embody new trends. However, it was the old trade unions that had adapted to changes in industrial structure. The LO had changed its organizational structure in accordance with the so-called industrial principle (i.e., all workers in one workplace should be organized by one union); the syndicalists, in contrast, had shown no interest in modifying their organization in accordance with such structural changes (Hansson 1923, 71, 74, 106; Hansson 1938b, 92–96). They lacked the maturity to do so, according to Hansson. The second line of argument attacked the federal system. The main idea of the SAC was to transfer as much power as possible to the grassroots. Giving the local level greater maneuvering room was referred to as federalism (Hansson 1922b; Hansson 1923, 85, 87), as opposed to the LO's characteristic centralism.

This decentralized system was the reason for the chaotic appearance of the SAC's organizational structure. In contrast to the SAC's stated determination to keep power at the local level, the syndicalists had in fact established a central organization. This, Hansson argued, made them rather inconsistent and contributed to the confused organizational structure (Hansson 1922b; Hansson 1922e, 313–17; Hansson 1923, 74; Hansson 1938b, 92–96). The confusion was accentuated by the Marxist class logic of the SAC, which called for the working class to be united against the capitalist class. Ideally, according to the SAC, there would not be several different trade union confederations organizing the struggle; rather, all the workers would be united in the same organization (Hansson 1923, 71; Hansson 1938b, 92). In other words, the SAC did not differentiate between different kinds of workers. Simultaneously, however, the SAC did pronounce its difference from the LO. In conclusion, in Hansson's description, the SAC's claimed organizational rationale comes across as contradictory.

The LO described the SAC as having no control over its members. This lack of discipline had highly negative effects on members of the LO, who were well-behaved, responsible, hardworking people who followed the rules and respected other organizations (and so were prone to being taken in by the impulsive syndicalists) (Hansson 1926a, 34). Once again, the comparison between centralized and decentralized systems was a way for LO to distance itself from the SAC. Moreover, while the materials do not say so explicitly, the reader gets the impression that it would be very difficult to combine decentralization with democracy (Hansson 1923, 84–87).

There are several other instances in which the LO's materials portray the syndicalists as irrational. For example, one minute the syndicalists attacked the reformist unions for concluding collective agreements, while the next minute they concluded their own agreements (Hansson 1923, 255–56; Hansson 1938b, 218–21). The SAC had also condemned the LO's strike fund, claiming that economic support would hamper the revolution, yet eventually decided to establish a strike fund of its own (Hansson 1923, 106, 111–12; Hansson 1938b, 143; Johansson 1924b).

One of the most striking characteristics of the syndicalists was their methods. They believed that strikes, sabotage, and obstruction were the only effective methods in the struggle against capital and would lead eventually to final victory. A revolutionary, antistatist, and non-parliamentary class struggle based on trade unions was the best way to go. Syndicalists were accordingly skeptical of parliamentary reformist work, believing that such methods might make workers lose faith in the possibility of revolution (Hansson 1923, 185–86, 290–91). The syndicalists and their supporters in the LO were usually radical young trade unionists. They were swayed easily by syndicalist rhetoric, and they believed in overthrowing capitalist society through a general strike, according to Hansson (Hansson 1923, 184–85). Here too, as the LO saw it, the difference between the organizations was clear. The SAC acted irresponsibly: it would go on strike at any time, without considering the consequences for other groups. Acting ruthlessly, it would put pressure on other groups, such as LO members, to undertake sympathy actions on its behalf (Hansson 1926a, 22, 29–30, 35–40). The misuse of sympathy strikes was an SAC strategy whose purpose was to create chaos in order to make the "reformist" organizations look bad (Hansson 1926a, 22). This sowed confusion among LO members over the meaning of solidarity and showed how self-centered the syndicalists were (Hansson 1925a; Hansson 1926a, 22).

The Political Right

Turning our attention to capital, the archenemy of the working class, we find two distinct actors: the political Right (the right-wing and conservative parties in Parliament) and the employers, which were treated separately in the LO's educational material.

The LO's relationship to the Right is described as a long struggle against the latter's attempts to constrain the labor movement through legislation intended to strengthen the employers. The first step in this struggle was the Åkarp Law, which made it illegal to prevent strikebreakers from working during a strike. Several other attempts to restrict workers' rights of association followed without success, according to the materials (Hansson 1923, 203, 207; Hansson 1938b, 248–52).

The political Right is depicted as an enemy of the workers. The employers, on the other hand, are not mentioned in Hansson's long account of how the Right tried to reduce union power through legislation. For example, in 1933 a major conflict started in the construction sector. The conflict caused both the Conservative and Liberal Parties to demand regulation of the right to start blockades. Such legislation would benefit the employers, according to Hansson, but the employers were never identified as the originators of the proposal (Hansson 1933b). (For a thorough analysis of the conflict, see Åmark 1989.) One might have expected some ire to be aimed at the employers for such legislation; after all, the chair of the Swedish Employers' Association (Svenska Arbetsgivareföreningen, SAF) was a member of Parliament for the Conservative Party. It would have been easy to treat the employers as a part of the political Right, to build a stronger class identity in opposition to them; Ragnar Casparsson, for example, did just that (Casparsson 1931).[9] However, the employers do not figure in the LO's materials in that context (Fackförenings-srörelsen 1936c; Hansson 1930c; Hansson 1930d).

Employers: History, Properties, and Actions

Finally, the third "other" that emerges in Hansson's texts is the employers. Being an old organization, like the LO, the SAF had considerably improved on its past immature behavior. For example, the SAF had formerly used strikebreakers to fight the unions and had even tried to organize company unions ("yellow unions") (Fackföreningsrörelsen 1930; Hansson 1923) but had since become much more accommodating. The employers offered company unions as an alternative to the reformist trade unions, but they never flourished. Furthermore, their harmful effects on the LO diminished, as working-class solidarity grew (Hansson 1923, 224–28). Hansson spent a great deal of time trying to explain the existence of strikebreakers in the past by stressing that organizations on both the labor and employer sides were not developed or powerful early on, compared with the situation in the early 1920s. This gave phony organizations such as "yellow unions" their chance. However, the major problem in the past had been that the considerable number of unorganized workers and unorganized employers made it hard for the parties to establish rules acceptable to both sides (Hansson 1923, 223–24). It seems there were some employers and some workers who refused to comply with the agreements reached by the relevant organizations. In this, Hansson's account of labor market history absolves the SAF of some of the blame. Certain employers had indeed tried to harm the trade unions, but the latter had been able to overcome such attacks.

This description of the use of strikebreakers may have been used to create an "us against them" attitude within the union movement; however, the approach taken in the educational materials is very objective. Most of the described incidents had taken place well in the past, signaling that this was how the employers *used* to behave, not how they behaved at the time Hansson was writing.

The reformist unions had always cherished labor market peace, their primary goal being to improve conditions for their members through negotiations. The employers, on the other hand, had not always been so forthcoming. They had tried to prevent workers from organizing, and this hostile attitude had led to work stoppages (Fackföreningsrörelsen 1930; Hansson 1923, 148–49). This too had changed over time (Hansson 1923, 150), indicating a degree of maturation on the employers' side.

Notwithstanding the efforts of both the workers' and employers' organizations to negotiate and find peaceful solutions, the number of work stoppages had gradually increased. Hansson tried to explain this in terms of the growth of the organizations: not only the trade unions but also the employers' organizations were getting stronger. As a result, the labor market organizations had been transformed into "fighting organizations" that were tempted to test their strength in conflicts (Hansson 1923, 152). This description of the past relationship between employers and workers is particularly interesting, since the Swedish labor market had been characterized by conflicts for many years; indeed, the number of work stoppages had steadily increased to become the highest in Europe in the 1920s (Tegle 2000, 165–69). However, this history of struggle is absent from Hansson's description of past relations between the labor market parties. He was clearly trying to avoid demonizing the employers in connection with work stoppages. Such stoppages, he argued, were an effect not of class conflict but rather of rising membership rates and the growing strength of the organizations on both sides. He mentioned the incidence of strikes and lockouts but ventured very few comments or interpretations of the figures (Hansson 1923, 162–66).

The similarities between the unions and the employers' organizations are emphasized in the materials: both are voluntary organizations (Hansson 1938b, 247–48); both have the same legal basis (Hansson 1938b, 247–48); both abide by the rule of law (Hansson 1923, 261–62); both are anxious to preserve labor market peace while collective agreements are in force (Fackförenings-srörelsen 1930; Fackföreningsrörelsen 1936a; Hansson 1938b, 252–56, 257); and both wish to resolve conflicts through negotiations (Fackföreningsrörelsen 1936c). Legislation on labor market issues, furthermore, had merely codified the customs created and practiced by the two sides (Hansson 1938b, 247).

However, the LO's description of the employers' side is not purely positive. The materials describe, for instance, how employers had drawn up blacklists of former employees who had been union members, intending to make it hard for them to get new jobs. Some of the LO affiliates had approached the employers' organizations on this matter because it represented a violation of the collective national agreements reached by the two main organizations that adopted agreements had to be followed (Hansson 1923, 193–94; Hansson 1938b, 197–201). This can be interpreted as an instance of the employers' untrustworthiness. On the other hand, the cited event had occurred a good deal earlier, in 1914, so it could be regarded as ancient history. The account in the materials is very objective, not being disparaging and expressing no bitterness. In some cases, individual employers tried to do harm to the union movement; for instance, one employer in Eksjö hired strikebreakers, leading to the breakdown of attempts to resolve the conflict. But the LO chose not to tar all employers with the same brush (Hansson 1933a).

The shared interests of employers and workers are obvious, according to the materials. In fact, even on issues on which the political Right had tried to restrict the powers of trade unions through unfavorable legislation, the employers and workers were able to find common ground (thereby making the Right look unreasonable) (Hansson 1938b, 261–62). Furthermore, as already mentioned, both sides wanted to keep the state out of the labor market. The state was not in a position to decide on labor issues or to secure labor market peace. It was the involved interest organizations that had the required competence as well as the will to make it work. They should therefore be entrusted with the task (Fackföreningsrörelsen 1936a; Fackföreningsrörelsen 1936b; Fackföreningsrörelsen 1936c; Hansson 1938b, 265).

This differentiates between the political Right and the employers, which did not have the same interests. Employers and unions, however, did have common interests, with both stressing the importance of the right of association and the need to keep the state out of the labor market. By separating the Right from the employers, the LO was able to combine support for the SAP with cooperation with the employers' side. Since employers and the Right were distinct actors, cooperating with the former was not the same as supporting the latter.

Who and What We Are and Are Not

What type of worker did Hansson depict? What was the ideal LO member like? From the analysis of the material, the main trait of a good worker appears to have been "responsible behavior." How does the responsible worker fit into the ideology of reformism? After all, the communists probably also wanted to have responsible members in the disciplinary sense (i.e., paying their membership dues on time, engaging actively in the organization, and so on), so how was the LO different from the other labor organizations?

According to its self-depiction in the materials, the LO was a "strong and growing organization with powerful resources." The workers had once been humble servants, but because of the formation of trade unions that was no longer the case. Assigning power to the working class, as Hansson's descriptions do, was not specific to the reformist labor movement, but it was important to build confidence in the workers, and, above all, it was important to maintain that the LO, not the new labor organizations, had given the working class these powers.

Another crucial trait of the organization was its adherence to the rule of law. Members were to obey whatever rules had been accepted by the organization—the centralized system required obedience—as democracy would not work otherwise. Hansson described the reformist unions as willing to take responsibility for labor market peace. The belief that the labor market could be made to work without the need for parliamentary legislation, but through negotiations with employers, is a notable feature of the LO's self-depiction in the materials. No doubts are entertained that the labor market parties could make it work. These descriptions clearly separate the LO from the left-wing organizations: the LO was an organization that

TABLE 4.3 Summary of the central and distinctive features of the LO relative to those of other organizations

	LO'S SELF-DEPICTION	LO'S DEPICTION OF THE SYNDICALISTS	LO'S DEPICTION OF THE EMPLOYERS
History and development of the organization	Strong and growing organization; long tradition; had evolved from liberal to social democratic; had matured	New movement; lacking history; had developed as a "disorganized organization"	Old like the LO; growing; had become increasingly friendly to unions; had matured
Properties, self-depiction, and description of the "others"	Centralist, democratic, reformist, responsible, mature; feared by the Right	Inconsistent, decentralized, complex, immature, inexperienced	Responsible; same legal basis as the LO; fairly trustworthy
Actions: view of how the LO and the "others" should act	Members should respect and follow adopted rules; should be responsible (e.g., should pay membership dues on time and engage actively in the organization); should display discipline and social responsibility	Irresponsible, selfish, irrational; disrespectful of adopted rules	Takes responsibility for the labor market

negotiated, and its members were workers who realized the benefits of negotiation as opposed to the paltry gains of always taking the path of conflict.

Acknowledgement of democracy as the best system was indeed a feature distinguishing the radical left-wing organizations from the reformists: the latter took the view that the labor movement should seek reforms through the democratic system to improve the living conditions of the working class. This was Eduard Bernstein's main criticism of Karl Marx: the premises on which Marx had based his theories were wrong, as the working class was not becoming more exploited. Bernstein dismissed revolution as the main instrument in the hands of the working class and argued instead that bourgeois society should be overcome through gradual reforms (Hansson 1991, 11–12). Hjalmar Branting adopted Bernstein's ideas at an early stage, providing Swedish social democracy with its ideological foundations. For the reformist branch of the labor movement, democracy was the most important tool for implementing reforms; indeed, democracy was a prerequisite for reformist success (Hansson 1991, 15–16). Bernstein's ideas, however, were above all applicable to political parties. In the political sphere, democracy was the key to success and the realization of socialism. However, the trade union movement was not a political party standing in elections, so reformist ideas had to be converted into practical trade union work.

Democracy within the union sphere referred to internal democracy, in which the members elected the union leadership (as in a representative democracy) and in most affiliates could vote to accept or reject wage agreements. However, the labor market could not be regulated by means of democratic institutions but only through negotiations or radical struggle (unless every single agreement on the labor market were to be governed by parliamentary legislation, which seemed unrealistic). Radical struggle was the path chosen by the left-wing organizations, not the LO. Creating a relationship with employers built on struggle would make it hard to carry out reforms, as Bernstein suggested. If the political parties used parliamentary democracy as means in the class struggle, negotiations were the means the unions should use, according to Hansson.

Of course, one could imagine a scenario in which certain labor market issues, such as the minimum wage, were decided on by Parliament. Parliament was elected, so letting it decide on key issues was indeed to trust in democracy. However, politics in Sweden had been unpredictable since the introduction of universal suffrage, and social democracy did not immediately become a dominant force. Relying on Parliament to decide on labor market issues could have had unpleasant consequences for the working class. Meanwhile, the union movement was big enough to pressure the employers in negotiations, so keeping the state out of the labor market as far as possible was indeed in the interest of the LO. Few other options remained for handling labor market issues besides negotiations, given that revolution was not an option. Because of the LO's internal democracy, LO leadership was given a mandate to do what it considered to be in the interest of the workers. This required that the workers behave responsibly. Unless the members followed orders from the leaders, the union movement would not speak with one voice, and its credibility would be lost. Discipline in the movement and a large number of members were prerequisites for the negotiation option to work best. The LO therefore needed to mobilize the working class but within the framework of negotiations. Hansson used democracy and the rule of law to justify member discipline and the centralization of the movement. This way, the spirit of consensus became a result of reformism applied to trade unions.

Surprisingly, the rhetoric of solidarity was almost absent. Hansson had written a booklet that was used in study circles on that very issue, aimed at proving that helping syndicalists through sympathy strikes was not an act of solidarity. In the main course book, however, solidarity was not discussed. This may seem a little odd; on the other hand, it was difficult to discuss the principle of solidarity and at the same time argue that it did not apply to syndicalist workers.

In addition, the materials are most accurate regarding what LO was *not*, that is, its organizational distinctiveness, with less attention paid to what LO *was*. The demonization of the syndicalists was meant to deter LO members from joining or helping them, and this mirrored the struggle to make trade unions a cohesive actor during this period. This is why the reformist unions did their best to crush their leftist rivals. Another noteworthy feature is Hansson's altered terminology when confronting the leftist enemy: suddenly words and phrases such as "class struggle," "methods of struggle," "oppression," "working class," and "revolutionary" make their appearance (Hansson 1923, 85, 149, 185–89, 291–92). The rhetoric of class is almost absent from *Den svenska fackföreningsrörelsen*, and the few times it does appear, moreover, it is used with reference to the syndicalists (not the employers). One might otherwise expect such language to be used to create a strong class identity, which could be a powerful tool for mobilizing the membership. If the LO had chosen to build its collective identity on class identity, however, it would have found it difficult to justify cooperating with the employer side. Instead, the syndicalists were made out to be a slightly irrational and rather ignorant revolutionary group. Quite often, words or concepts with connotations of class conflict were cited in a highly condescending way, within quotation marks. The message conveyed to the reader is this: the syndicalists are a *so-called* revolutionary organization, which is trying to conduct a *so-called* class struggle. Reading between the lines, one might easily conclude that the syndicalists were poseurs who were not to be taken seriously. The LO probably intended to convey the notion that joining the syndicalists meant joining a meaningless struggle. Staying in the LO, on the other hand, meant being part of a growing organization with powerful resources and a promising future. This could also explain why the LO refused to describe its history as socialist. The apparent stress on distinctive features in contrast to the left-wing organizations suggests that the organizational logic had superseded the more ideological ideas of class struggle within the leadership, and that creating an *organizational* identity that clearly referred back to and distinguished the LO from other working-class organizations was the primary aim of the study material.

Moreover, one cannot help wondering what happened to the communists. There is very little in the materials about them, though we do know that the LO perceived them as a threat. One possible explanation is that the communists did not organize their own trade unions but were members of LO affiliates. The syndicalists, on the other hand, had their own trade unions, so they constituted a clear target and a rival. Demonizing communists, by contrast, would actually mean criticizing many members of the LO. In the worst-case scenario, such members might then leave the organization. An article in *Fackföreningsrörelsen* by Johan-Olov Johansson, member of the LO Secretariat, testifies to such opinions.

Johansson criticized the idea of revolution among unions and political parties and condemned the SAC, but revolutionary ideas in the political sphere were, he concluded, hard to separate from the LO because there were many communists among its members (Johansson 1924a).

Finally, what is clear in the materials is the emphasis on common interests with the employers' side. A distinction is drawn between the political Right and the employers, which opens up the possibility of cooperating with the latter without being "unfaithful" to social democracy. If the materials did have an impact on the grassroots, it is not hard to see why the Swedish model of organizing the labor market found support among the grassroots. After all, the materials essentially encourage the readers to welcome closer cooperation with the employers. A remarkable finding from analyzing the educational materials is that the descriptions of the LO, employers, and syndicalists did not change notably over time. This is remarkable because the close cooperation with the employers, an element that has made the Swedish labor market famous, was sealed with the Basic Agreement in 1938. As early as 1923, however, when the first edition of *Den svenska fackföreningsrörelsen* was published, the spirit of consensus was already presented as the ideal way of organizing the labor market, according to the LO Secretariat.

Relations with Employers

The self-image of the LO depicted in the educational materials indeed embraced negotiations and reformism. The LO's interpretation of the reformist ideology took the shape of applied reformism, exhorting specific actions, which can be summarized as *the spirit of consensus*. The spirit of consensus, one of the most prominent features of Swedish labor market relations, was entrenched by the study materials provided by the LO leadership. However, to argue that the leadership strategically constructed this particular image of the organization requires additional analysis of the LO leadership and its relationship to the employers. Was it a mere coincidence that Hansson's descriptions of the movement encouraged friendly relations with the employers? Did the leadership make any other efforts to promote the spirit of consensus?

The LO Secretariat and the Spirit of Consensus

Undoubtedly, the Secretariat had particular motives for trying to make the LO's members more friendly to employers, to which the challenges to the movement presented in chapter 2 bear testimony. Sigfrid Hansson was among the first to articulate these quite controversial ideas, and we can date such attitudes to as early as 1921, at least on Hansson's part (Hansson 1928a; Hansson 1938a). Was Hansson alone in holding such a view of employers? The remaining sources do not allow us to answer this question in detail. In Hansson's own diary it is claimed that other parts of the Secretariat shared his views (e.g., see Edvard Johansson's speech at the meeting with the LO Representatives in October 1921). Johansson, who at that time was secretary of the Secretariat and would become the president of the LO after Thorberg died in 1930, was the person who initiated the negotiations in Saltsjöbaden, which started in 1936 and resulted in the Basic Agreement. According to Hansson, Johansson stated: "They [the workers] ought to try to make the best of it [the economic crisis] for *their own and the industry's sake*, and above all they ought to protect their trade unions and wait for better times that will enable the working class to focus their efforts on new, positive tasks related to the democratization and socialization of economic life" (Hansson 1921, 10 October, my italics).

According to Hansson, Johansson's point of view was common among the trade union elite. There are, however, no traces of explicit statements in favor of cooperation with the employers in the minutes from the LO Representatives that year. Johansson talked about the economic crisis and the need to act cautiously and not misuse strike funds, but the minutes do not say anything about considering the interests of employers. That does not necessarily mean that this idea was not well established in the trade union elite.

Nevertheless, it is unlikely that Hansson acted on his own without the support of the LO Secretariat. Hansson's influential book was published in the LO's own booklet series, implying that the Secretariat had approved the manuscript: the Secretariat was invested with the power to stop publication, and it did review drafts of items in the booklet series before publication. For example, Per Bergman's booklet *Vår fackliga kamp* (Our Trade Union Struggle) was distributed to the entire Secretariat for review before it was published (Landssekretariatet 1921c). In the event, the book was used in the most common study circle course for almost twenty years.

Actions of the LO leadership in the Late 1920s

Whereas the LO's main concern in the 1920s had been the left-wing organizations and the large number of strikes, resulting in outreach and educational efforts focusing on the syndicalists and communists, this focus shifted somewhat in the late 1920s. This was partly because of the increased interest of the Swedish Parliament in labor conflicts. The industrial actions in the 1920s disrupted the Swedish economy to the extent that addressing work stoppages was strongly prioritized by Parliament. In 1926 the social democratic government initiated a public investigation of what was needed for sustainable labor market peace (SOU 1927: 4), and the Liberal government that succeeded it proposed a bill on collective agreements that had profound impact on labor conflicts. This new law bound the parties entering into collective agreements to peace, so conflicts were prohibited while an agreement was in place. If one party did start a conflict, the individuals involved would be prosecuted, and the organization could be sued. In other words, the organizations were responsible for making their members comply with the agreement. The members, on the other hand, were forced by the law to accept an agreement reached by the organization; and even if they left the organization, they could be sued for contravening this requirement (Casparsson 1951, 107–11).

Since any type of regulation of the labor market was regarded with suspicion in the labor movement, the law on collective agreements passed in 1928 was preceded by protests unprecedented in the history of the LO. The law might seem fairly uncontroversial in retrospect, but in 1927–1928 it was strongly contested by the labor movement because it constrained the right to strike. The law also put pressure on the unions to impose discipline in the movement. Complaints about the law poured into the LO Secretariat; protests were directed toward the government, but many local sections demanded that the Secretariat take action. The LO's official standpoint was to oppose the law, as the SAP did, but this was done with little result.

The law may have helped the communist project, the Unity Committee (Enhetskommittén, see chapter 2), to obtain more support among Swedish workers, and its 1929 conference attracted almost twice as many local sections as did the first one (Casparsson 1951; Kennerström 1974, 10; Schüllerqvist 1992). Indeed, the law made it easy for the left-wing organizations to argue that the bourgeois state was trying to suppress the working class.

In response to the strong reactions to the law on collective agreements, the government attempted to improve labor relations in 1928 by organizing a labor market peace conference. Inspired by the Mond-Turner talks in Britain (McDonald and Gospel 1973), the conference's purpose was to improve relations between workers and employers. The LO Representatives were torn regarding the peace conference. Some, including Sigfrid Hansson as the main proponent, defended the conference, claiming that employers and unions had common interests. However, meeting only when conflict had already escalated would never deepen the common interests, according to Hansson. Others strongly opposed such an approach (Casparsson 1951, 142–43). The conference resulted in the appointment of a new committee whose aim was to improve labor relations (Hansson 1928b). Hansson referred to the conference as the "consensus conference" in *Fackföreningsrörelsen.*

Threats of even greater interference in the labor market came in 1934. The SAP leader and prime minister (1932–46) Per Albin Hansson participated in the LO Secretariat's meeting in December and made it clear that the state would interfere in the labor market unless other solutions to the conflicts could be found (Landssekretariatet 1934b).

The pressure from Parliament and the government more widely must indeed have given the LO an incentive to change the prevalent situation in the labor market and above all to change the image of the employers among the members. What was actually done besides creating employer-friendly content in the educational materials?

Getting to Know the Enemy

If the strategy was not only to actively address identity formation but also to change the image of the employers among the workers, what would be the best way of doing that? Sigfrid Hansson's answer was to inform the LO members of the employers' perspective on various labor market issues. If the demonized "other"—the enemy of the workers—was given the opportunity to tell the workers about their views of particular problems and their experiences of production, attitudes toward the employers could change.

Employing this strategy, Hansson invited managers of big companies to talk about their situation (and the production problems they faced) at meetings with trade union members. Information about these events is sparse, so it is hard to tell how often such events were arranged and whether the strategy was successful. In the correspondence between Hansson and Gerhard de Geer, the manager of Lesjöforsen AB in the Värmland region, we can ascertain that de Geer had been invited to talk about "work from the employers' perspective" at least twice in 1934 and 1935. In 1934 the meeting had taken place in Viggbyholm, Stockholm, and workers' reaction to de Geer's speech had not been positive (de Geer 1935; Hansson 1935c). De Geer was an atypical and controversial representative of the employers, which might well have been why he was chosen. In the numerous attempts to reduce wages in the early 1920s, de Geer was one of the prime advocates of lowering wages. Representing the classic school of liberal economic theory, de Geer was one of the men who had provoked the LO to initiate a new general strike in 1920, which he asserted could "solve the union problem" once and for all (Casparsson 1951, 26–27).

Regardless of the results of such attempts, the whole idea of inviting managers to talk to union members in order to improve relations with employers illustrates how important it must have been for the LO to facilitate a change in attitudes.

The SAF at Brunnsvik

It was at Brunnsvik, again, that Hansson's ideas came to be realized with the best possible effect. The SAF manager, Gustaf Söderlund, was invited to the LO school at Brunnsvik in 1935. Söderlund gave two lectures, one on the organizational structure of the SAF, a lecture that, in his own words, "was hardly likely to give rise to discussion" (Söderlund 1935b), and one with the title "The Contradiction between Capital and Labor." In the latter, which treated the relationship between workers and capital, Söderlund pointed out that the struggle between the labor market parties was inevitable because of the very nature of the labor market organizations. However, the antagonism between the two could be handled in different ways. He dismissed the syndicalist way and industrial democracy, saying that they would only empower the workers, not resolve the antagonism. He also criticized the option of letting the state resolve labor conflicts. The best way, according to Söderlund, was if the labor market parties could handle the conflicts on their own, without state interference. However, such an approach required that both parties restrain themselves, which would be easier if they learned more about each other (Söderlund 1935c). The symbolic value and importance of having the leader of the employers lecturing at Brunnsvik, a location intimately connected to the labor movement, should not be underestimated.

The reactions were not long in coming. Söderlund's appearance at Brunnsvik caused reactions in the left-wing press, and Hansson had to defend the lectures in *Fackföreningsrörelsen* (Hansson 1935a). Later on that summer, Söderlund commented on the debate in a letter to Hansson in which he stated that "we may well rejoice that the critics essentially are named *Ny Dag* and *Nya Dagligt Allehanda*" (Söderlund 1935a). The newspaper *Ny Dag* was a communist newspaper and *Nya Dagligt Allehanda* was a conservative one. In other words, the speech was not publicly criticized by the LO affiliates or members of the SAF. Instead, it was the supposedly "natural"—in terms of class structure—friends of the employers (the political right) and the LO (the left-wing parties) that opposed cooperation. In 1935, the controversial de Geer was also invited to the LO school in Brunnsvik (de Geer 1935; Hansson 1935c).

Once again, Sigfrid Hansson appears to have played an important role in the LO. In a letter to Sigfrid Hansson after Söderlund's speech at Brunnsvik in 1935, Stefan Oljelund, editor of the social democratic newspaper *Ny Tid*, pointed out: "I think that the spirit that breathes in your words, which testify to extensive experience and keen judgment of human nature, in the long run is more beneficial for those we want to serve than revolutionary or dogmatic speeches. Surely, we can have a good conscience that we are truly serving the working class. It will probably be more obvious what you meant in that regard" (Oljelund 1935).

Oljelund, like Hansson, appears to have been convinced that closer cooperation with the employers was the best way of serving the interests of the working class.

Inviting representatives of the employers' side to talk about the common interests of the labor market parties was hardly a random act. Moreover, the correspondence between Hansson and Söderlund testifies not only to two men with common ideas as to "what had to be done" to solve the labor market issues but also to friendship. It is possible that the friendship emanated from the different committees on the National Board of Health and Welfare (the first Swedish government agency in which the labor market parties had representation, not only in the executive board but also in a number of committees) in which Hansson and Söderlund served as representatives of their organizations (see Statskalendern 1931–1938). Irrespective of how Söderlund and Hansson became acquainted, because of his success Söderlund was invited to give lectures at the LO school in Brunnsvik again the following summer (Söderlund 1936).

The Enterprise from the Worker's Perspective

Brunnsvik was not only the venue where personal connections were forged between the elites of the labor market parties; the summer school classes also treated specific themes in line with the employer-friendly policy. In the summer of 1935, the course on trade union studies contained an essay competition on the subject "The Worker and the Enterprise." Söderlund's appearance at Brunnsvik, lecturing about "the enterprise from the employers' perspective," was followed by an essay competition intended to complement that perspective with the workers' standpoint. Approximately ten essays were entered, seven of which have been preserved. The winner, Tore Flyckt, also gave a speech on the subject (Landsorganisationen 1935, 148).

Analysis of the students' essays indicates that the course genuinely tried to address the relationship between workers and employers. The essays all try to explain why workers held a particular view of the enterprise and what affected their perceptions. Structural factors such as type of employment (long-term vs. short-term), sector (export vs. domestic industries), and wages were all presented as factors affecting workers' attitudes toward the enterprise (Andersson 1935; Flyckt 1935; Jakobsson 1935). Moreover, the perceived use of the production in which the workers were involved had an important impact on loyalty and commitment to the enterprise. When workers thought favorably of what they were producing and how it would be used, the workers would take responsibility for production (Flyckt 1935; Jansson 1935; Svensson 1935).

The essays also make it clear that course participants recognized how important it was that the enterprise should prosper. If the management assigned itself a disproportionately high wage, the workers had a right to complain, but it was in the interest of the workers (and the employers) that the enterprise should deliver good results. In a company with efficient production, the workers could perceive themselves as important and thus feel a stronger connection to the company. Furthermore, under such circumstances, workers would show loyalty toward the employer. The essay writers considered rationalization a natural aspect of an enterprise (compare Johansson 1989) that was not necessarily harmful for the workers: if the enterprise rationalized its production, the workers could be sure that this was of use to society, and the work could become more meaningful for them (Andersson 1935; Flyckt 1935).

The essay writers all emphasized the importance for the workers and employers both developing a sense of belonging to the enterprise; in theoretical terms, the essays stressed the importance of an organizational identity in relation to production.

One argument made in favor of cooperation and consensus between the labor market parties was that of usefulness for society as a whole (Flyckt 1935). The idea that the labor market parties should stop focusing on narrow self-interest and instead consider Swedish society implies that the parties were *co-responsible* for the societal economy. This is hardly surprising, since this line of thought runs through Hansson's book: "It is therefore of great importance that any conflict that might arise ought to be settled by peaceful means, if possible. On the whole, that is the approach generally taken. Since both parties are largely sympathetic to one another and are well aware of what conflict can lead to, in the long term they always seek to avoid open conflict" (Andersson 1935).

The history of the trade union movement was also described by the students. Initiated by perceived oppression, the trade union movement had a tense relationship with the employers during its first phase. However, because of better social insurance systems, for example, tensions had declined (Flyckt 1935).

Finally, the most important factor that affected the workers' view of the enterprise was the enlightenment of the working class (Andersson 1935; Flyckt 1935; Håkansson 1935):

> A worker with a high level of awareness sees the importance of the enterprise that employs him to society. In this way workers foster a positive attitude to the company . . . workers who are less aware, however, are unable to appreciate the significance to society of the company they work for. This means that they often have a negative attitude to the company, which then mostly appears to be a predator seeking to "exploit" the worker. Thus, both society and companies should make every effort to raise the workers' educational standards as much as possible. (Flyckt 1935)

The importance of popular education for the maturation of the working class and therefore the insight that consensus could bring gains to the working class strongly confirms the thesis of the present study. One essay writer even recommended that the workers follow the "excellent" syllabi the ABF provided: "With regard to popular education in general, we cannot appreciate enough what the ABF has accomplished. The best way of doing so is, if we haven't already done so, to join the ABF elite team and continue [the work] and thus strengthen the movement, whose aims are immensely valuable, not only for the workers themselves but also for society as a whole" (Andersson 1935).

Are the essays a measure of the outcome of workers' education? The essays doubtless mirror what was taught at Brunnsvik. The course transmitted a view of the employers compatible with the new relationship based on consensus that the LO Secretariat tried to establish among LO members. The essays also confirm the link between popular education and the behavior of the workers, seeing that an educated and enlightened worker would not act irresponsibly. The students, on the other hand, were unlikely to have been random members but rather were probably local activists occupying central posts in the labor movement in their home communities. What was taught at Brunnsvik cannot therefore be freely generalized to the rest of the study activities organized in the 1920s and 1930s. We can, however, assume that the ideas expressed in the essays were ideas held by the study leaders who had attended the LO school. Flyckt, the winner, was clearly the essay writer who most accurately expressed Hansson's ideas. As the

FIGURE 4.2 Sigfrid Hansson (*center, with open jacket*) in front of the students in Brunnsvik, 1937. *Source:* 3331/0845 Fotosamling Brunnsviks folkhögskola, ARAB, Stockholm.

quotation above demonstrates, he both advocated cooperation with the employers and condemned the behavior of the SAC, while praising popular education.

Reformism and Consensus

Organizational members can indeed be controlled through identity formation. Matts Alvesson and Hugh Willmott noted that the morals and values defined by the organization can be used to establish a distinct set of rules of the game by which "norms about the 'natural' way of doing things" are established (Alvesson and Willmott 2002). "Natural" ways of doing things create a logic of appropriateness, and if such norms are established among the members, they will create discipline in the movement. The expounded morals and values with regard to how reformist trade unions have acted and how trade union members in general *should* act, which were entrenched in the study materials, contained all the right elements to set up such rules of the game.

The routinization of charisma, which promotes identification with an organization (Ashforth and Mael 1989), was not achieved through the idealization of the leaders (e.g., as "heroes," a common view in communist communities); rather, the ideal everyday worker became the norm. This ideal member, the ordinary worker, had internalized the values important to the organization, particularly regarding his or her relationship to the employers and the left-wing organizations.

The actions taken by Hansson in the 1930s testify to the effects of strategic action taken to accomplish a change in attitudes using different kinds of education. Hansson appears to have played a central role in the LO and seems to have had few rivals. He was the editor of *Fackföreningsrörelsen* and was appointed commissioner of the board of the LO school at Brunnsvik in 1924, board chair of the ABF in 1928, and director of the LO school at Brunnsvik in 1929. He also wrote histories of many LO affiliates, as well as the memorial publication for the LO's first twenty-five years. He was the author of several titles in the LO's booklet series. He was assigned the task of giving a lecture course on trade union studies that was broadcast on radio in 1931 (the ABF had an agreement with Radio Sweden to broadcast for thirty minutes every Sunday).[10] In other words, he occupied a key position in the system of workers' education. Besides his various positions in the educational sphere he was also, in the capacity of editor, a member of the LO Secretariat as well as being an SAP member of Parliament. As the brother of Per Albin Hansson, the SAP leader, he was likely well informed about the party's internal affairs. He had not, unlike the other members of the Secretariat, gained his position by working for his local union; rather, he had risen from the ranks of the SSU and made a career as a trade union intellectual, despite limited experience of labor market conflicts. This might have allowed him to take an alternate ideological perspective on the problems facing the LO.

Did popular education indeed instill reformism and the spirit of negotiation in its participants? Hansson had a very objective writing style. Even though the content was radically reformist, it was presented as science rather than propaganda, increasing the likelihood that the workers would take it seriously. The next chapter examines in greater detail how popular education was perceived by workers.

IMPLEMENTING THE EDUCATION STRATEGY

Identity entrepreneurs acting strategically always face certain dilemmas: Do the grassroots really accept being told how to act and what to think about a movement? Can identity formation processes really be managed without compulsion? (If force is resorted to, the movement will inevitably be transformed from a social movement to authoritarian rule.) Can perceptions of the movement and, more importantly, the behavior of the members really change through study activities?

Doubtlessly, the LO Secretariat was forced to consider this dilemma, as overly strict identity management would scare off members and violate the democratic principle of the movement. Democracy was entrenched in all spheres of the labor movement and was, as chapter 4 shows, characteristic of the LO's organizational identity. Under such circumstances, it would be very difficult to employ compulsory ideological schooling of the membership or force anyone to study certain subjects or read certain books. However, the popular education system that had become the solution was inescapably "free and voluntary." In concrete terms, this meant that the local Workers' Educational Association (ABF) body, the education committee, and the local unions had great autonomy in shaping the education programs—for instance, in the choice of literature and courses to offer. The composition of the local education committee certainly influenced the topics of the study circles and the lectures. The only feedback from the grassroots to the LO was through the annual reports, submitted by the study circles to the ABF at the end of the year, detailing the subjects treated by the circle and the number of meetings held during the year.

Meanwhile, the educational sphere had an organizational logic of its own, and, as the workers' education movement grew stronger, two aims crystallized for the study activities. On the one hand, workers' education was supposed to compensate workers for their comparatively low level of prior education, improving their knowledge and skills in various subjects. On the other hand, following Gramsci, others emphasized the importance of "enlightening" and raising the awareness of the working class, since without proper insight and cultural knowledge the working class would never be able to seize power (Arvidson 1985, 142). These theorists and practitioners stressed not the appropriation of specific skills but rather the ability to analyze and appreciate the arts; the working class should be transformed from "individuals into human beings" (Gustavsson 1991, 29–30). Popular education offered one route to such enlightenment and could liberate the working class from the oppressive burden of ignorance. Neither of these strains of thought was clear in the LO Secretariat's education strategy. The Secretariat could only establish an institutional setting that would facilitate and encourage members to participate in certain study activities and then hope for the best. Scrutinizing how this strategy was received by the grassroots of the labor movement is therefore crucial for any assessment of the success of the education strategy, so this exercise constitutes the final part of this study.

Examining the Implementation

The LO Secretariat may have considered at least three crucial matters when trying to implement the education strategy: first, local-level steering (involving both the ABF education committees and the local unions); second, sufficient member participation for the strategy to have an effect; and, third, appropriate study activity content. These elements of implementation need further elaboration before we analyze the empirical material.

The first step in analyzing the education strategy implementation is to examine *the steering of the local organizations*. Soft steering, such as information distribution and encouragement, was the only means at the LO Secretariat's disposal. Meanwhile, an effective steering process for the local units was a prerequisite for the education system to take the form the LO leadership wanted. Did the steering approach work? As a first step in analyzing steering implementation, the development of the education committee in the industrial town of Skutskär and the relationship between this committee and the central ABF organization is examined. By mapping the composition of the education committee and its activities, we can establish whether the local unions and their education committees followed orders from above. The ABF was a meta-organization whose members were other organizations. At the local level, the organizational principle was the same: the local association (i.e., the local education committee) was an umbrella organization with other local associations as members, and those organizations depended on the local associational environment. Which local association took a leading role in the study activities affected the direction of the educational programs, influencing, for example, the subjects of the study circles, the books in the local ABF library, and the lecturers invited. If the reformist unions did not engage in the education programs, the education committee could have been spreading left-wing organizations' ideas or just presenting popular education in general subjects, such as mathematics, literature, and Swedish.

It has been established in previous chapters that the LO became more engaged in the ABF after 1920 when the shift in LO leadership took place and Thorberg attained power. If the strategy had been implemented correctly, the work of the local ABF should have changed around 1920–21. At least, the LO affiliates' local associations would have tried to change the study activities around that time. Thus, developments of *the local study activities should match the time order at the national level.*

Related to the steering of the local level is the attitude toward popular education among the local trade union sections. The idea of popular education might have been important at the central level but could have been a second-order priority at the local level. The local units may have considered the education programs a waste of time that diverted attention from ordinary trade union work. To what extent the grassroots—especially the activists—in the trade unions appreciated the popular education has implications for its execution as well as content. If the local unions were indifferent to workers' education, it is hard to argue that the popular education affected the workers. A second indicator of the local unions' commitment to popular education is whether or not the local sections subscribed to *Fackföreningsrörelsen.* As stated in chapter 3, the LO leaders defined the magazine as a means of educating the workers and establishing a new channel of information dissemination between members and leaders. If the education strategy was implemented properly, we would expect the union members to read the magazine.

The second step of the implementation analysis is *to scrutinize the scope of the study activities.* The scope of the education programs obviously indicates how well the local associations implemented the strategy. A shift in the activities from individual study forms, such as library services only, to collective forms of study, such as lectures and study circles, should have increased after 1920–21. At the national level, an increase should be discernible in the numbers of education committees, study circles, and circle participants around the country.

Moreover, the impact of the education could also depend on *who* participated. The ideal scenario would be that all workers did so, but this is unlikely. For the LO Secretariat, however, the most important group to reach was the local activists— that is, the trade union members who occupied positions of responsibility

TABLE 5.1   Summary of the analysis of the education strategy implementation

IMPLEMENTATION OF THE EDUCATION STRATEGY		EXPECTATIONS ACCORDING TO THE THESIS	THE THESIS DOES NOT HOLD IF . . .
1. Steering the local level	- Composition of education committees? - Time order compared with national level? - How did the unions perceive the education programs? - Were the trade union members encouraged to join study circles? - Subscriptions to the journal *Fackföreningsrörelsen*?	- The education committee was dominated by the reformist unions. - The local ABF's activities should have changed around 1920–21. - Shift in activities from libraries to collective forms of study activities. - The unions participated in the local educational activities.	- An education system was established but was inactive. - The education system was dominated by syndicalists and communists. - There was no or weak participation in the education programs.
2. The scope of the education programs	- Number of participants? - Number of study circles? - Who participated?	- The number of circles and lectures increased over time. - Union members participated in education programs. - Participants held important positions in the unions.	- The number of study circles did not increase. - The participants in the education programs were not active in the unions.
3. Content of the education	- Appropriate subjects? - What educational materials were used? - Did the study circles follow the syllabi?	- Majority of the circles and lectures had a reformist message. - The study circles studied what they set out to study.	- Only general subjects increased. - The field of trade union studies was marginalized. - No reformist literature was used. - The study circles did not follow the syllabuses.

in local associational life—because this group could steer the grassroots and was in a favorable position when it came to mobilizing workers in strikes. If these potentially important actors in the labor movement were involved in the popular education program, it is fair to assume that they would bring the skills they had learned and the ideas they had developed in the study circles to their work in the unions. This way, ideas about reformism and consensus could spread through these people to the members of the labor movement who did not actively engage in study activities. Inducing the activists to participate in the study activities could thus be decisive for changing the unions' way of interacting on the labor market. It must therefore be determined who attended the study circles and whether they had important roles in the local unions.

Finally, *the content of the study circles* is decisive for their possible effect. If study circles in mathematics had increased, for example, this would hardly have turned the workers into disciplined reformists. An increase in general knowledge among the workers could probably have other positive effects on the movement, but for the formation of an organizational identity a certain kind of education had to increase—namely, the study programs designed by Sigfrid Hansson. In the third step of the implementation study, accordingly, the content of the education program is analyzed. Ideally, if the education strategy was implemented flawlessly, the book *Den svenska fackföreningsrörelsen* or any of Hansson's other books with the same content would have been used in the study circles at the local level. If the unions did arrange popular education programs but none had any connection to the reformist doctrine, the thesis of the present book would lack support. Therefore, as a final step of the analysis, the study circles' work is investigated.

Table 5.1 summarizes the structure of the analysis. It also specifies the ideal circumstances in which the thesis of this book would gain support and the circumstances in which the thesis can be questioned. The last two columns should be seen as conveying ideal types; reality is far more complex and likely lies somewhere between these two.

Steering the Local Education Committees in Skutskär and Nationally

Examining these three steps of implementation requires not only an analysis of statistics from the national ABF but also a case study in order to trace the behavior of the unions at the local level. The case selected for the in-depth analysis of popular education at the local level is that of Skutskär. This typical industrial town is illustrative of the circumstances applicable to most places in Sweden at the time, as the reformist branch of the labor movement had not yet won the battle for the workers in the 1920s.

Skutskär is located near the coast in the municipality of Älvkarleby, in the northern part of the region of Uppland in central Sweden, between Uppsala and Gävle. Skutskär developed into a stronghold of social democracy in the twentieth century (Socialdemokraterna 2002, 14–15). Skutskär had approximately six thousand inhabitants in 1921 (including Harnäs), but by 1932 its population had fallen to approximately fifty-five hundred and by 1941 to five thousand (Nordisk Familjebok 1932; SCB 1942a).

Skutskär is best known for its impressive industrial complex situated on the coastline, near the Dalälven estuary. In the 1920s, this industrial complex, owned and run by Stora Kopparbergs bergslags AB (later Stora Enso), consisted of a sawmill and a pulp mill. The sawmill and pulp mill industries were important industries in Sweden. At that time, the mining and metal industry was the biggest industry in Sweden in terms of number of employees; the second biggest was the wood industry, including sawmills, followed by the paper mill industry (SCB 1921, 101–5; SCB 1928, 126–30; SCB 1933, 110–14).

In the late nineteenth century, the sawmill was the main employer in Skutskär and Harnäs. Founded in 1869 by a Norwegian company, the sawmill was sold to Stora Kopparbergs bergslags AB in 1885. Stora Kopparberg had plants in Domnarvet, Falun, and Korsån but concentrated its production in Skutskär after 1885 (Nordisk Familjebok 1932; Rolfsson et al. 1989). Skutskär's location was attractive to the sawmill industry because Dalälven—Sweden's second longest river—reaches the sea in Skutskär and was perfect for transporting lumber from the forests in the county of Dalarna to the sea. The port was located in the village of Harnäs, which also had a small ironworks dating from the seventeenth century (Rydbeck 1995, 157–58). The sawmill industry expanded greatly in Skutskär during the late nineteenth and early twentieth centuries to include sulfite and sulfate mills, a turpentine mill, an alcohol factory, and the paper industry (Nordisk Familjebok 1932; Rolfsson et al. 1989). Sweden had long been a prominent paper producer and in 1927 was the second biggest producer of chemical pulp behind the United States, making the paper industry important to both the domestic and world markets (Pappersindustriarbetareförbundet 1928, 24–25). Stora Kopparberg was a progressive company and at an early stage established a laboratory at its factory to improve pulp production (Jönsson and Gens 1993, 126–27; Rolfsson et al. 1989, 68–69). The industries connected to the pulp mill employed several occupational groups, including sawmill workers, paper mill workers, wood industry workers, lumberyard workers, electricians, and longshoremen.

The Trade Union Sphere in Skutskär

Skutskär was dominated by various branches of the wood industry, and the number of different unions was comparatively low in the 1920s and 1930s. Seven union sections were present: the Sawmill Workers' Union sections 2 and 54, the Paper Mill Workers' Union Section 2, the Longshoremen's Union Section 11, the Foundry Workers' Union, the Painters' Union, and the syndicalist local association (*lokal samorganisation*, LS) of Skutskär.

The unions in Skutskär had close relationships with one another, which is understandable considering that the various industries in Skutskär were all owned by the same company, Stora Kopparberg. The sawmill workers, lumberyard workers, and factory workers were all organized in one union in 1897, the Sawmill Workers' Union Section 2, but shortly afterward they split into different unions. The lumberyard workers kept the name Sawmill Workers' Union Section 2, whereas the actual sawmill workers became Section 54 in 1898 (Rolfsson et al. 1989, 136–37). In 1940, the sawmill workers' and lumberyard workers' unions reunited into one union, the Sawmill Workers' Union Section 2. August Lindberg, who signed the Basic Agreement as the president of the LO, started his career in the Sawmill Workers' Union Section 2 in Skutskär. He left Skutskär in 1920 to become an ombudsman in the central organization of the Sawmill Workers' Union. He was well regarded among the local workers, and a certain pride can be discerned in the minutes whenever they mention Lindberg— a son of the community who made it all the way to the headquarters of the Sawmill Workers' Union and later the LO, defending workers' rights. The industrial workers founded their own organization in 1900, the Factory Workers' Union Section 60, which in 1920 became the Paper Mill Workers' Union Section 2. The Sawmill Workers' Union sections 2 and 54 and the Paper Mill Workers' Union Section 2 cooperated frequently and regularly held joint meetings. The syndicalist trade union Skutskär's LS was founded in 1919.

As table 5.2 shows, the reformist unions organized the majority of the organized workers in Skutskär. During the 1920s, however, the syndicalists clearly constituted a viable alternative to the reformist unions (organizing up to 25–30 percent of the organized workers), so the community cannot be regarded as reformist from the start. On the contrary, the critical mass of syndicalist members makes Skutskär a suitable case for examining the implementation of the education strategy.

The three other unions in Skutskär—the Longshoremen's Union, Foundry Workers' Union, and Painters' Union—were smaller sections that have left little material behind. The Foundry Workers' Union existed for only six years (1919–25). No documentation of the Painters' Union remains; we know it existed only

TABLE 5.2   Union memberships in Skutskär, 1915–1940

	SAWMILL WORKERS' UNION SEC. 2 (LUMBERYARD WORKERS)	SAWMILL WORKERS' UNION SEC. 54	PAPER MILL WORKERS' UNION SEC. 2	SKUTSKÄR'S LS
1915	74	–	106	–
1916	83	67	130	–
1917	133	83	258	–
1918	149	107	311	–
1919	176	111	305	79
1920	157	87	302	233
1921	175	122	409	319
1922	192	148	307	198
1923	215	154	357	162
1924	253	242	397	159
1925	275	275	418	174
1926	273	269	447	149
1927	272	254	468	148
1928	285	241	500	132
1929	311	254	530	119
1930	324	283	573	80
1931	300	294	603	66
1932	238	289	599	95
1933	212	279	574	99
1934	191	270	591	85
1935	166	257	566	77
1936	144	232	576	80
1937	126	211	615	78
1938	122	201	648	81
1939	118	192	639	75
1940	303*	–	649	67

*In total, 192 workers were transferred from Section 54 to Section 2.

because it was a member of the local ABF section. These three smaller unions have been left out of the analysis, which instead focuses on the major unions: the Paper Mill Workers' and Sawmill Workers' Unions.

Industrial Conflicts in Skutskär

There were several major worker-employer conflicts in Skutskär in the 1920s and 1930s. The number of work stoppages was not extraordinarily high compared with that in other sawmill-dominated communities elsewhere in Sweden. In general, the conflict level in Skutskär followed the national pattern in the sawmill and paper mill industries. There were work stoppages (strikes or lockouts) approximately every second year in the 1920s. In between, there were small conflicts almost constantly, but they did not escalate into work stoppages. It seems to have been unusual for a conflict to last less than a month (Pappersindustriarbetareförbundet 1917–1940; Sågverksindustriarbetareförbundet 1917–1940). Most conflicts started in the Paper Mill Workers' Union and spread to the sawmill workers. In the second half of the 1920s, many of the conflicts involving the unions were caused by breakdowns in wage negotiations; in most of these cases, the employer locked the workers out.

In 1925, the Swedish Employers' Association (Svenska Arbetsgivareföreningen, SAF) launched a nationwide lockout in order to reduce wages in several trades, and the paper mill and sawmill workers in Skutskär were affected. The workers responded by announcing strikes. The lockout ended after only one month and was described as a major victory for the workers in the unions (Casparsson 1951, 26–41; Sågverksindustriarbetareförbundet avd. 2 1925), which boosted the workers' confidence and self-esteem. The fact that the workers could mobilize such a large number of participants in the conflict forced the employers to the negotiation table in the conflict of 1925, according to the unions' analysis.

The next major conflict came in 1928 in the paper mill industry. Once again, it started at the national level, when the employers' organization again tried to reduce wages during the wage negotiations that year. The workers rejected the wage offer, and the reaction of the paper mill employers' organization was to proclaim a lockout, first against the paper mill workers but a few weeks later expanding to include sawmill workers, in an attempt to put pressure on the paper mill workers. The lockout was again described as a failure for the employers: after ten weeks, the employers agreed to extend the agreement from 1927, retreating from their intention to reduce wages (Eling 1989, 85; Sågverksindustriarbetareförbundet avd. 2 1928). Once again, the victory strengthened the workers' side. After this confrontation, the paper mill industry was spared from conflict for two years.

In 1932, however, a new conflict started that would turn out to be more comprehensive than any before. In that year, the Great Depression had started to severely affect the Swedish economy. The crash of the New York Stock Exchange in the autumn of 1929 had revealed an unstable stock market system, and the crisis spread to the wider financial market. As the paper industry belonged to the traded sector, highly dependent on the world market, the decreased global demand in the autumn of 1931 hit the paper mill industry. As in previous conflicts, the employers were inspired by liberal economists, so the solution was to reduce wages (Unga 1976, 49–54). After negotiations, the employers canceled the existing collective agreement, and the Paper Mill Workers' Union responded by initiating a strike in February 1932. Skutskär was one of eight factories in the country where workers put down their tools, so the strike was not a local conflict but a nationwide one. A proposal for resolving the conflict came in March, but it was rejected by the members (the paper industry workers always held membership referenda on agreements and strikes). Among the union sections that voted in favor of accepting the offer was that in Skutskär. However, since most sections in the country voted against the proposal, the conflict continued until September that year. By that time, the strike funds were completely exhausted and the workers had to accept an offer inferior to the one in March. The defeat was devastating. The union movement suspected that the employers had purposely prolonged the conflict, enabling them to cut back production without layoffs (Olsson 1980; Pappersindustriarbetareförbundet 1932, 21–25). After 1932, the level of conflict decreased in Skutskär, as in most parts of the country.

Syndicalist Conflicts and Sympathy Actions in Skutskär

The syndicalist organization Skutskär LS was formed in 1919. The syndicalists in Skutskär had never had particularly good relations with the employer Stora Kopparberg. In 1920, Stora Kopparberg falsely accused the syndicalist leader Viktor Eriksson of stealing, and he was arrested in humiliating circumstances. A trial was held, and Eriksson was found not guilty. Stories from 1920 portray Eriksson as returning to Skutskär from the trial in Gävle as a hero, with a marching band greeting the David who had stood up to Goliath (Eling 1989, 74). This incident has a symbolic value that should not be underestimated. It lived on in the memory of the workers in Skutskär and pushed the reformist workers closer to the SAC, uniting all workers against the common enemy. The leader of Skutskär LS during the 1920s was Axel Lindberg, the brother of August Lindberg.

The reformist unions supported the LS through sympathy actions from time to time. At the beginning of the 1920s, all the reformist unions in Skutskär participated in a sympathy strike for the LS. Stora Kopparberg had repeatedly harassed syndicalist workers, resulting in the mobilization of support for the syndicalists among the reformist trade unions. The reformist trade unions also supported the syndicalists by negotiating with the employer on their behalf in some cases when syndicalists had been harassed.[1] However, support actions for the syndicalists decreased in the 1930s, possibly because of rationalizations: Stora Kopparberg tended to lay off syndicalists and unorganized workers in the major rationalizations around 1928–32 (Pappersindustriarbetareförbundet 1920–1940; Sågverksindustriarbetareförbundet 1910–1940; Sågverksindustriarbetareförbundet avd. 2 1922) rather than LO members, as it caused too much trouble to fire the latter. Nevertheless, sympathy actions for the syndicalists were not unusual, and the actions in Skutskär are typical in this regard.

The Party Sphere in Skutskär

Political party organizations, especially the youth organization of the SAP, were also involved in the popular education system. The SAP was established as early as 1901 in Skutskär, and in 1913 a local group of the SDU, the SDUK, was formed.[2] When the SAP split in 1917, the local social democratic organization in Skutskär also split. One part, led by August Lindberg, joined the Left Party and started a local section, a so-called Left Party commune, in Skutskär with the SDUK. When the Left Party became the Communist Party in 1921, the local party organization split into a Left Party fraction and a communist fraction, and the youth organization joined the Communist Party and started the communist Workers' Commune in Skutskär. The Left Party was represented in the municipal council in Älvkarleby until it rejoined the SAP in 1923. These local developments followed the pattern at the national level described in chapter 2 and are illustrated in figure 5.1. In 1924, the Social Democratic Workers' Commune started a new

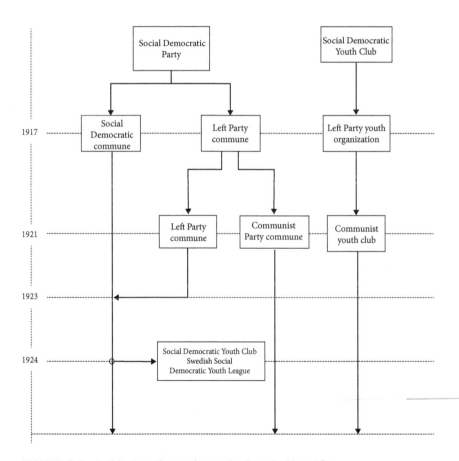

FIGURE 5.1 Political parties and organizations in Skutskär

youth organization in Skutskär and reclaimed the old name, the SDUK, even though the national youth organization by this time was called the SSU.[3] The SAP had been in power in the municipality ever since the introduction of universal suffrage in 1921 (and it is still in power today).

After the split of the SAP in 1917, there was significant support for the Social Democratic Left Party within the unions in Skutskär, especially within the Sawmill Workers' Union Section 2. August Lindberg, the chair of the Sawmill Workers' Union Section 2, founded the Social Democratic Left Party in Skutskär. Lindberg was not the only one to support the Left Party; all the reformist trade unions in Skutskär paid membership fees to the Left Party from 1917 until it reunited with the SAP in 1923 (Vänsterkommunen Skutskär 1917a). The fragmentation of the labor movement experienced at the national level was certainly reflected in Skutskär.

Organizing Popular Education at the Local Level

The first step in analyzing the education strategy implementation is to examine the steering of the local organizations—that is, both the education committee and the local unions. The popular education would likely have the desired impact if the institutions promoting it at the local level were controlled or at least dominated by the reformist trade unions. Moreover, the organizing of popular education at the local level should also be consistent with the time order at the national level. The establishment of local education committees all over the country would have been in vain unless the unions embraced the idea of education. For the strategy to be implemented successfully, the unions had to be involved and to have perceived study activities as important.

The Constitution of the Education Committee

On the initiative of the Nytt Hopp (New Hope) lodge of the workers' temperance organization Nykterhetsorden Verdandi (NOV), the local education committee in Skutkär was formed in February 1917. As in most other places in Sweden, establishing a library (here, ABF library number 246) was the main task of the local ABF section during its first years (ABF Skutskär 1917b; ABF Skutskär 1920c; Eling 1989, 81–82).

The founding organizations, besides the NOV lodge, were the Paper Mill Workers' Union Section 2, the Sawmill Workers' Union sections 2 and 54, Skutskär's Longshoremen's Union Section 11, the Social Democratic

Commune in Skutskär, and the Social Democratic Youth Organization, SDUK (ABF Skutskär 1917b).[4] The latter had joined the Left Party in the same month as the education committee was established (Larsson 1964). The reformist organizations were clearly in a majority position during the first year. The initial influence of NOV over popular education in Skutskär was quickly phased out, and the NOV lodge was no longer a member of the education committee after 1924 (ABF Skutskär 1926).

Each member organization of the local ABF body had one representative on the education committee (i.e., the local ABF board). The organizations paid a membership fee in accordance with their own membership rates of ten öre per member per year (Sågverksindustriarbetareförbundet avd. 2 1917b). It appears that the membership fee was uncontentious for the unions; in Section 2 of the Sawmill Workers' Union the matter was not even debated but simply voted through at the annual meeting (Sågverksindustriarbetareförbundet avd. 2 1917c), suggesting that the unions had already considered popular education a natural part of labor movement activities.

The local syndicalist organization, the Skärskär LS, joined the education committee in 1923, shortly after the central syndicalist organization, the SAC, had joined the ABF in 1922 (ABF Skutskär 1923b; SAC 1922, 12–13). Information about the syndicalists is sparse, but, judging from the annual reports on membership fees paid to the education committee, the LS was the fifth-biggest organization in the local education committee by the end of the 1920s (ABF Skutskär 1928b).

Neither the Left Party nor the Communist Party joined the education committee, but the Left Party's youth organization, the SDUK, was a member of the education committee, keeping the Left Party informed of the position of the local ABF and allowing it to use the local facilities. After the SDUK became the Communist Youth Organization in 1921, it participated in the study activities in Skutskär and even arranged a study circle in 1921–22 under the leadership of John Sandberg (ABF 1921b). The influence of the left-wing organizations on the study activities does not seem to have been particularly strong in the 1920s, though there was some indirect influence. For example, the chair of the Left Party Commune also occupied the position of chair of the Sawmill Workers' Union Section 2, which meant that it could influence the education indirectly without being a formal member of the education committee.[5]

There is little sign of conflict between the members of the education committee. The entrance of the syndicalist LS did not cause any controversies either. The closest to a conflict found recorded in the minutes of the committee's meetings concerned scholarships to go to Brunnsvik. These scholarships were established in 1929 in response to the concerns of representatives in the education committee that Skutskär had too few study circles. The committee claimed that one reason for this deficiency was the lack of study circle leaders. To solve this problem, two scholarships to finance the study leader course at Brunnsvik were established, and anyone could apply for them (ABF Skutskär 1929). Axel Lindberg, who represented the LS on the education committee, applied for a scholarship but was not permitted to take the courses he was interested in, as the scholarship was intended primarily to educate study circle leaders in trade union studies and fiction. Lindberg declared that he had been overridden by the other representatives in the committee. The education committee denied that that was the case; instead, the other representatives stated that the need for study circle leaders in these two subjects had been the basis for the decision (ABF Skutskär 1930). Whether or not this was true, or whether this incident actually indicated serious conflicts in the education committee, is shrouded in history. Besides this incident, however, there are no traces of conflict in the education committee; instead, the representatives in the education committee appear to have been united in their mission to motivate and educate the workers in Skutskär.

Time Order

Between 1917 and 1920, the education committee held only one meeting each year, the annual meeting in which the preceding year was discussed and the committee's bookkeeping was approved. Also, the operational plan for the coming year was discussed and approved. If other meetings were held between the annual meetings, their minutes have not survived, but nothing indicates that the education committee was particularly active during the first three years of its existence. In December 1920, however, the pattern changed. An extra meeting was held, even though the operational plan had already been approved. At this extra meeting, the local education committee decided to nullify a decision made at the annual meeting only two months earlier. Instead of using the budget to buy new books for the library, the local committee decided to make changes in their activities; in particular, the committee decided to start arranging lectures (ABF Skutskär 1920b; ABF Skutskär 1920c). This decision led to a fairly sudden change in the local education activities in Skutskär. During the committee's three years of existence, running the library had been its main task, so the focus on lectures after 1920 represented a clear break.

Another meeting followed shortly after the extra meeting at which potential lecturers were discussed. The education committee showed enthusiasm for arranging lectures and had grand visions of their work. For example, the committee decided unanimously to invite Rickard Sandler to give a talk on socialism and decided that if Sandler was unavailable, Ernst Wigforss would be a good replacement (ABF Skutskär 1920a).[6] At that time, Sandler and Wigforss were already central figures in the Swedish labor movement, so the committee was not ready to settle for just any lecturer.

How well does this change correspond to developments at the national level? As illustrated in chapter 3, the idea of education as a means to stabilize the movement seems to have originated with Arvid Thorberg when he became the president of the LO in February 1920. Other researchers have also noted the change in the education programs around 1919–20 (Johansson 2002, 298; Åberg 2008, 66). In other words, the developments in Skutskär fit the processes within the LO at the national level quite well.

Controlling the Education Committees?

As shown in chapter 3, the reformist organizations dominated the ABF Representatives from 1919 onward, but that did not give the reformist branch control over the grassroots organizations per se. Rather, it gave them prerequisites for influencing the local committees and preventing the left-wing organizations from taking control of the ABF.[7] The matter of steering the local bodies is important, because if the education committee had started to live a life of its own without any connection to the central organization, it would have been very difficult for the LO to use the education system as a means to control the grassroots.

Organizational steering can be done through economic means. For example, the grants from the ABF to the local education committees could have been made on a conditional basis, though the ABF did not do so in any way. The ABF's principles regulating financial support for study circles seem to have been simple: the circles should study subjects that would improve the workers' ability to run labor movement organizations, be good citizens, and develop as human beings. These principles were formalized as rules in 1935 (Heffler 1962, 158).

The study circles were obliged to contribute financially, and the ABF would contribute the same sum as the study circle members had collected among themselves. This was also the case in Skutskär. According to the accounts of the education committee in Skutskär, the local committee's work was financed through the member organizations, the ABF, and grants from the county council; the study circle members also contributed small sums (ABF Skutskär 1914; ABF Skutskär 1933). However, there was no way to force the study circles to study certain topics. It was therefore hard to steer the local organizations by economic means. The only study circle subjects that seem to have been rejected for funding were vocational subjects (Heffler 1962, 158; Hellblom 1985, 192). This was doubtless part of the ABF's organizational design that was impossible to change: the various member organizations were free to use the means put at their disposal by the

ABF—their activities were to match those of the ABF, but they would never have to renounce their own identities.

Another way of exercising influence and steering was to guide the education committees on how to organize activities. This kind of steering, through distributing information that provided encouragement to behave in a certain way, probably helped make the study activities more alike around the country. Two instruments for informing the grassroots on issues related to popular education were the journal for the study circles, *Bokstugan*, published jointly by the ABF and a temperance organization (the IOGT), and *Studiekamraten*, the ABF's own magazine for "free and voluntary *bildung*." One of the most vital features of these magazines was the publishing of syllabi for study circle courses. Through the journals, the syllabi adopted by the central bureau and the ABF Representatives were disseminated throughout the country, spreading the central organizations' ideas on how study circles should act and what they should study to the grassroots.

Turning to developments in Skutskär, we know that the reformist unions in Skutskär appear to have had control over the education committee, and the expected change in the work of the local ABF accordingly came in 1920. However, did the local education committee obtain and consider information from the ABF? The library in Skutskär started to subscribe to *Bokstugan* in March 1920 (ABF Skutskär 1917a). This is significant because it gave the workers in Skutskär access to the syllabi approved by the central ABF body. *Studiekamraten* was also subscribed to by the education committee in Skutskär (ABF Skutskär 1928a). Whether the syllabi were used and followed by the workers in Skutskär is examined below.

Education Activities in Skutskär

Skutskär's education committee perceived its work as essential for the local labor movement. Besides trying to engage the workers in study circles, the committee offered one or two lectures targeting a broad audience in Skutskär every year during 1920–34. The topics varied, including fiction, the Swedish economy, sexual hygiene, and old-age pensions. In addition to these lectures, several lecture series on socialism were held at different times, and one lecture series on trade union studies was offered. The education committee managed to arrange for several famous activists and educators to visit Skutskär and give lectures, including Johan Sandler, Carl Cederblad, Frans Severin, Gunnar Hirdman, and the syndicalist and sexual education pioneer Elise Ottesen-Jensen (ABF Skutskär 1923a; ABF Skutskär 1928c; ABF Skutskär 1931; ABF Skutskär 1934).

Despite some well-attended lectures (Ottesen-Jensen's lecture in 1934, for example, attracted 194 attendees; ABF Skutskär 1934), the committee members were deeply concerned about the lack of interest in popular education among the workers in Skutskär (ABF Skutskär 1922; ABF Skutskär 1937). In particular, the education committee appears to have been worried about the study circles. Judging from the minutes and reports left behind by the education committee, a great concern among the members of the committee was the number of study circles and their quality, which was intimately tied to access to study circle leaders (ABF Skutskär 1930). Establishing scholarships to attend the LO school in Brunnsvik (ABF Skutskär 1929) was one action taken to address the problem. However, the scholarships already specified what subjects were to be studied by the applicant, as decided by the committee. In other words, the committee soon started to express its own will and opinion regarding which subjects *should* be studied in the study circles.

Education Activities in the Unions

Unsurprisingly, the education committee was determined to make the popular education programs work in Skutskär. However, a far more delicate issue was the *unions'* attitudes toward popular education. How important was such education to the unions?

Educational issues were not debated very often in the trade unions in Skutskär during the 1920s and 1930s. Union meetings in the local sections concerned roughly four categories of issues. The first category was negotiations with employers, above all about wages and collective agreements but also about the workplace environment. This category included most of the local sections' work. Second, the local sections discussed letters from their central organizations, the LO, and the ABF. These letters concerned conflicts, agreements, and general issues regarding the union movement. Third, the unions discussed fund-raising for various purposes—for example, solidarity funds for other union sections or for labor movements in other countries (e.g., Germany and Spain). Finally, union meetings devoted considerable time to reports by individual members who had attended meetings such as ones with other unions or organizations (the ABF, the People's Houses, etc.).[8] Debates on education were usually instigated by individual members who raised specific issues about the education programs or by letters from the ABF or the LO (see, for example, Pappersindustriarbetareförbundet avd. 2 1923; Pappersindustriarbetareförbundet avd. 2 1931; Pappersindustriarbetareförbundet avd. 2 1935).

The lack of debate and discussion at union meetings of popular education and study activities should not be taken as a sign of indifference to such activities.

Examining the actions of the unions clarifies the extent and type of their engagement in local ABF activities. The Paper Mill Workers' Union Section 2 and the Sawmill Workers' Union Section 54 initiated their own study circles in 1922 and 1926, respectively. The LS also had a study circle from 1927 onward (ABF Skutskär 1928b). These study circles were established and then kept going year after year, every year addressing new topics and involving new participants. The local sections did not talk much about the study circles. The Sawmill Workers' Union Section 54 mentioned the study circles in its annual reports, but the section does not seem to have intervened in their activities (Sågverksindustriarbetareförbundet avd. 54 1927; Sågverksindustriarbetareförbundet avd. 54 1930; Sågverksindustriarbetareförbundet avd. 54 1931). Technically, the study circles constituted small associations in themselves, independent of the unions. However, the union sections kept themselves informed about the work of the circles, which was possible because the study circle participants usually also attended the section meetings (these networks of activists are examined later in this chapter). Reports on the whereabouts of the study circles came informally from circle participants who attended union meetings. For example, in 1935 the study circle leader of Section 54's circle moved away from Skutskär; a new leader was needed if the study circle was not to be dissolved, a fact that the remaining circle participants reported to the section (Sågverksindustriarbetareförbundet avd. 54 1935). Moreover, if study activities declined, the section took action, advertising to persuade more members to attend and participate in the study activities arranged in Skutskär (Sågverksindustriarbetareförbundet avd 54 1935; Sågverksindustriarbetareförbundet avd. 54 1934). Other education formats, such as correspondence courses and lectures, were also monitored by the unions (see, for example, Pappersindustriarbetareförbundet avd. 2 1925) and advertised at union meetings (Pappersindustriarbetareförbundet avd. 2 1932).

Although the local union sections do not seem to have discussed the education programs much, keeping the study circles alive was desirable, and the unions appear to have taken responsibility for this. An important actor in this process was the SDUK. As previous chapters have shown, the youth organizations—both the Social Democratic Youth League, the SSU, and the Left Party's youth organization—attached great importance to popular education. This was also the case in Skutskär.

Education Activities in the SDUK

Both the Social Democratic Youth League (SSU) and the Communist Youth Organization (KUF) valued "enlightenment" and awareness-raising (see appendix tables 2 and 3, which present the number of study circles organized by each member organization in the ABF). Active youth organizations therefore became a vehicle for the development of the education system at the local level.

After its rebirth in 1924 as the youth league of the Social Democratic Party, the SDUK in Skutskär spent a lot of time and resources on education. In fact, this group became the driving force of the local ABF and the study circles. The SDUK formed an education council whose aim was to engage members as well as workers in general in popular education (SDUK Skutskär 1933a; SDUK Skutskär 1933b).

One SDUK strategy to increase its influence over the local ABF education committee (and thereby control the orientation of the educational activities offered in Skutskär) was, as with the Communist Party, to act through the unions. Indeed, the SDUK had a strategy of endeavoring to influence the unions and carefully recorded how many positions in the local unions were held by SDUK members (SDUK Skutskär 1928). This explicit strategy of getting its members into important positions in local associations would allow the SDUK to spread the social democratic message (SDUK Skutskär 1932). The SDUK's education council stated in 1928 that the educational work had proceeded satisfactorily during the short period it had been operating but that more members should be more involved: "No, comrades, our solution should be that all club members must participate in the study activities. Remember that without a knowledgeable and purposeful working class we can never achieve our goal, a more equal and just distribution of the goods of the world, a socialist society" (SDUK Skutskär 1928). The SDUK had approximately one meeting per month at which "knowledge quarters" were held. Knowledge quarters were short lectures, usually given by an SDUK member. The subjects varied, but most were about labor movement subjects such as "the principles of organization in trade unions," "the issue of a world language," "women and work," and "unemployment" (SDUK Skutskär 1930; SDUK Skutskär 1933b).

In 1932–33, Skutskär's SDUK had three study circles—on Swedish, organizational studies, and labor movement history—but it also reported that several members had attended study circles held by other organizations (SDUK Skutskär 1933b). Participating in study circles was highly valued, and the organization repeatedly expressed dissatisfaction at the small number of members participating in the SDUK's own education programs. Finding qualified study circle leaders was a recurring problem. The SDUK's 1933 annual report reveals that the association had managed to recruit study circle leaders for the subjects of socialism and trade union studies (SDUK Skutskär 1933a).

The SDUK was an important part of associational life in Skutskär, and the youth organization attributed great value to education. In its annual report on educational activities in 1932, the SDUK reported that 117 club members had participated in study circles (SDUK Skutskär 1933a). That year, 179 people in Skutskär had participated in study circles overall (see table 5.6), meaning that the majority of the study circle participants were SDUK members. These figures could have been overestimated, as the youth organization definitely wanted to frame itself as an advocate for enlightening the working class, but it is safe to say that the SDUK was a key actor in popular education in Skutskär. During the 1930s, the SDUK became increasingly disappointed with its members' lack of interest in popular education: "The club members' laziness and indifference to studies are as indefensible as they are inexplicable, when there are opportunities to gain the knowledge necessary to become practically and socially qualified citizens through the study circles virtually without cost" (SDUK Skutskär 1935c). To the SDUK, enlightenment was a cornerstone in making the labor movement effective, and popular education was the way to facilitate such enlightenment.

The Magazine *Fackföreningsrörelsen*

After its first trial issue in 1920, *Fackföreningsrörelsen* started publication as a weekly journal in 1921. *Fackföreningsrörelsen* was frequently promoted by the LO, which sent letters to its sections about the magazine, urging everyone to subscribe. Normally, the LO's correspondence with local union sections went through the affiliated unions, and the most common subjects, naturally, were wage negotiations and labor market conflicts. From 1921 onward, the magazine was a recurrent theme in communication with the sections. The LO Secretariat argued: "It is of great importance for the whole trade union movement and for the activities of each and every affiliate that the members' knowledge of trade union issues be intensified and expanded. Landsorganisationen has, because of this, tried to disseminate knowledge of trade union issues by establishing the magazine *Fackföreningsrörelsen* and Landsorganisationen's booklet series" (Landsorganisationen 1923b). The LO leadership seemed very eager to convince the sections to buy the magazine. Eventually, the LO even subsidized subscriptions, paying some of the costs of production to lower the price for the local sections (Landsorganisationen 1923b; Landsorganisationen 1924d; Landsorganisationen 1925c; Landsorganisationen 1927a; Landsorganisationen 1927b; Landsorganisationen 1928a; Landsorganisationen 1937). The magazine was described as a means of "caring for the members" and was meant to tie the workers to the movement, which in turn would increase its power (Hansson 1936a).

It would be very useful to know the size of the print runs, but unfortunately these figures cannot be traced. Nevertheless, we can examine whether the sections in Skutskär bought the magazine and, more importantly, whether it was read.

The Sawmill Workers' Union sections 2 and 54 and the Longshoremen's Union Section 11 all subscribed to the magazine. As early as December 1920, after the trial issue and before weekly publication had started, the LO sent a letter to the sections encouraging them to subscribe. The circular prompted debate among the members of the Longshoremen's Union section. The union's board suggested at a section meeting that the section should buy five subscriptions, mainly for the board members themselves, arguing that it was important for them to keep up with trade union issues. The meeting participants did not agree, however, and opponents suggested that the section should buy ten subscriptions because the magazine would probably interest all members, not only the board. "It was unfair that only the board should read it; the members should also have copies," they argued. In the end, the section bought only three subscriptions (Stuveriarbetarefackförbund 1920). All participants in the meeting agreed that the section should buy the magazine; the debate concerned how many copies were needed.

The Longshoremen's Union Section 11 was the first local section to subscribe, followed by the Sawmill Workers' Union Section 54. A decision was taken at a 1922 meeting of sawmill workers to buy three subscriptions for 1923. The same meeting also decided to subscribe to the magazine *Industria* (Sågverksindustriarbetareförbundet avd. 54 1922), the magazine of the employers' organization, the SAF. Obviously, the sawmill workers not only wanted information from the union movement but also wanted to keep up to date with the employers' analyses of labor market issues. The lumberyard workers in Skutskär also subscribed to *Fackföreningsrörelsen* (Sågverksindustriarbetareförbundet avd. 2 1926; Sågverksindustriarbetareförbundet avd. 54 1927).

How many workers did the magazine reach? Did only the section boards read it? The dissemination of the magazine's information and messages to the masses constituted an important part of the education strategy. Who read Sigfrid Hansson's essays in *Fackföreningsrörelsen*? In Skutskär we know that the information conveyed by the magazine did spread among the workers. For example, in the annual report of the Sawmill Workers' Union Section 2 from 1926, the section's board wrote that, during the preceding year, the section had read aloud from the magazine at meetings to raise awareness of trade union issues (Sågverksindustriarbetareförbundet avd. 2 1926). This appears to have been a habit for the section, part of its culture: even during August Lindberg's time as the section's chair (1915–19), reading aloud was integral to union meetings (Sågverksindustriarbetareförbundet avd. 2 1916; Sågverksindustriarbetareförbundet avd. 2 1917a). Obviously, the trade unions were not only interest organizations defending the workers in relation to the employers but also an environment in which workers could learn about politics and improve their education. In other words, the concept of enlightenment and the need for education so important to socialist theorists were actually practiced in Skutskär.

The Sawmill Workers' Union Section 54 donated two of its three *Fackföreningsrörelsen* subscriptions to the local ABF library after its members had finished reading them, so, from 1927 and onward, all issues of the magazine were available in the library for anyone to read. This donation is important because, aside from the book *Den svenska fackföreningsrörelsen*, articles from the magazine constituted the course material for several study circle courses, including ones in trade union studies (ABF Skutskär 1917a; Sågverksindustriarbetareförbundet avd. 54 1925). A prerequisite for anyone to follow Hansson's syllabus for trade union studies was therefore access to the magazine, which everyone indeed had in Skutskär.

Were the Unions Engaged in Popular Education?

The unions did not spend much time talking about popular education, which could indicate that it was not important to them; on the other hand, the sections monitored the study circles without interfering in them. It was important to keep the study circles alive, although the reasons for that are unclear. It seems that education was considered a natural part of union work, something union sections *should* engage in. In other words, promoting popular education was one of the norms of the union movement. The subscriptions to *Fackföreningsrörelsen* and, above all, the fact that the unions read aloud from the magazine indicate a willingness among the unions to engage in educating their members. In the SDUK, popular education was perceived as very important to the organization and the whole labor movement. The SDUK was not the same as the union movement, of course, but its members were also workers and trade union members. Its engagement in and enthusiasm for popular education was just as important as the unions' involvement. Since the LO affiliates dominated the education committee in Skutskär, the reformist unions were in a good position to control the study activities. The developments in Skutskär fit developments at the national level, so it seems the LO Secretariat could control or at least steer the local bodies solely through information provision.

The Scope and Participants of Popular Education

Engaged unions were not in themselves enough to ensure implementation of the education strategy. If study activities were successfully used to establish an organizational identity in the labor movement, the number of study circles and other collective forms of education should have increased over time. Likewise, if only a small minority of the workers attended the education programs, the thesis of this book would be called into question. An increased number of study circles should also follow the suggested time order, and study circles should increase in number after 1920. In this step of the analysis, it is both meaningful and feasible to go beyond the case of Skutskär to also consider study circle activities at the national level and then move on to the development of popular education in Skutskär.

Number of Study Circles at the National Level

The number of study circles arranged by the ABF grew rapidly in the 1920s. Figure 5.2 illustrates the total number of study circles offered during 1912–45 (black line) and the number of study circles specifically organized by the LO sections

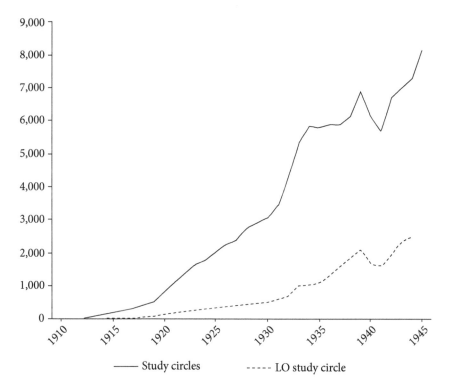

FIGURE 5.2 Number of study circles offered by the ABF, 1912–45. *Note:* The black line indicates all study circles offered by the ABF regardless of which organization specifically organized them. The dashed line indicates the number of study circles organized by the LO sections within the ABF. *Source:* data reported in ABF annual reports.

(dashed line). Examining the trend over time, two breaks of the time series are visible: the first is a rapid increase in the number of study circles in the 1920s, and the second is another sharp increase starting around 1930. The number of study circles continued to grow in the 1930s, though the numbers temporarily declined in 1938–42, reflecting the Second World War. Many men were conscripted into the military during these years, especially during the Finnish Winter War (1939–40), negatively affecting participation in popular education.

Table 5.3 presents the number of study circles offered by the various member organizations of the ABF, categorized according to their ideological affiliation. The members of the SAP and its affiliated youth organization, SSU (and consequently the participants in the study circles arranged by these organizations),

TABLE 5.3   Number of study circles offered by the main member organizations of the ABF

YEAR	TOTAL NUMBER OF STUDY CIRCLES	REFORMIST ORGANIZATIONS	LEFT-WING ORGANIZATIONS	OTHER UNIONS	KF AND NOV	MIXED CIRCLES
1922	1,387	37% (514)	25% (344)	7% (98)	9% (131)	22% (300)
1923	1,636	39% (640)	24% (391)	3% (52)	9% (143)	25% (410)
1924	1,783	42% (754)	24% (426)	4% (67)	10% (171)	20% (365)
1925	2,005	41% (813)	21% (422)	3% (62)	8% (156)	27% (552)
1926	2,251	44% (985)	19% (430)	3% (70)	8% (177)	26% (589)
1927	2,390	44% (1,058)	18% (421)	2% (56)	7% (166)	29% (689)
1928	2,737	43% (1,180)	17% (468)	2% (58)	6% (154)	32% (877)
1929	2,905	46% (1,343)	4% (124)	2% (58)	5% (152)	42% (1,228)
1930	3,060	49% (1,509)	3% (78)	2% (70)	6% (171)	40% (1,232)
1931	3,430	53% (1,815)	2% (80)	2% (65)	6% (194)	37% (1,276)
1932	4,306	49% (2,104)	2.5% (115)	1.5% (71)	5% (208)	42% (1,808)
1933	5,309	55% (2,922)	3% (172)	1% (31)	4% (213)	37% (1,971)
1934	5,826	55% (3,211)	3% (169)	1% (32)	3% (193)	38% (2,221)
1935	5,793	60% (3,461)	1.5% (96)	0.5% (21)	3% (198)	35% (2,017)
1936	5,886	58.5% (3,465)	2% (132)	0.5% (19)	4% (223)	35% (2,047)
1937	5,894	66% (3,870)	1.55 (75)	0.5% (35)	3% (216)	29% (1,698)
1938	6,136	66% (4,022)	1% (46)	1% (58)	3% (213)	29% (1,797)
1939	6,896	63% (4,368)	1.5% (88)	0.5% (22)	3% (206)	32% (2,212)
1940	6,138	58% (3,544)	1.5% (71)	0.5% (29)	3% (214)	37% (2,280)

Note: The various organizations have been sorted into categories: "Reformist organizations" are the LO, SAP, SSU, and Unga Örnar (Young Eagles, a social democratic youth organization for children founded in 1930); "Left-wing organizations" are the SAC, the Communist Party (SKP), the Communist Youth Organization (KUF), and SUP; "Other unions" are unions not belonging to the LO; the KF and NOV have been aggregated because these organizations were neither political nor labor market organizations.

Sources: ABF annual reports, 1922–1940.

were probably also union members. From the analysis of study activities in Skutskär we know that union members participated in study activities through the youth organization. Thus, even though the LO was not the organization that arranged most study circles, it is safe to say that its members participated in them no matter what group organized them. The reformist organizations arranged approximately 40–45 percent of all ABF study circles in the 1920s. This proportion increased in the 1930s, and in the second half of the decade ABF study circles arranged by the reformist organizations accounted for two-thirds of the total.

The increased proportion of study circles arranged by the LO, the SAP, and the SSU indicates the growing importance of education for the reformist organizations. The SSU was by far the most ambitious organization in this respect, arranging more study circles than did the LO in the 1920s even though the LO was a much bigger organization.

The left-wing organizations arranged a fairly large share of the study circles in the 1920s, but their proportion decreased drastically starting in 1929, even though study activities were as important to the left-wing organizations as they were to the reformist organizations, and for the same reasons. The Communist Party and the Communist Youth Organization arranged no study circles between 1929 and 1938 (see appendix table 3) due to the exclusion of the organizations from the ABF. After yet another split of the Communist Party in 1929, the ABF Representatives concluded that it was impossible to decide which of the new parties was the rightful heir of the old Communist Party and thus a member of the ABF. Combined with the fact that the communist organizations had had trouble paying the membership fee to the ABF, the party split caused the ABF Representatives to suspend the organizations' memberships (ABF Representantskap 1926; ABF Representantskap 1930; KPU 1926). Subsequently, between 1929 and 1938 the communist organizations were denied access to the ABF's study facilities.

The most popular type of study circle was the so-called mixed circle. These circles contained participants from various organizations and were usually arranged by the local ABF educational committee, which also provided the study circle with a leader and a place to meet. Unfortunately, information on the composition of the mixed circles is sparse, but it is safe to assume that many of them consisted of participants from the SSU and some of the local unions in the community. We would therefore expect the composition of many of these circles not to deviate significantly from the composition of circles arranged by the LO sections alone. Of course, in some of these mixed circles we would expect to find communists as well, which the analysis of the study circles in Skutskär also confirms.

Table 5.4 shows the number of participants in study circles organized by the reformist and left-wing organizations in 1922–40. The figures indicate that a fairly large part of the Swedish population at that time attended study circles of some kind. On average, 37,500 workers attended the reformist organizations' study circles every year in the 1930s; the corresponding figure for the 1920s is 12,000.

The ABF kept track of the numbers of participants attending the study circles organized by the various member organizations. However, since the mixed circles were very common, constituting almost half of the circles in the 1930s, a more germane figure is the total number of participants each organization had in *any* organization's study circles (LO members are shown in table 5.5).

If we look at the number of LO members who attended study circles arranged by *any* organization, we find that approximately thirty-three thousand LO

TABLE 5.4   Number of participants in study circles offered by the main member organizations of the ABF

YEAR	REFORMIST ORGANIZATIONS		LEFT-WING ORGANIZATIONS		OTHER UNIONS		OTHER ORGANIZATIONS		MIXED CIRCLES		TOTAL
1922	7321	39%	4070	21%	1478	8%	1588	8%	4603	24%	19,060
1923	8295	38%	4339	20%	800	4%	1731	8%	6520	30%	21,685
1924	9338	41%	4584	20%	1015	4%	1779	8%	6260	27%	22,943
1925	10,435	41%	4854	19%	831	3%	1740	7%	7697	30%	25,496
1926	12,650	44%	4825	17%	1109	4%	2067	7%	8224	28%	28,757
1927	13,366	45%	4754	16%	758	2%	1761	6%	9342	31%	29,893
1928	14,867	42%	5454	15%	980	3%	1746	5%	12,664	35%	35,648
1929	17,728	46%	6101	16%	964	2%	1806	5%	12,129	31%	38,695
1930	19,320	46%	842	2%	1005	3%	2086	5%	18,499	44%	41,752
1931	23,307	49%	890	2%	1065	2%	2620	5%	19,893	42%	47,775
1932	27,411	45%	1397	2%	1324	2%	2696	4%	28,547	47%	61,316
1933	38,885	50%	2155	3%	759	1%	2881	4%	32,839	42%	77,433
1934	41,486	52%	1999	2%	530	1%	2542	3%	33,941	42%	80,391
1935	41,232	54%	1102	1,5%	318	0.5%	2351	3%	31,806	41%	76,809
1936	40,567	53%	1270	1,5%	306	0.5%	2505	3%	31,722	42%	76,370
1937	48,170	61%	732	1%	530	1%	2543	3%	26,869	34%	78,844
1938	44,933	57%	466	1%	687	1%	2395	3%	30,615	38%	79,096
1939	46,915	92%	1329	2%	355	1%	2460	5%	-	-	51,059
1940	40,721	92%	731	2%	339	1%	2121	5%	-	-	43,912

Note: The various organizations have been sorted into categories: "reformist organizations" are the LO, SAP, SSU, and Unga Örnar (Young Eagles); "left-wing organizations" are the SAC, the Communist Party (SKP), the Communist Youth Organization (KUF), and SUP; "other unions" are unions not belonging to the LO; "other organizations" are the KF, the NOV, and a few other small working-class organizations. The table shows the proportions of the study circle participants belonging to the different organizational categories, as well as the total number of participants.

Source: ABF annual reports, 1922–1940.

TABLE 5.5   LO members participating in any kind of study circle, 1922–1940

YEAR	NUMBER OF LO MEMBERS IN ANY STUDY CIRCLE	NUMBER OF PARTICIPANTS IN STUDY CIRCLES ORGANIZED BY THE LO	PERCENTAGE OF LO MEMBERS PARTICIPATING IN STUDY CIRCLES
1922	8,457	3,269	2.89%
1923	9,697	3,411	3.10%
1924	10,300	4,117	2.86%
1925	12,469	4,590	3.24%
1926	14,668	5,591	3.54%
1927	15,247	6,048	3.48%
1928	17,579	6,019	3.74%
1929	18,445	6,508	3.63%
1930	19,609	6,652	3.54%
1931	22,958	7,922	3.90%
1932	28,474	9,549	4.46%
1933	34,529	13,621	5.45%
1934	35,960	14,306	5.50%
1935	32,446	13,308	4.63%
1936	32,884	16,147	4.34%
1937	35,336	20,571	4.21%
1938	38,738	20,280	4.31%
1939	44,577	23,702	4.64%
1940	39,907	20,093	4.11%

Source: ABF annual reports, 1922–1940.

members attended study circles of some kind every year in the 1930s, whereas only approximately fifteen thousand participants per year attended study circles arranged by the LO, so it appears that LO members in particular participated in mixed circles. Overall, 2.86–5.5 percent of the LO membership participated in study circles every year. This may not seem like much, but the accumulated number of workers who had participated in educational programs arranged by the ABF throughout the examined period is considerable. The corresponding figure in Britain for all types of education organized by the Workers' Educational Association (the WEA) and National Council of Labour Colleges (the NCLC) during the same time period is only approximately 1.1 percent of these organizations' memberships per year (Jansson 2018).

A potential problem with these figures is the lack of information on overlapping participants—workers who participated in several study circles at the same time or who attended study circles several years in a row. This is a potential problem because overlapping may lead to overestimation of the number of participants. It is impossible to control for this because there are no complete listings of participants in the study circles. In Skutskär, at least one person participated in two study circles in the same year, Carl Hyllengren in 1932 (Möteskultur 1932a), and we also know that many workers continued to participate in circles for many years. Moreover, *who* these participants were and what role they played in local associational life were equally important in determining the effects of popular education.

Scope of the Education Programs in Skutskär

How many people attended the study circles in Skutskär? Unfortunately, there are no records of the participants for the entire period, but starting in 1924 the circles reported their number of participants to the education committee. We know from the study circle reports sent to the ABF central bureau that two study circles had existed from 1916 onward, though they were not particularly active until the 1920s.

Table 5.6 presents the numbers of participants and study circles in Skutskär. The unions in Skutskär claimed that the increase in the number of study circles

TABLE 5.6   Numbers of participants and study circles in Skutskär

YEAR	PARTICIPANTS	NUMBER OF STUDY CIRCLES
1922–1923	—	2
1923–1924	10	2
1924–1925	10	2
1925–1926	20	2
1926–1927	46	5
1927–1928	84	7
1928–1929	108	9
1929–1930	52	6
1930–1931	74	7
1931–1932	119	10
1932–1933	179	11
1933–1934	97	8
1934–1935	154	10
1935–1936	150	11
1936–1937	140	12
1937–1938	196	15
1938–1939	155	12
1939–1940	100	8
Total	1694	137

Source: Annual reports of the ABF education committee in Skutskär and the study circle reports sent to the ABF central organization, 1923–1939.

in the early 1930s was an effect of unemployment and labor market conflicts—more spare time led to greater engagement in popular education. That is partly true, but the increased number of study circles could also be an effect of the education campaigns carried out by the ABF in the 1930s and of increased funding from the state, as a new 1930 law allowed study circles to obtain grants directly from the state (Arvidson 1985, 117). Pamphlets admonishing the workers to use their spare time wisely on popular education were sent out in the 1930s (ABF 1930; ABF 1933a).

It is hard to tell whether the figures are high or low, as a reference point of some kind is needed. The population in Skutskär was approximately 5,000–5,500 in the 1930s, and the average number of circle participants every year was 124. Consequently, on average 2–2.5 percent of the population in Skutskär attended study circles every year, but among trade union members this rate rises to an average of 11 percent.[9] In other words, more than a tenth of the trade union members in Skutskär attended a study circle between 1923 and 1939, which is considerably higher than the average number of LO members participating in study circles and accounts for a considerable share of the union members.

The Local Associational Elite and the Study Activities

Who participated in the popular education programs? Although the statistics on participants indicate that a large number of workers participated in study activities during the examined period, it was not a majority. However, *who* participated might be more important than how many. From the LO's point of view, the most troublesome activist segment in the organization constituted local trade union activists with powers to organize strikes and sympathy actions for the syndicalists, not ordinary trade union members.

Clearly, not everybody participates in social movements or in social movement organizations. Often the "believers" in a movement—individuals with faith in its goals and ideologically convinced—are those who take active roles. If these individuals are more radical than the grassroots or the leaders of the organization, tensions will arise. Very little supports the idea that every union member in Sweden was radical, not even in areas where communists and syndicalists had strong support. For most workers, conflicts were costly and led to loss of income. It was therefore crucial to identify and reach the active members.

It is reasonable to assume that the LO leaders particularly wanted to target the local activists to make sure they were loyal to the organization. The communist infiltration of the reformist unions took place at the local level, and the support for syndicalists was strong among the grassroots. Meanwhile, many unions used the strike referendum, a procedure susceptible to manipulation by radical local agitators that could mobilize the rank and file to support conflicts, including sympathy measures for the syndicalists. However, even official union leaders who too often got involved in work stoppages could drive workers from the unions simply because they were tired of strikes and could not afford the loss of income. Consequently, the activists were a group that LO leaders would have wanted to control: radical local leaders who could incite the members to vote for work stoppages or to join syndicalists in conflicts. Committed reformist labor leaders in the sections could stabilize the movement, and, in case the grassroots wanted to initiate imprudent work stoppages, these leaders could prevent them by talking sense into the members. The activists also held positions that allowed them to spread ideological messages to the members; they were nodes in the local associational networks, crucial for the LO leadership to control and the main target group of the study activities.

Examining minutes and annual reports from Skutskär's local sections reveals a clear pattern of who engaged in union work. Local union leaders indeed handled all member contacts and often knew the members personally. The Sawmill Workers' Union Sections 2 and 54 and the Paper Mill Workers' Union Section 2 all had boards (small groups of people with executive powers) that occasionally held closed meetings. The boards each consisted of approximately five people, and a recurring pattern was for the same people to be elected to a given board several years in a row. The post of board chair was often passed between board members (as was the post of study circle leader) but was sometimes occupied by the same person for several years.

Another group of activists with good access to the members comprised those who collected the union dues, which were paid every month to *uppbördsmän*, appointed activists who met every single member to collect the dues. The identities of these *uppbördsmän* were not unimportant: because their personal contacts with members were more frequent than the leader—member contacts in any social movement today, these *uppbördsmän* activists were well known to the members. While paying their dues, the members could ask about work- or union-related concerns, and at the same time the activists could inform the members about various issues. The board members of the local union usually also served as dues collectors.

Another interesting category of activists is those who served as study circle leaders. Information about these leaders in the 1920s is sparse; at least fourteen different study circle leaders were active in Skutskär during the 1920s, and that number more than doubled in the 1930s (the numbers are likely greatly underestimated due to a lack of sources). Of these study circle leaders, five had positions in the local unions—John Sandberg, Karl Hammarström, Helge Lindberg, Otto Westerholm, and Carl Hyllengren. Some of these five grew to become important figures in the associational life of Skutskär in the 1930s, while others moved away from the town. In particular, Karl Hammarström was a central figure in the 1920s, being active in the Left Party (he was one of the party's founders, together with August Lindberg), the Social Democratic Party, and the SDUK, and occupying positions in all the local unions at some point (apparently he changed jobs and thus unions). In the 1930s, he is not visible in any organization, likely having moved away from Skutskär.

John Sandberg occupied a position in the education committee as the representative of the Paper Mill Workers' Union Section 2, and between 1917 and 1936 he was the leader of a study circle for each of the SDUK, the Communist Youth Organization, and later the Paper Mill Workers' Union Section 2. He was also one of the activists who started the Left Party, though he rejoined the SAP later in the 1920s. During his years as study circle leader, he was also a member of the board of the Paper Mill Workers' Union Section 2. Sandberg, in a way, exemplifies how the transformation of the workers was supposed to happen: he started his career in the youth organization, left the SAP for the Left Party, later returned to the reformist party, and in the 1930s become a study circle leader in association studies, teaching younger unionists how a good reformist worker should behave.

Otto Westerholm was also a member of the Paper Mill Workers' Union Section 2 and served on the board of the Social Democratic Workers' Commune. He was a study circle leader in the 1920s but resigned from working in popular education in the 1930s to devote his time to politics.

There were more study circles in the 1930s than in the 1920s, but the number of study circle leaders was still limited; it appears that people who became study circle leaders would continue in that role for several years. Some of the study circle leaders, particularly those in association studies and organizational studies, were recruited from the boards of the local union sections. It was not uncommon for the chair of the local section to also be a study circle leader.

Some new names appear in activist networks in the 1930s. Bertil Sundman, Viktor Hansson, Bror Larsson, Birger Larsson, and Gunnar Johansson were all deeply involved in the study circles as well as the education committee, the boards of the unions and the SDUK, or the local party associations. Their activity pattern resembled that of John Sandberg and Karl Hammarström. The claim that some activists tended to be active in several different arenas concurrently appears to have been very true in the case of Skutskär.

One methodological problem when analyzing the activists in Skutskär is that no lists of study circle participants have been preserved. The only information we have are the names of the study circle leaders (for most of the years) and the names of some participants in the four study circles whose minutes are preserved. Our information about the participants besides the study circle leaders is therefore very limited. It is likely that far more of the activists than rank-and-file union members attended study circles; we know for a fact that 11 percent of the members of all unions attended study circles. The yearly average of 124 study circle participants in Skutskär could in fact contain a large proportion of the activists (who were not all that numerous in Skutskär—after all, the town had only 5,000–5,500 inhabitants), of course affecting the impact of the educational program.

Number of Participants and the Elite at the Grassroots Level

The study circles indeed drastically increased in number in the 1920s and even more so in the 1930s. Consequently, the number of LO members who participated in popular education also increased. Even though the communist organizations also engaged in popular education, arranging a large number of study circles compared to their relatively small memberships, their education programs still did not reach the majority.

The development of education programs in Skutskär followed the same trend as that identified at the national level: the number of study circles and of workers engaging in popular education increased over time. Mapping the networks of activists in Skutskär reveals a common pattern typical of the time, in that a few key people in the town were active in several different arenas simultaneously. They attended meetings as well as educational activities, and they played critical roles in the development of the local labor movement. Not only did the local party organizations, particularly the SDUK with its "knowledge quarters," have an explicit strategy of endeavoring to influence the unions, but these groups also valued the educational ideal and the idea of enlightenment. It was not enough for reformist purposes for the study circles to be common; rather, a particular kind of study circle was needed. To address this matter, we proceed to the final step of the implementation analysis: examining the content of the study circles.

Content of the Education Programs

Increasing workers' general knowledge through educational campaigns would not necessarily promote class formation or make trade union members committed to the goals of the reformist labor movement. General education would also not make workers distance themselves from the syndicalists and communist organizations. A *certain type of study circle* would need to proliferate for the education strategy to be implemented successfully. Consequently, the study circles' subjects and content should be scrutinized, at both the national and regional levels. Finally, a focused investigation of the content of study circles in Skutskär provides specific insights into the work of the study circles.

The Study Circle Subjects

Various study circle subjects were prevalent in the 1920s and 1930s, between twenty and fifty subjects being treated every year. To simplify the analysis, the study circle courses have been clustered in accordance with their content as treating *general, organizational, ideological, hobby, current political,* and *reformist* issues.

At the national level, the subjects most commonly offered during the first ten years were Swedish, mathematics, and macroeconomics (ABF 1913; ABF 1915; ABF 1916; ABF 1920b; ABF 1921b), which are here classified as *general subjects*. Esperanto has also been put in this category.[10] So has macroeconomics.[11] The vast number of circles focusing on general subjects has several explanations. First, the circles were intended to improve the general educational level and promote the enlightenment of the working class, which was the primary goal of the ABF from the start. Second, the introduction of universal suffrage prompted debate about whether or not the workers were educated enough to be responsible citizens, as to vote they should have a certain level of knowledge. Parliament even earmarked funding for the provision of citizenship courses in 1923 (ABF 1920a, 1; ABF 1924b, 13). It was not only the desire of bourgeois forces to educate workers, as the labor movement soon needed educated representatives to fill posts in various governmental bodies after the introduction of universal suffrage. A similar pattern emerged in most countries after democratization: when the workers gained political rights, the working class soon entered leading positions in society. To create personnel able to discharge such responsibilities, labor movements needed to educate their activists (Goldman 1999; Landsorganisationen 1924e).

In the 1920s, the study circle courses in *general subjects* remained popular but were increasingly in competition with other categories of subjects. The number of courses with an *ideological* aim grew, as did those intended to improve *organizational* skills, to ensure that the rank and file knew how to run an organization. Such circles provided the workers with basic knowledge of meeting protocol (e.g., raise your hand if you want to talk, stand up when talking, etc.) and the function of the chair and the secretary or of how to undertake bookkeeping for an organization. The *organizational* study circles were crucial for organizational development at the grassroots level. The trade union movement had fought for the right to freedom of association, but to retain that right and not give the employers or the political Right any reason to demand its withdrawal, the workers had to manage their associations properly, especially the bookkeeping. This category of study circle courses includes bookkeeping, rhetoric, and meeting culture.

There were also study circle courses with *ideological* content, such as courses in communism and syndicalism. Courses in socialism, which were common in the 1920s, were designed by Ernst Wigforss and have been categorized as *reformist* study circle courses, since their content resembled that of the course designed by Sigfrid Hansson. The absence of study circles in social democracy is worth noting; socialism was the subject that came closest to treating social democratic ideas.

Ideological study circles were usually organized by the syndicalist movement or the communist organizations. On some occasions, the LO arranged lectures on syndicalism from a reformist point of view. Of course, the LO's approach to syndicalism differed from that of the courses offered by the SAC. The range of ideological study circle courses was never as wide as those of the other categories of courses, a fact hardly surprising given the size of the communist and syndicalist movements.

In the 1930s another type of study circle appeared, *the hobby circle*, the main aim of which was fun and recreation (for example, singing, theater, and gymnastics). Other courses placed in this category are ones very specific to a particular community or occupation, circles that cannot be classified as raising general knowledge among the workers or having an ideological content. The trade unions did not appreciate study circles intended to improve occupational skills: the Metal Workers' Union section in Söderfors, for example, was refused funding by the union for a study circle course on technical issues. The Metal Workers' Union maintained that it was better if the sections instead attended association studies or macroeconomics circles (Hellblom 1985, 192). Accordingly, very few study circles had occupational skills content. The hobby circles should not be underestimated, however, as they contributed to the construction of identity and organizational culture in the local community. Unison singing, for example, had a particularly important position in the associational life of the working class. The syllabus for association studies designed by the SSU suggested that every trade union meeting should start with unison singing, and that suggestion was followed by at least one of the study circles in Skutskär (SDUK Skutskär 1935b).

There were also circles on *current political issues*; these circles were "problem-based," inspired by and treating particular societal problems or reforms.[12] These circles normally did not last very long; they were intended to inform the workers of various complex issues that were deemed important to understand or particularly intriguing to the participants. For example, such study circles considered aspects of the social insurance system (e.g., the pension system) that was under construction in the 1920s and 1930s or legislation on labor market or international issues that engaged the organized labor movement worldwide.

Finally, there were study circle courses treating *reformist issues*, the courses most relevant to this study. These were the courses intended to teach the workers about the labor movement and trade unions and included subjects such as trade union studies, organizational studies, and association studies (all of which used books by Sigfrid Hansson). Less popular subjects with reformist content, such as the history of the Swedish labor movement and socialism, have also been placed in this category.

The LO Circle Subjects

The first step of the analysis is to examine the study circles arranged by the LO in order to establish which subjects were the most popular within the organization.

Figure 5.3 clearly shows that the most common study circles treated general subjects and that by the end of the period the number of reformist circles had surpassed the general ones in popularity. The time series is unfortunately only sixteen years, the reason being lack of information: the ABF did not keep a record of the different subjects the circles had studied before 1921–22 or after 1937–38.

The five most common subjects in LO-affiliated study groups are presented in table 5.7, which shows that trade union studies and association/organizational studies were equally popular, with the third more popular study circle subject, political science or municipal studies, lagging significantly behind. At first, macro-level glance, the "right" type of subject had increased over time in these study circles.

Regional Differences

Shifting our attention from the national level, this section examines regional differences in study circle subjects. Not only does the analysis give us some perspective on the kind of case Skutskär represents, comparing different regions allows a detailed examination of differences between regions where the communist/syndicalist movement enjoyed strong support and regions where social democracy was strong. The counties chosen are Norrbotten, Gävleborg, Uppsala, and Skåne (represented by the two cities Malmö and Lund). As mentioned in chapter 3, northern Sweden was targeted by the LO's organizers because of the strength of the left-wing organizations in Norrbotten. In the northern Swedish county of Norrbotten we would therefore expect communist and syndicalist organizations to dominate organizational life in the towns and villages. Gävleborg was

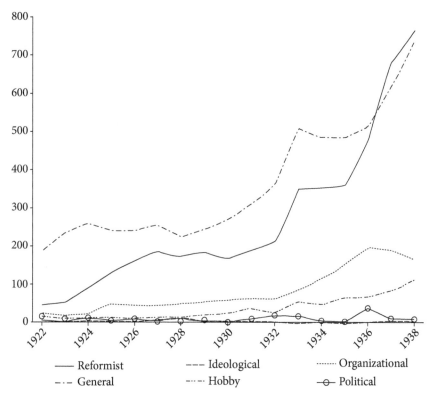

FIGURE 5.3 Study circles offered by LO affiliates by subject, 1922–1938. *Note:* The graph shows all study circles offered by the LO affiliates' sections as reported to the ABF. The circles are sorted by subject. *Reformist circles* consisted of courses on association, organizational, and trade union studies, as well as the trade union movement, labor movement history, industrial democracy, the history of the Swedish working class, socialism, and the labor movement. *Organizational circles* consisted of courses on rhetoric, meeting culture, cooperation, and bookkeeping. *Ideological circles* consisted of courses on syndicalism and communism. *General circles* consisted of courses on stenography, biology, geography, philosophy and religion, governmental and municipal studies, English, Esperanto, German, Swedish, mathematics, fiction, macroeconomics, sociology, literary history, and history. *Hobby circles* consisted of courses on singing and music, women's and men's handicrafts, amateur theater, construction techniques, astronomy, design, electronic techniques, gardening, botany, food studies, and gymnastics. *Circles on current political issues* consisted of courses on socialization, Swedish work life, workplace safety legislation, other current legislation, and current social issues. Because of the lack of data for 1934, I have used a mean for that year. The subjects for which values are missing are labor movement history, rhetoric, macroeconomics, sociology, women's handicrafts, amateur theater, electronic techniques, and gymnastics. *Source:* All figures come from ABF annual reports, 1922–1938

TABLE 5.7   The five most popular subjects in LO-affiliated study circles, in terms of number of study circles

YEAR	TRADE UNION STUDIES	ASSOCIATION/ ORGANIZATIONAL STUDIES	POLITICAL SCIENCE/ MUNICIPAL STUDIES	MATHEMATICS	BOOKKEEPING	ENGLISH
1922	14	13	37	33	23	21
1923	16	23	52	44	16	20
1924	48	31	63	39	20	26
1925	67	52	50	46	29	24
1926	93	48	46	31	25	30
1927	94	68	56	36	26	26
1928	85	67	40	34	24	34
1929	98	68	38	37	39	29
1930	86	69	37	37	36	58
1931	104	71	41	53	40	52
1932	124	68	68	37	39	54
1933	188	139	102	66	55	67
1934	186	134	113	72	89	64
1935	152	180	102	83	133	76
1936	176	274	93	107	177	100
1937	266	388	115	159	164	125
1938	322	401	116	194	144	203
Total	2119	2094	1169	1108	1079	1009

Source: ABF annual reports, 1922–1938.

also a region where communists enjoyed support (Horgby 2012, 42–43). Malmö and Lund are cities where the reformist branch early on enjoyed strong support; it was the region where the party originated and the Hansson brothers started their careers, and this should be reflected in the choice of study circle subjects there. Finally, the county of Uppsala where Skutskär is located should end up somewhere between the reformist stronghold Skåne and the left-wing Norrbotten. Study circle subjects in the four regions have been mapped for two study years: 1927–28 and 1936–37. The lack of material for some years during the study period affected the years selected for this examination.

General subjects clearly were the most popular study circle category in 1927–28, although in Skåne the reformist issue came a close second. As illustrated in table 5.8, Norrbotten differs distinctly from the cities in Skåne. Only 7 percent of the total number of circles arranged in Norrbotten were reformist circles in 1927–28, whereas 27 percent addressed communism and syndicalism; the corresponding figures for Malmö and Lund were 31 percent reformist circles, with only a single study circle on communism, offered by the Food Workers' Union section in Malmö. This pattern confirms the LO Secretariat's apprehension that communists and syndicalists enjoyed support in northern Sweden and that workers in Skåne were already committed to social democracy.

Gävleborg had fairly large proportions of reformist circles (18 percent) and ideological circles (16 percent) in 1927–28, suggesting that the region had both reformist and left-wing communities. Uppsala County displays a partly expected, partly surprising pattern. The proportion of the reformist circles is somewhere between those of Gävleborg and Skåne, which is not surprising; however, regarding ideological circles, Uppsala region is much closer to the Skåne towns than it is to Norrbotten. This could be because most of the study circles in Uppsala region were held in the city of Uppsala, where neither the communists nor the syndicalists had gained any noteworthy influence.

This analysis of regional differences regarding subject and the choice of syllabus indicate that, with few exceptions, study circles on communism were organized by the Communist Party or the Communist Youth Organization, and study circles on syndicalism were organized by the SAC.

Comparing the two years reveals some interesting trends. First, the number of reformist circles increased tremendously in Norrbotten. This can be partly explained by the suspension of the communist organizations' memberships in the ABF but might also be the effect of successful outreach by the LO in the region. Regardless of the reason, it is a fact that reformist circles increased in number in the 1930s in Norrbotten. The number of reformist study circles increased in all regions except Skåne, where hobby circles instead gained in popularity. One possible interpretation is that the workers were well-behaved reformists: they had attended study circles in trade union studies in the 1920s and, for the union movement to maintain these workers' interest in popular education, it offered study circles on hobbies.

One obvious change in the ideological circles is probably a direct effect of the suspension of the Communist Party's membership in the ABF. One might suspect this suspension to have hit the communist movement hard, since it did not possess sufficient resources to organize study activities to any great extent on its own. Somewhat surprising, however, are the poor results from the syndicalist movement. This could indicate the importance of a political movement having a branch that competed in elections and thus regularly mobilized during election campaigns. Overall, the regional comparison between the two years confirms that the study circles in the "right subjects" increased over time and highlights important regional differences. The next step in the analysis of study circle subjects is to examine the study circles in Skutskär more closely.

TABLE 5.8 Study circle subjects in four regions, 1927–1928

	REFORMIST CIRCLES		ORGANIZATIONAL CIRCLES		IDEOLOGICAL CIRCLES		GENERAL CIRCLES		HOBBY CIRCLES		POLITICAL ISSUES		SUBJECT UNKNOWN		NUMBER OF CIRCLES	
	NO.	%	NO.	%	NO.	%	NO.	%	NO.	%	NO.	%	NO.	%	NO.	%
Gävleborg County	18	18%	7	7%	16	16%	56	57%	1	1%	–	–	1	1%	99	100%
Norrbotten County	4	7%	3	6%	14	27%	24	46%	3	6%	1	2%	3	6%	52	100%
Uppsala County	16	24%	9	13.5%	3	5%	29	44%	5	7.5%	–	–	4	6%	66	100%
Lund and Malmö	37	31%	6	5%	1	1%	46	39%	23	19%	5	4%	–	–	118	100%

Note: 1927 was the year Hansson's syllabus for trade union studies was published, although a shorter version existed previously.

Source: Annual reports sent to the ABF by the study circles (ABF, 2831/E/04/12, ARAB, Stockholm).

TABLE 5.9 Study circle subjects in four regions, 1936–1937

	REFORMIST CIRCLES		ORGANIZATIONAL CIRCLES		IDEOLOGICAL CIRCLES		GENERAL CIRCLES		HOBBY CIRCLES		POLITICAL ISSUES		SUBJECT UNKNOWN		NUMBER OF CIRCLES	
	NO.	%	NO.	%	NO.	%	NO.	%	NO.	%	NO.	%	NO.	%	NO.	%
Gävleborg County	43	27%	13	8%	2	1%	86	53%	14	9%	2	1%	2	1%	162	100%
Norrbotten County	42	31.5%	11	8%	1	1%	48	36%	28	21%	2	1.5%	1	1%	133	100%
Uppsala County	37	42%	8	9%	2	2.5%	29	33%	9	10%	3	3.5%	–	–	88	100%
Lund and Malmö	34	21%	9	5%	–	–	79	48%	37	22%	–	–	7	4%	166	100%

Source: Annual reports sent to the ABF by the study circles (ABF, 2831/E/04/35-38, ARAB, Stockholm).

Study Circles in Skutskär

Compared with the national level, the workers in Skutskär organized study circles in trade union studies comparatively early on, and in 1925 the SDUK already reported holding a study circle on the subject (ABF Skutskär 1914). As illustrated by figure 5.4, however, the subject never became very popular in Skutskär, possibly because of the lack of study circle leaders. The most frequently offered study circle subject in the 1920s was a course with apparent similarities to trade union studies—namely, association studies.

Various subjects were discussed in the study circles in Skutskär. The second-most-popular study circle subject was Esperanto, the workers' universal language. Esperanto was popular in Skutskär in the 1920s and 1930s, when there was even a local Esperanto association (ABF Skutskär 1928c; ABF Skutskär 1931; ABF Skutskär 1932; ABF Skutskär 1933; ABF Skutskär 1934; ABF Skutskär 1937). Other subjects repeatedly offered were mathematics, bookkeeping, Swedish language, rhetoric, and macroeconomics. In table 5.10, the study circles in Skutskär are clustered into the same categories as used in the national-level analysis.

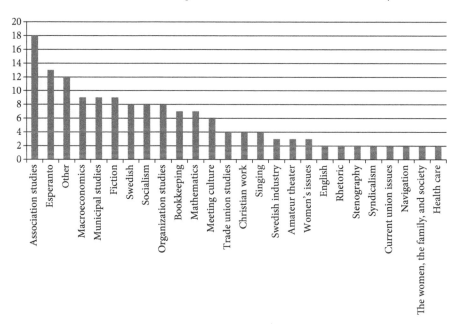

FIGURE 5.4   Study circle subjects in Skutskär, 1916–1940. *Note:* The "Other" category consists of thirteen study circle courses offered only once: theory of life, labor movement history, psychology, health care, carpentry, workplace safety legislation, SSU history, legislation on paid vacation time, biology, geography, history of civilization, and citizenship studies. *Source:* Annual reports of the ABF education committee in Skutskär, 1916–1940

TABLE 5.10 Study circle subjects in Skutskär

	REFORMIST CIRCLES		GENERAL CIRCLES		IDEOLOGICAL CIRCLES		HOBBY CIRCLES		ORGANIZATIONAL CIRCLES		POLITICAL ISSUES		SUBJECT UNKNOWN		TOTAL	
	NO.	%	NO.	%	NO.	%	NO.	%	NO.	%	NO.	%	NO.	%	NO.	%
1921–1925	-	-	9	82%	1	9%	-	-	-	-	-	-	1	9%	11	100%
1926–1930	2	7%	15	52%	-	-	2	7%	10	34%	-	-	-	-	29	100%
1931–1935	13	28%	28	61%	2	4,5%	1	2%	2	4,5%	-	-	-	-	46	100%
1936–1940	25	44%	11	19%	-	-	8	14%	3	5%	10	18%	-	-	57	100%

Source: Annual reports of the ABF education committee in Skutskär and the study circle reports sent to the ABF central organization, 1921–1940.

Table 5.10 presents the development of the study circles in Skutskär according to subject, showing that the pattern deviates somewhat from that at the national level. At the national level, the number of general and reformist circles steadily increased. In Skutskär the general circles dominated in the 1920s and early to mid 1930s but then decreased in number by the end of the decade. Simultaneously, the number of reformist and hobby study circles increased in the 1930s. Eventually, all unions except the Longshoremen's Union Section 11 had their own study circles. These circles focused on organizational skills or general subjects in the 1920s and early 1930s. From 1935 onward, the subject association studies completely dominated the unions' circles. One possible explanation is that the first members to attend study circles in the 1920s were true activists who were already sufficiently skilled in running associations; in the 1930s, however, the increased number of circles in association studies could be explained by the increased participation of non-activist union members. Of course, the campaigns of the ABF and the LO to persuade people to attend study circles also contributed to this pattern.

Most of the circles arranged in Skutskär were mixed circles having no parent or sponsoring organization, and most of the study leaders had connections to the SDUK (ABF Skutskär 1937; ABF Skutskär 1940). The number of circles increased through the 1930s up to 1939, when the outbreak of the Second World War interrupted the expansion. The education committee in Skutskär wrote in the annual report for 1939 that seventeen circles had been prepared at the beginning of the year but that only eight carried out their activity plans (ABF Skutskär 1940).

Do the study circle activities of Skutskär's workers indicate that the LO Secretariat's education strategy was implemented successfully? As already stated, if the strategy were successful, we would expect the reformist circles to be dominant, but they were not in a majority until the end of the 1930s. This could be explained by a time lag: in other words, it took some years to establish a local education committee and even longer to engage the unions in the education programs. The lag could also be due to stronger support for the left-wing organizations among the workers of Skutskär, support that rapidly decreased in the 1930s. In 1928, the local education committee stated that increasing interest in popular education had been noticed during the preceding year. The committee's conclusion was that its efforts to engage the workers of Skutskär had started to pay off. However, the committee also suspected that this sudden increase in the numbers of study circles and lecture attendees was caused by the big lockout of the paper mill and lumberyard workers at Stora Kopparberg in the winter of 1928; the unions noticed the same trend regarding participation in union meetings (ABF Skutskär 1928c; Sågverksindustriarbetareförbundet avd. 2 1928). The drastic increase in study activities in the 1930s could similarly be explained by the major lockout in 1932. Table 5.6 offers some support for that possibility, as the number of participants in study activities in 1932–33 was the second-highest throughout the examined period. Whether it was a general trend for workers to use their spare time during a labor market conflict to engage in education is hard to tell. Despite these participation numbers, the education committee perceived the level of study activity to be low. In evaluating the previous ten years of education activities, the education committee declared despondently that it was difficult to motivate the workers (ABF Skutskär 1928c; ABF Skutskär 1931; ABF Skutskär 1932; ABF Skutskär 1934; ABF Skutskär 1937).

Books and Materials in Skutskär

The prevalence of the "right" study circle subjects indeed increased over time at the national, regional, and local levels, suggesting the successful implementation of the education strategy. A detailed examination of course content would convey more than statistics on number and subjects of the study circle courses, however. More details on the actual work in the study circles as well as the literature used would provide a deeper understanding of the content of the study activities. What did the study circle members actually read? What did they discuss?

Whether or not the right kind of literature was used in the study circles is hard, not to say impossible, to determine at an aggregated level. There are no central records of the books in the study circle libraries, but we can examine what books were used in Skutskär. The ABF library in Skutskär was established in 1917 when the education committee was founded. The inventory list ends in 1933, so no extant records document what books were bought and used after that time. In the inventory list, the author's name Sigfrid Hansson appears several times, and the main book used in trade union studies, *Den svenska fackföreningsrörelsen*, is listed in 1933. Besides that book, other books and booklets by Hansson are found in the library list: *Arbetarrörelsen, Minneskrift Landsorganisationens första kvartsekel 1898–1923*, and *Skråtidens gesäller* (ABF Skutskär 1917a). *Arbetarrörelsen* (The Labor Movement) was a short version of *Den svenska fackföreningsrörelsen*; it conveyed the same ideas and image of the LO and was used in organizational studies. The Sawmill Workers' Union Section 54's regular donation of the magazine *Fackföreningsrörelsen* to the ABF library constituted an important contribution to both the library and the study circle activities (ABF Skutskär 1917a; Hansson 1927c).

It seems that some books bought by the study circles never ended up in the library, so the inventory list may well not reveal the full picture of the literature used. For example, the SDUK was granted money to buy books for a study circle in trade union studies in 1925, but these books were never listed in the inventory (ABF Skutskär 1925).

Besides the books found in the library list, we also know that the booklet *Solidaritet eller monopolism?* by Hansson, which was also mandatory in trade union studies, was sent to its two sections in Skutskär by the Sawmill Workers' Union. The union decided in 1926 to send a copy of the booklet, which expressed serious criticism of the syndicalist movement, to each one of its local sections (Sågverksindustriarbetareförbundet 1926, 12).

The fact that some of Hansson's books were present in the library indicates that some of the study circles must have used them, though the library did not own many copies. In comparison, a study circle in trade union studies organized by the Hospital Workers' Union in Uppsala bought one copy of the prescribed book for each participant (ABF Uppsala 1927). The size of the library holdings means that the books did not necessarily have the desired impact, though the preconditions for Hansson's writings to influence the workers of Skutskär were fulfilled.

Study Circle Activities

The composition of the study circles held by the ABF varied depending on who organized them. As already mentioned, the ABF study circles were open to participants from any member organization. This in turn meant that the temperance movement, the trade unions (including the syndicalists), and the labor movement's political parties could all participate in the same study circles. Each study circle became a small local association with a particular number of participants and could exist for several years. In fact, the circles were encouraged to continue their activities for several years, though they usually changed the subject of study. The circles were intended to become a permanent element and a natural part of the workers' lives, and this was encouraged in many ways. For example, in the association studies syllabus, the last assignment was for participants to write an essay about what they would like to study the next semester (Socialdemokratiska Ungdomsförbundets studieråd 1930).

Two types of documents were generated by each study circle meeting: formal minutes and a report describing the discussion. Because of this documentation, it is possible to identify who said what during discussions of the course literature. Two people wrote the two documents, and since the circle was organized democratically, all participants were sooner or later appointed to write either the minutes or the report (the position of chair also rotated). This procedure of rotating responsibilities was covered by exercises in the association studies syllabi, as the circles were intended to be a training camp for democracy.

The first study circle in Skutskär was held in 1916 by the temperance movement, and the following year the SDUK also started a study circle. These early circles were not particularly active, providing their members with books but rarely holding meetings. In 1925, a study circle organized by the Paper Mill Workers' Union Section 2 offered a course in trade union studies (ABF Skutskär 1914). The circle participants asked the education committee for funding to buy books, and this funding was granted (ABF Skutskär 1925). Hansson's syllabus was used by this circle the first two years of its existence, and the local library supplied the circle with the necessary literature (ABF 1926; ABF 1927).[13] The education committee also sponsored the study circle participants to join them on a trip to the nearby town of Gävle to listen to a lecture given by Sigfrid Hansson himself (ABF Skutskär 1926).

Very few minutes have survived from the study circles. In total, 152 study circles were held in Skutskär between 1916 and 1940, and from all these circles only four sets of minutes have been preserved. Nevertheless, these four circles have different characteristics, making a comparison of them interesting.

One set of minutes comes from the SDUK's study circle. This circle had existed for quite some time, so the participants knew one another very well and had been studying together for many years. Consequently, the study circle meetings would sometimes be used to discuss strategies for the organization's activities (e.g., outreach strategies) or would sometimes be mere social events. This circle was mature, so to speak, and exemplifies how we would expect study circle participants to act or talk after attending study circles in organizational studies or association studies and then other courses in subsequent years. We would also expect the participants to be convinced reformists.

The second set of minutes comes from a circle studying meeting culture. This was a mixed study circle comprising participants from different organizations, and nothing indicates that the circle existed before 1931. The circle changed its subject of study to socialism in 1932, when some participants were continuing from the meeting culture circle and others were new.

The third set of minutes comprises remnants from a study circle in organizational studies. This study circle seems to have been a typical introductory circle for union members who wished to become active in union work. The circle was starting from scratch on the subject and exemplifies the endeavor to educate workers in the skills necessary to make the union movement effective. From this study circle's reports, we know that organizational studies and association studies were offered every year starting in 1931; moreover, the study circle leaders were the same people—Bertil Sundman, Viktor Hansson, Helge Lindberg, Bengt

Bengtsson, and Gunnar Johansson, all of whom were important figures in the unions and political organizations in Skutskär.

The SDUK's Study Circle (457 and 2697)

We know from its records that the SDUK had a study circle, number 457, from 1914 onward (ABF Skutskär 1914). The SDUK came to play an important role in the associational life of Skutskär. The members of the youth organization were active in the unions, the SAP, and the local education committee. After the split of the SAP in 1917, the old youth organization, the SDU (Socialdemokratiska ung-domsförbundet), joined the Left Party at the national level, changing its name to the Left Party's Youth Organization. This was also the case in Skutskär, where the SDUK became the youth organization of the Left Party. Later in 1921, the organization affiliated itself with the Communist Party and changed its name to the Communist Youth League (KUF) (KPU Skutskär 1921). For several years, the circle fell under the control of the communists. In 1925, the SAP—which parts of the Left Party had rejoined—decided to start a new youth organization in Skutskär. Different names of the youth organization appear in the archives, but it seems that the new organization reclaimed the old name, the SDUK (*Socialde-mokratiska ungdomsklubben*). The circle continued but changed its sponsor in accordance with the changes in the youth organization (ABF 1921a; ABF 1933b).

The remaining documentation of the SDUK circle's activities is sparse, and minutes of circle meetings have been preserved only for the years 1934–36. During the 1934–35 study year, the circle followed a syllabus for some kind of organiza-tional studies. The earliest dated meeting minutes differ from the other minutes, describing how one of the participants, Henry Holmgren, presented a project allotted to a small group of the circle participants that he chaired. The group was supposed to simulate a committee whose task was to come up with a sugges-tion for the construction of a public bath in the fictitious town of Skråköping. Holmgren as chair presented the proposal, after which the other participants discussed the suggestion and criticized it in several respects. Holmgren then had to defend the proposal. The circle decided that the proposal needed further inves-tigation, and a new committee was appointed to do that. However, no follow-up to this is recorded in the minutes. The meeting appears to have taken the form of role-playing. The concept of "teaching" in this context meant self-teaching, and what better way to learn how to behave in an official position than through role-playing? Many of these activists were or became involved in local politics, and for many of them imagining such a scenario and deciding how to act in it was indeed a good exercise. Similar exercises were also recorded as occurring in the study circle course on meeting culture, and the idea probably originated in the syllabus for association studies designed by Holme. This syllabus had "practical exercises" for suggesting and presenting proposals at meetings (Holme 1928; Möteskultur 1931b).

Generally, the meeting procedures were strictly followed in the SDUK's circle. Standard procedure: an introductory presentation followed by questions and criticism concerning the presentation and finally debate on how to resolve the issue. When a conclusion or consensus could not be reached (e.g., the members could not agree on where to place the public bath), the conclusion was, as is typical in Swedish politics, to have the issue further investigated instead of bringing it to a stalemate. This pattern is visible in the other circles as well.

At the start of 1936, the character of the circle's minutes changed, being filled with participants' comments about each other. Since the minutes were always read aloud at the next meeting, the participants could comment on how they had described one another. These parts of the minutes are of little relevance when it comes to examining the substance of the discussions, but they do tell us something about the participants. They all knew each other very well and had been attending the study circle for quite some time. Even though it was more of a weekly social event—a night spent with friends—they never compromised on the meeting procedure that they had learned. At one meeting in December 1935, one participant suggested that the circle should change its meeting procedure and allow everyone to sit when talking; this suggestion met with severe resistance (SDUK Skutskär 1935a). Despite the fact that the meeting was more of a social than a working event, maintaining the proper forms was still deemed very important.

The meetings always had a theme, and a presenter, assigned to provide an introduction, was always appointed beforehand. In 1936, the theme was "current political issues." This points to a potential problem with the data on the courses: in the reports to the ABF, the circle was said to be an organizational studies circle, but in reality the circle studied something else. The current issues discussed mainly concerned equality, such as "equality in the home," "should women be allowed to do sports," and "male-female friendship." Other study circle meetings centered on the issue of the party press, the labor movement's relationship to sports in general, the labor movement's relationship to the temperance movement, and the world language question (Esperanto vs. English). Some meetings were devoted to strategic debates on how to develop the SDUK; for example, the circle discussed how to organize propaganda in upcoming elections. The participants also discussed how they could motivate more workers to join the study circle (SDUK Skutskär 1936). There were no discussions of ideological issues, such as reformism versus syndicalism or communism; the participants all seem to have adopted reformism.

What can we learn from this study circle about the implementation of the education strategy and about identity formation in study circles? First, the circle was mature: the participants had been studying together for quite some time, and mature circles tended to establish a certain internal mentality or culture; the people attending the meetings knew each other and the tone was familiar, friendly, and often bantering. Although these characteristics have no real connection to reformism, they do testify to the centrality the labor movement came to have in working-class lives and leisure time, which affected working-class culture. Second, since the circle was organized by the SDUK, it is no surprise that the participants already were convinced reformists. This circle must therefore be contrasted to circles that were sponsored by other organizations.

Study Circle on Meeting Culture

The study circle on meeting culture started in 1931 and was a mixed circle. It bears a resemblance to the SDUK's circle in that it used the same meeting procedures: an introductory presentation followed by questions and criticism concerning the presentation and finally debate on how to resolve the issue.

Some of the new circle's participants may have participated in study circles before—for example, studying general subjects—but most of the participants appear to have been new to meeting protocol and to the obligations of organization members. This study circle also had a social aspect, but it took education and exercises more seriously than did the SDUK. Even though the study circle consisted of workers from different branches of the labor movement (most of the participants appear to have been Communist Party members), they all seem to have known each other and the atmosphere was friendly. Once again, the study circle must be considered a hobby for the participants: the circle members held parties, had their own representative in the People's House (probably because the study circles needed a place to meet), and always had a break, during which they often drank coffee (Möteskultur 1931a).

The topics discussed by the study circle were parliamentarianism, the chair's obligations, and how to make a proposal. The characteristics desirable in a meeting chair were discussed, and the participants concluded that a chair "creates authority through maintaining discipline in the assembly as well as maintaining self-discipline" (Möteskultur 1931a). A good chair should also have mastered the Swedish language, according to the participants.

This study circle conducted practical exercises, including role-playing on several occasions. The same role-playing exercise conducted by the SDUK circle was conducted here—namely, proposing the construction of a public bath. In this case, as in the previous one, the participants had a hard time agreeing on one suggestion, so they decided that the issue needed to be investigated further before a decision could be made, exactly as in the SDUK circle (Möteskultur 1931b).

Doubtlessly, the disciplining elements that the LO wished to transfer to the grassroots were present in the study circle course, but the circle did not explicitly discuss reformism. One reason for this might have been that the study circle was a mixed circle, and as long as the participants followed the syllabus, the study circle meetings would not devolve into "partisan debates."

The members of the study circle expressed concerns about their fellow union members who did not engage in study activities, as described in a report on educational activities written by Bengt Bengtsson, one of the true study circle advocates in Skutskär: "With awareness comes success in life. But if the people continue to worship [the sport of] bandy, they will be transformed into sporting couch potatoes, and this cannot in any way foster citizens useful for society. Thus, the local inhabitants should, to a greater degree than they do today, spend their spare time on popular education activities in order to become important cogs in the big machine that is society" (Bengtsson 1931). Education was defined as a way out of the oppression of ignorance. Through education, the workers could change their situations. The quotation also reveals a belief that the main purpose of the workers as a collective was to serve society, and this idea that the workers were important to (and consequently should take responsibility for) society is familiar from Sigfrid Hansson's writings. These ideas were certainly evident in the study circles in Skutskär.

Study Circle in Socialism

The circle on meeting culture changed to studying socialism in the autumn of 1932, continuing its work until the spring of 1933. It was also a mixed circle, whose participants came from different organizations and seemed to have different ideological backgrounds. The circle leader was Gustaf Jansson, who has not been identified in the materials from the reformist organizations and likely belonged to the Communist Party. He often talked about communism in positive terms and framed reformist organizations as old organizations that had "bourgeoisified" (Möteskultur 1933b). Because of the mixed character of this circle and its ideological topic, this study circle conducted many debates in which the participants offered contrasting opinions.

This study circle discussed various aspects of socialism. The point of departure at most meetings was Marx and Engels's *Communist Manifesto*. The meetings always started with a speech about a subject agreed on at the previous meeting. After the speech, the participants took a short break, which was followed by a debate. In other words, this circle followed the same procedure as the others.

The participants and, in particular, the study circle leaders really seem to have wanted to debate. The communists appear to have outnumbered the reformists in the circle, and if the reformists in the circle did not speak up at the meeting, someone from the Communist Party would try to provoke them to enter the debate (Möteskultur 1933a).

Issues discussed included the main ideas of Marx, the Soviet Union, the five-year plan in the Soviet Union, population, utopia, and Bernstein's reformism and its distinctive features. In a debate on revisionism, the introductory speaker read aloud from Karl Kautsky, prompting debate on whether Kautsky was the best proponent of revisionism. One participant stated that Kautsky was too superficial and that Ernst Wigforss's book on materialism was much more worth reading (Möteskultur 1932c). At another meeting, cooperation was debated, clearly revealing the left-wing elements in the study circle. Some participants stated that cooperation had become bourgeois, like the reformist unions (Möteskultur 1933b). The breakdown of capitalist society foreseen by Marx was, according to the speaker, close at hand. Bernstein's criticism of Marx's catastrophe theory was no longer applicable; the reformist path was not sufficient for changing society: "The crisis that at the moment is sweeping the world is the greatest hitherto, and the unemployment that comes in its aftermath must unconditionally impel the working class to more united action, which means that one must leave the old reformist paths in order to achieve better results" (Möteskultur 1933b).

This statement was not left unanswered, and a lively debate ensued. One of the participants, Ekberg, replied by questioning whether catastrophe theory was indeed true. Ekberg thought that the former speaker had failed to present evidence, making the theory sound too good to be true. The debate reveals an interesting dilemma for the communists. A revolutionary organization needs to conduct a revolution to be a revolutionary organization, otherwise it will by definition become reformist. One can only credibly defend the idea of revolution to a certain level, and mixed circles offered an arena in which the communists' arguments could be thoroughly surveyed, to the advantage of the reformists.

The debates on the Soviet Union also revealed the left-wing supporters in the study circle: Jansson stated that Leninism was the true (and best) realization of Marxism. This statement was, however, challenged by other participants, who questioned whether Stalin's politics were a successful implementation of Marxism (Möteskultur 1932b).

The communist wing in the study circle appears to have claimed most space in the debates. The two main proponents of this point of view were Jansson (the study circle leader) and Rask. The latter has also not been mentioned in the materials from the reformist branch of the labor movement, so he was likely a

Communist Party comrade of Jansson. Some of the participants could also have been organized in the LS.

Although the participants clearly had different ideological standpoints, the minutes give the impression that the participants took their studies seriously, showing up at the meetings prepared to talk about the chosen subjects. Moreover, the participants also remained friends despite their differences of opinion, and a harsh tone is not discernible in the minutes. The study circle also held social events, seemingly obligatory in the labor movement at this time, as the labor movement was not only a place for politics but also a way of life.

The subjects were unquestionably theoretical, and quite often some of the participants commented on the difficulty of reading and actually understanding the texts. However, the records of debates that survive in the minutes suggest that the main ideas were understood by the participants. Most importantly, the workers actually discussed the foundations of the theory of socialism, indicating that the study circles certainly had potential to be the identity-constructing vehicle that the thesis of this study suggests.

Finally, the mixed nature of this circle raises some questions. Apparently, the circle included many communists, but since the Communist Party had been shut out from the ABF when this circle existed, the communist element is a little surprising. One possibility, however, is that the communists participated in mixed circles through their union memberships during their time of formal exile from the ABF.

Study Circle in Organizational Studies

The study circle on organizational studies concerned basic information about how to run an organization. Like the previously discussed study circle on meeting culture, this circle discussed the obligations and rights of the chair and members of an organization (Organisationskunskap 1935a), how to make a proposal, how the chair should respond to proposals (Organisationskunskap 1935c), and the importance of unison singing for the movement (Organisationskunskap 1935b).

In a debate on what organization a worker should first and foremost join, two positions emerged. One side advocated the temperance movement, as sober people, I was argued, could better defend the interests of the working class. On the other side, the debaters advocated the union movement: without workers' organizations, the working class could never defend its interests (Organisationskunskap 1935a). This circle mixed organizational studies with labor movement issues.

The participants were eager to engage more people in the study circle, so they appointed a committee whose main task was to recruit new members (Organisationskunskap 1935c). This circle, like the others, also held social events. After one semester, the participants decided to discuss current political issues at their meetings instead of organizational studies. This is understandable, as organizational studies was not a topic that the same people could study several semesters in a row. This circle's activities stopped in 1936.

Trade Union Studies

There are no remaining minutes from any of the study circles engaged in trade union studies in Skutskär. However, since this particular course is important for the argument made in this book, there are reasons to examine relevant material from other local education committees. Two study circles in trade union studies, one organized by the Hospital Workers' Union in Uppsala and the other by the local educational committee in Föllinge in the county of Jämtland, serve as cases. The syllabus for trade union studies was interpreted quite literally in both cases.

In Föllinge, the study circle was active in 1936–37 and seems to have possessed only one copy of the book *Den svenska fackföreningsrörelsen*, so the study circle read the book, chapter by chapter, in its meetings. The established procedure was that the circle would decide who would read aloud at the next meeting so that participant would have time to prepare. After the chapter had been read aloud, the circle would discuss the topic of the chapter (ABF Föllinge 1936).

In Uppsala, study circle number 1450 started in 1927 and in its first year focused on association studies. The procedure was that the participants wrote a short essay before each meeting on a topic decided beforehand. For example, at a meeting in October 1927, the theme was how to keep proper minutes; the participants brought their essays on the subject, which were read aloud and discussed (Studiecirkel 1450 1927).

The study circle started to address trade union studies in November 1930. The circle had at least nine participants, of whom three were women. The circle met once a week, on Thursdays at 7:30 p.m. (Studiecirkel 1450 1930). The ABF library to which the circle belonged had acquired Sigfrid Hansson's syllabus for trade union studies as well as the required books. The study circle participants read Hansson's book and, just as in 1927, the participants wrote thorough essays on the topic of each meeting. Both these cases clearly indicate that trade union studies was a course taken seriously by the participants and that Hansson's book was in fact read.

Study Circle Content in Skutskär and Beyond

What conclusions can we draw from analyzing the minutes of the study circles? To start with, whether or not the study circles actually studied what they were supposed to study (based on what they reported to the ABF) depended partly on how old the study circle was. The older the study circle, it seems, the less politically serious its activities.

Furthermore, the workers seem to have embraced the educational ideals of the ABF and the LO, and the study circles contained elements that could have had a disciplining effect on the participants. Through discussions at the study circle meetings, the workers were instructed on how to behave. Since the common meeting procedure appointed one participant to give a speech on the topic of the day, the disciplining elements came from a fellow participant, not as a dictate from above. This increased the likelihood that the message conveyed would be taken seriously. If some piece of information in the educational material was questioned, the participants would discuss it and try to come up with a solution or an interpretation that suited everyone. The whole concept of learning together and from each other was probably decisive for what arguments the participants accepted and what arguments they disregarded.

Most study circles appear to have discussed politics and workers' living conditions, which increased the likelihood that the study circles helped construct a particular image of workers. The experience of the organizational studies study circle indicates that not only trade union studies had course content that was useful in spreading reformism.

Implementing the Education Programs

The implementation of the education system was crucial for the LO's education strategy. Analysis of the content and spread of the popular education by examining nationwide data as well as the Skutskär case indicates that program implementation was successful in many ways. The time order follows the changes at the national level; the education programs were perceived as important to the unions in Skutskär; the magazine *Fackföreningsrörelsen* and the main books from Hansson's syllabus were in the library collection; and the number of study circles increased over time, as did the number of circles treating the "right" subjects. The idealistic view of popular education as a means to enlighten the working class had support among the local union elite, which could promote education among the rank and file. The preconditions for successfully implementing the education strategy were all there. Managing identity formation from above through internal popular education may have worked, its seems. Connecting ideological schooling of the grassroots to the much bigger issue of working-class education likely helped make the education strategy a success.

The impact of this popular education on the working class cannot be determined today, as it is impossible to measure changed perceptions of the movement before and after participants joined study circles. That said, the presented descriptions of popular education's role in the labor movement testify to the efforts and sacrifices made by local activists to mobilize and engage the working class in workers' education. It is very likely that the study activities had the impact that the LO Secretariat strove to realize.

6

CRAFTING THE LABOR MOVEMENT

In December 1938, August Lindberg, the president of the LO, signed the legendary labor market peace agreement known as the Basic Agreement, in the small town of Saltsjöbaden. The turbulence that had dominated the labor market for four decades came to an end. The agreement, which forced the labor market parties to negotiate whenever conflicts arose, heralded a new era in Swedish labor relations, which became known internationally as the Swedish model. August Lindberg, with Gustaf Söderlund of the Employers' Organization (SAF), came to embody the spirit of consensus: they made negotiations seem like a natural and wise way of resolving conflicts.

However, Lindberg's life history shows that consensus had not always been his preferred way of resolving labor market conflicts. Lindberg was born in 1885 in Harnäs, a small village on the outskirts of Skutskär, the location of the sawmill and pulp mill company Stora Kopparberg AB. Lindberg started to work in the lumberyard at an early age, and at the age of seventeen he joined the Sawmill Workers' Union Section 2, of which he eventually became chair. Lindberg's passion for politics was also awakened; he joined the Social Democratic Party and shortly afterward became chair of the local party association. Lindberg sympathized with the radical opponents of Branting and the party leadership and sided with the left wing of the labor movement when the party split in 1917. Subsequently, Lindberg left the Social Democrats and formed Skutskär's Left Party Commune, which only a few years later became the Communist Party of Sweden.

It is unlikely that Lindberg could have guessed in 1917 that he would go down in history as an advocate of consensus and the man who signed the Basic Agreement. The journey from left-wing activist to disciplined reformist is truly remarkable, not only for Lindberg personally but also for the thousands of other workers and their organizations that underwent the same transformation. The reformation of the Swedish working class laid the groundwork for the extraordinary development of Swedish social democracy.

The internal development of the LO and its relationship to its members reveals some important yet heretofore unexplored aspects of the development of the Swedish labor movement, either ignored or tacitly assumed by previous studies. The assumption that there existed discipline and ideological cohesion in the movement is an oversimplification of reality. The vital left-wing organizations constituted a real problem for the reformist labor movement. It is too easy to dismiss the left-wing organizations as not being influential, an aside in Swedish history, because of the marginalized role they were forced into from the late 1930s onward. This marginalized role originated mainly from the complete dominance of the Social Democratic Party and the LO. However, this does not mean that these fractions were unproblematic in the 1920s and 1930s. The left-wing organizations indeed caused problems for the LO, both by competing to organize workers in unions and, perhaps even more troublesome, by creating tensions within the LO. In 1920, the problems of an ideologically split labor movement culminated, forcing the LO Secretariat to either take action or watch the movement wither away. The year 1920 was what path-dependency theorists would refer to as a critical juncture. The identity problem that followed the rise of different ideological branches of the labor movement, organized in separate bodies, not only in Sweden but in the labor movement worldwide, had to be dealt with. The new organizations forced the LO to position itself relative to them and thus to define its own characteristic traits. More important, however, is that the Secretariat had this insight.

The LO Secretariat turned to popular education to find a solution to these problems. Popular education, with its long traditions in Sweden, allowed reformist messages to be delivered to the workers, ostensibly for enlightening the working class. With the right educational material and with suitable methods, themes important not only for the labor movement but also for the consolidation of Swedish democracy came to be discussed in study circles all around the country. The backbone of the reformist union movement was democracy and the rule of law: for democracy to work, union members simply had to follow the lead of those elected (i.e., the trade union leaders). The content of the educational materials depicted a particular kind of worker, one who applied the ideas of reformism to trade union work by embracing nego-tiations with the employers.

From Movement to Organization

The formation of classes cannot be fully understood without taking labor lead-ers into consideration. This thesis, which has guided the empirical analysis of this book, is based on two assumptions: first, labor organizations will follow an organizational logic, and, second, social identities need to be activated in order to become power resources.

In their famous article from 1966, Mayer N. Zald and Roberta Ash claimed that social movement organizations should be analyzed from an organizational perspective. As soon as social movements form organizations, the organizations will adopt the goal of organizational maintenance (Zald and Ash 1966). This is also true for labor organizations. Marxist theoretical analyses, which have dominated the field of labor studies, usually assume that labor organizations are sui generis, but labor organizations, like any organization, also follow an organi-zational logic. Ignoring that fact will make us overlook the internal dynamics of the labor movement, when in fact the internal battle needs to be won in order to pursue mobilization against others and to gain political power. Identity is vital for the organizational logic: it defines who belongs to the in-group and the out-group, it gives members a sense of meaning, and it constitutes the glue that keeps the organization's parts together. For organizations, organizational identity will always trump more inclusive social identities, such as class, that people can carry without joining an organization. Many organizations claim these social identi-ties, which are often based on structures such as class, gender, and ethnicity, using them for mobilization. Social identities based on such structures can be very efficient in mobilizing people for a cause, because such identities, when activated, engage fundamental and deeply rooted elements in individuals. For example, the women's movement clearly used gender as a mobilizing identity during the struggle for universal franchise, and the labor movement used the notion of the oppression of the working class when forming unions. Structural identities make people want to join a movement, but as soon as the movement needs to specify its goals, ambitions, and program for action, the dilemma of organizational identity emerges. It is difficult to materialize structural identities into political programs. Some issues will inevitably be prioritized over others, creating different factions, and once different factions exist, the emergence of different organizations is a possible next step. Although identities based on such structures have mobilizing effects, it is difficult to convert them into organizational identities, as this book has illustrated. The transition from mobilizing movements to *movement organizations* often calls for identity reformation. The emergence of more than one labor organization signals the existence of various notions of what a worker is. For their organizations to survive, members need to understand why they should be members of particular class-based organizations. How well labor organizations manage such transitions will affect the cohesiveness in the movement—in other words, how labor organizations transform class identity into organizational identity is crucial for our understanding of cross-national differences.

Some problems currently facing the trade union movement emanate from this tension between structural class identity and organizational identity. It is well known that the international union movement has been in a state of crisis for the past thirty years (Gumbrell-McCormick and Hyman 2014; Waddington 2014): union density has declined, especially among the working class, and bargaining power and political influence have subsequently decreased. Even though the economy has gone global and the need for unions to protect workers' rights is as important as ever, unions do not seem to be able to mobilize and recruit members. Meanwhile the class structure has changed profoundly in the Western world. While the industrial era was a period dominated by the working class, the post-industrial era has been dominated by the middle class. The working class is shrinking in size. Meanwhile, insecure employment contracts have created a new stratum of well-educated individuals forced to take employment for which they are overqualified under insecure conditions, a stratum called the "precariat" by Guy Standing (Standing 2011). The "new" working class in Europe has become more heterogeneous in terms of ethnicity and gender, and the changed labor market relations have blurred the perceptions of class belonging. Yet class has been and still is the mobilizing identity for many unions, so many unions have found themselves trapped in a class identity with members who do not primarily identify with class or who hold very different notions of what class entails. This is the reverse of the problem in the 1910s, when class identity superseded organizational identity, but in both cases it calls for unions to think in terms of organizational identity rather than class when recruiting members. Labor leaders need to take responsibility for managing, upholding, and reproducing identity.

This leads us to the second assumption of the thesis in this book—namely, that social identities need to be activated by leaders. Karl Marx's account of the class formation process, in which class becomes class *for itself*, has influenced labor leaders *ideologically* and class formation research *theoretically*. In both cases, Marxist interpretations have led to a focus on structures. Marxist class formation research has focused on structural explanations of class formation processes, often resulting in analyses of technical developments and their implications for class identity, neglecting the actor's role in the class formation process. The actor is ignored or regarded as subject to external forces. Likewise, social movement research has focused primarily on "the collective," neglecting leadership issues (Stutje 2012, 2–3). However, labor leaders can take an active part in the construction of a sense of "we" in the movement. Leaders in a class organization can act in order to steer the members toward perceiving the organization in a particular way. How leaders talk and act has an impact on organizational identity because of the leaders' position in the organization. The dynamic nature of social identities can be used by an attentive leadership to construct and activate identity processes. Acting as identity entrepreneurs is indeed, as Mills (1948) claimed, an important task for labor leaders. All organizations need managers of discontent, but for voluntary organizations this may be particularly true, because members stay members only if they identify with the organization and can easily leave if they do not.

However, far from every labor leader would come to this insight, especially not those who were ideologically devoted to Marx. The leaders of Marxist labor movements would less actively seize the identity entrepreneur role because of the inherent structural analysis of labor movement's development offered by Marxism. Berman's 1998 empirical analysis of the Swedish and German social democratic parties during the interwar period confirms such conclusions: dogmatic Marxist thought guided the actions of the SPD, Sozialdemokratische Partei Deutschlands, so the German labor movement found itself trapped in an ideological framework that limited its maneuvering room. The Swedish labor movement, on the other hand, had less at stake ideologically and could handle political problems pragmatically (Berman 1998, 201–30).

Workers' Education and the Ideological Schooling of the Working Class

Identity entrepreneurship entails not only understanding that organizational identity can be managed, but also that leaders have an idea of where the organization and the movement are heading. Core values must be defined and presented to the organization's members. In such a process, internal education constitutes an important strategy that any identity entrepreneur can use in creating cohesion in an organization. Indeed, internal education constitutes a good opportunity to define an organization, to foster and to discipline members. This argument resonates with the wide range of research that has mapped the socializing effects of education in general. In particular, civic education has been ascribed great importance for the establishment of democratic values, political participation, and trust (Dudley and Gitelson 2002; Galston 2007). Even though formal education differs from popular education in its pedagogy, participants, and organization, some commonalities do exist: the mechanisms of identity formation and the transfer of values between participants in the study activities are the same.

The educational sphere of the labor movement became a vehicle for the development of working-class culture. This work's description of study circle activities in Skutskär reveals that the educational sphere offered a meeting place for the other spheres of the labor movement—unions, political parties, youth associations, women's organizations, and temperance associations—all of which participated in popular education. Indeed, workers' study activities became a crucial part of everyday working-class life. This finding is not limited to Sweden (e.g., Friesen and Taksa 1996), and Jonathan Rose's famous book on the British working class testifies to the importance of workers' education for working-class culture in Britain as well (Rose 2001).

For identity management—that is, steering perceptions of the movement—it is not enough to have just *any* education; rather, the type, content, and scope of the education are important. Based on the present findings, the generalizability of this claim requires two reflections: first, on the uniqueness of the Swedish popular education system, and, second, on the effects of workers' education. Workers' education grew in extent all over Europe during the first decades of the twentieth century (Holford 1994; Jansson 2015; Steele 2007). Education programs organized by and for the working class quickly assumed different forms in different countries due to different ideas of the usefulness and aims of workers' education. According to many contemporary activists and educators, the main aim of organizing such education was to emancipate and empower the working class— in other words, enlightenment and *Bildung* (education) were the core ideas. The aim of workers' education for the proponents of such ideas was to lift the masses out of ignorance and compensate the workers for low formal education. Enlightening the working class usually meant providing general education to the broader public. The workers' institutes that emerged in most countries toward the end of the nineteenth century provided these types of popular education and often had a slightly patronizing underlying attitude toward the working class (e.g., Società Operaia in Italy, mechanics' institutes in Britain, and the Workers' Institute in Sweden) (Johansson 2015; Kelly 1952; Shapin and Barnes 1977; Steele 2007, 28–29). These institutions for educating the working class often adopted what Bernt Gustavsson has called "the civic education ideal," which claimed that education for the working class should be pursed for the benefit of *society* (Gustavsson 1991). Such arguments were often made to lobby for increased public funding for popular education institutions. This tradition of popular education from above was soon challenged by *the neo-humanistic school* (Gustavsson 1991), in which workers' education was intended to liberate and raise the working class, so the *individual worker* and one's gains became the focus. These ideas led to the establishment of educational institutions by and for the working class, such as the Workers' Educational Association (Arbetarnas bildningsförbund, ABF).

However, as this study suggests, there is a third perspective on workers' education. Following the thesis of identity entrepreneurship, education for the working class could also be organized by labor organizations for the purpose of *ideologically and organizationally schooling* their members. This might be the missing link in understanding national differences between labor movements. It is safe to say that workers' education played different roles in different countries, as the institutional framework, funding, pedagogical view, content, and scope of the popular education systems all differed across countries. Key elements of the success of workers' educational efforts in Sweden were not only insightful leadership but also the main study activity: study circles. Study circles were interactive and nonhierarchical, and their main strength was the acceptance of a diversity of ideas: everybody, including the study circle leader, had to defend their opinions. It would be wrong to assume that poorly educated workers would accept anything said to them in the study circles. On the contrary, the analysis of the study circles in Skutskär found deliberation over theoretical issues and critical discussions of the literature. In the study circle, rational argument had primacy. These types of study activities should be contrasted to activities in other countries. In Britain, study activities through the Workers' Educational Association (WEA) rapidly increased in the 1920s and 1930s, as such activities had in Sweden. Comparing the Swedish study circles with study activities in Britain suggests that the more hierarchical British learning situation (the WEA had tutors with university degrees running the tutorial classes) influenced identity formation in workers' education (Jansson 2016). The British study activities closely resembled formal education: they were teacher-led, with specified learning goals, regular written assignments, et cetera, whereas the Swedish study circles can be classified as informal learning situations in an informal institutional setting (Eshach 2007) in which the participants learned from each other through deliberation. Hierarchical education tends to turn students into passive listeners, whereas active, participatory, and nonhierarchical study activities can be the seedbed for identity formation in the small group of study participants and in the movement as a whole.

Comparing the Swedish popular education system with workers' education in other countries highlights the causal relationship between the study circles and the development of the Swedish labor movement. It is impossible to measure the effect of the workers' education at an individual level, as no material is preserved that would allow such an analysis. Nevertheless, two remarks that support the thesis that the study activities did have an impact warrant mention. Following research into socialization and popular education, it seems that participating in informal study activities positively influences bonding in organizations. In a comprehensive evaluation of Swedish social movements and the popular education offered by them carried out in the 1990s (Andersson et al. 1996, 65–66), participants in various study circles were interviewed. The study concluded that the participants perceived the circles as helping deepen their interest in the subject of study and as strengthening self-esteem, social skills, and fellowship among the participants. The circles helped to uphold and develop "citizens' values" such as forming and expressing personal opinions and arguing for them in the group, taking responsibility, and making decisions collectively (Andersson et al. 1996, 65–66)—in other words, many of the skills that Hansson wanted to inculcate in the membership. Study circles clearly had a profound impact on their participants in the 1990s, and there is little reason to suggest that the effects of popular education in the 1920s and 1930s would have differed.

Causal analyses are difficult to pursue in historical studies of changes in social identities due to the scarcity of relevant material. However, for some *individuals* such material is preserved that is worth mentioning. In 1932, twenty-two-year-old Arne Geijer started to study at the Brunnsvik People's High School, and in 1933 he entered the LO summer school. Geijer belonged to a different generation of trade union activists from that of August Lindberg. Although Geijer (according to himself) had been very critical of the LO's actions, particularly regarding assistance for the unemployed, Sigfrid Hansson, obviously impressed by the young Geijer, recommended that he apply for a position at the LO (Geijer 1935). The rest is history. In 1956, Geijer became president of the LO, a post he would have for almost twenty years, during which Swedish social democracy flourished: the comprehensive welfare state was constructed, unemployment was low, and the Swedish model—the industrial relations and corporatist system—peaked. Few personified the consolidation of the consensus model of Swedish industrial relations as well as Arne Geijer.

The Swedish reformist labor movement underwent a thorough transformation in the 1920s and 1930s. The spirit of negotiation is indeed characteristic of the Swedish labor market, and the Basic Agreement became the ultimate symbol of the willingness to make compromises and negotiate. The agreement with "the enemy" became a major success. By the time Geijer assumed office, the spirit of consensus was institutionalized and the norms of industrial relations established in Sweden. The former student of Sigfrid Hansson was representing the LO in the regular tripartite meetings in Harpsund between the LO, the Swedish

Employers' Association (Svenska Arbetsgivareföreningen, SAF), and the host: the Swedish government. Of course, Geijer could have applied these visions and ideas elsewhere, as the self-image of the LO as an advocate of negotiations was not delimited to the study circles. These ideas had evidently become rooted in the generation of union activists who gained power in the 1940s and 1950s, and it is not a far-fetched suggestion that the educational work of the LO played a role in socializing the labor leaders into a particular type of organizational culture and therefore into adopting a particular identity.

Consensus Culture, Saltsjöbaden, and the Swedish Model

The intriguing dominance of the Swedish Social Democratic Party (SAP) in Swedish politics has engendered numerous studies. In explaining the SAP's success, cross-class electoral strategies, the electoral system, and ideological pragmatism have all been emphasized as important variables (Berman 1998; Przeworski 1980, 1985; Svensson 1994; Therborn 1989). The role of the labor movement's other branch—the trade union movement—has as yet been over-looked in this scholarly discourse, perhaps for good reasons: political parties and trade unions are different types of organizations. Competing in elections, the success of political parties is often measured by the number of votes, and mobilizing voters requires visions of political reforms. For trade unions, mobi-lizing members requires considerable identity work on an everyday basis: union mobilization is less about convincing many people to support unions on one particular day than about a union proving itself useful every day. However, if and when such identity work in unions is connected to ideology, it can be very useful for political parties. By constructing an organizational identity based on reformism, the LO undoubtedly helped mobilize workers to vote for the SAP. By identifying that dynamic, this study presents one more piece in the puzzle of understanding the strength of the SAP. However, this book's main contribu-tion to understanding Sweden concerns labor market relations rather than the political party sphere.

Cross-class coalitions and cooperation have received ample attention from researchers (Afonso 2012; Korpi 2006; Swenson 1989; Swenson 1991; Åmark 1994), who have considered why parties with opposed interests would cooper-ate. In the Swedish case, the spirit of consensus is central to understanding such cooperation. The spirit of consensus, embedded in the culture of negotiation, entails finding solutions that all parties can accept, without letting labor dis-putes escalate into full-fledged conflicts. This characteristic of Swedish labor relations has been seen as the source of labor market peace in the postwar period. The road to the Basic Agreement has been analyzed multiple times (Lundh 2009). It is easy to turn to the elites in the LO and SAF in striving to understand the agreement. The elites are important, as Sweden is a small country, and networks obviously play a role. Regardless of political affiliation, the members of the elites would know one another, and the elites of the labor market parties were no exception to that. Before he became the SAF manager, Gustaf Söderlund had worked at the Swedish Government Offices as, for example, state secretary for Ernst Wigforss, the minister of finance, and was a representative on the Stockholm City Council together with Arvid Thorberg (Statskalendern 1926, 75; Statskalendern 1928, 391). Together with the labor movement elite, Söderlund was a representative of the SAF on various committees of the National Board of Health and Welfare (Socialstyrelsen), one important committee being the Social Council (Sociala rådet) (Statskalendern 1931). After the negotiations in Saltsjöbaden started in August 1936, Gustaf Söderlund wrote to Sigfrid Hansson (who was not part of the LO delegation), complaining that the process was progressing slowly because the LO and SAF representatives had not yet reached the same conclusions as he and Hansson had, though he was convinced they would "come to their senses in due time" (Söderlund 1936). The meaning of these personal connections between the labor market parties should not be overestimated, but we can be sure that these nested networks helped build trust between the men who pursued the negotiations. Judging from the correspondence between Hansson and Söderlund, at least parts of the elites of the labor market organizations had already realized the advantages of the spirit of consensus, even before the negotiations had started. This in itself is not a novel finding. The novel aspect that this study brings to industrial relations research in general, and to understanding Swedish industrial relations in particular, is that the spirit of consensus was established among the workers *before* the Basic Agreement was reached. Indeed, this study has demonstrated that the spirit of consensus was part of the conscious construction of an organizational identity within the LO, an identity that was transmitted through popular education long before the agreement was signed. The spirit of consensus was not an effect of the agreement but a precursor.

Grassroots consent was a key factor in the success of the Basic Agreement, for three reasons. First, the agreement represented formalized cooperation with the employers' organization, signaling an employer-friendly approach that was provocative to some Swedish workers. The new policy could indeed alienate members of the LO, which risked losing members because of its new pragmatic (and ideologically somewhat diluted) position. This threat was particularly real since the syndicalist Swedish Workers' Central Organization (Sveriges Arbetares

Centralorganisation, SAC) and the Communist Party constituted organizations that were alternative to the LO. Moreover, the syndicalists and communists enjoyed strong support among the grassroots in the reformist labor movement in the 1920s, support that could be mobilized against the Basic Agreement. The interpretation of the agreement prevalent among syndicalists and communists was that it represented "the labor movement's surrender to capitalism." In other words, the LO had given up the idea of pursuing socialism when it cooperated with capital. The syndicalist movement in Sweden today still refers to the Basic Agreement as a way for the state to limit the power of the working class and in that way strengthen the employers. Indeed, the Basic Agreement deviated from the prevalent traditional interpretation of how class struggle could and should be conducted.

Moreover, and even more importantly, successful implementation of the Basic Agreement would have been difficult without grassroots consent. The culture in the LO in the first decades of the twentieth century encouraged the use of the strike as a weapon, whereas the aim of the agreement was to control and restrain strikes. Strikes were perceived as the workers' main weapon against the employers and thus were untouchable and indisputable, so renouncing the right to use them when deemed necessary was a major surrender of power. If LO members had been dissatisfied with the agreement and the ensuing limitation of use of the strike, they could easily have prevented the implementation of the agreement simply by ignoring it and continuing to start strikes; this was in fact an already established culture in the LO.

Finally, entering into the Basic Agreement without support from below would have put the LO leaders in an awkward position on the labor market, damaging their credibility with the employers' side and perhaps forcing the state to intervene. It would also have badly weakened the LO's position among its own affiliates and members. Such an outcome was something that the LO leaders dearly wanted to avoid, especially after the loss of half the membership after the failed general strike in 1909.

However, there were no mass protests against the Basic Agreement, no uprisings. The agreement should be compared with the law on collective agreements passed in 1928. That law regulated conflicts during periods when collective agreements were in force. It does not appear to be a particularly controversial law from today's perspective, but it mobilized protests rarely seen in Sweden since the general strike. Indeed, reaction to the law on collective agreements demonstrates that the will to mobilize and protest against perceived injustices, especially any type of regulation of industrial actions, was strong in the grassroots. Had the grassroots not supported or at least accepted the agreement, they could have ended the cross-class cooperation. But the grassroots behaved "responsibly," obeyed their union leaders, and probably saw the benefits of the agreement—in other words, they applied what they had learned in the study circles.

When August Lindberg signed the Basic Agreement in December 1938 on behalf of the LO, he knew it would be controversial, but he also knew that it would be accepted by the members. Acceptance of the regulation of labor market conflicts through negotiations became a crucial element of the Swedish model, which in turn has deeply affected the development of Swedish society and the comprehensive welfare state during the twentieth century.

Appendix

TABLE A.1 Number of affiliates, sections, and members in the LO

YEAR	AFFILIATES (FÖRBUND)	SECTIONS (AVDELNINGAR)	MEMBERS
1900	21	787	45,575
1901	25	856	42,329
1902	24	797	39,545
1903	25	880	47,820
1904	30	1,172	81,736
1905	30	1,291	86,635
1906	30	1,726	144,395
1907	28	2,144	186,226
1908	28	2,172	162,391
1909	17	1,829	108,079
1910	27	1,576	85,176
1911	26	1,449	79,926
1912	27	1,392	85,522
1913	26	1,433	97,252
1914	27	1,478	101,207
1915	27	1,502	110,708
1916	28	1,672	140,802
1917	28	1,953	186,146
1918	30	2,305	222,185
1919	31	2,652	258,996
1920	31	2,799	280,029
1921	32	2,783	252,361
1922	33	3,207	292,917
1923	33	3,448	313,022
1924	34	3,810	360,337
1925	34	3,901	384,617
1926	35	4,042	414,859
1927	36	4,247	437,974
1928	36	4,386	469,409
1929	36	4,546	508,107
1930	37	5,064	553,456

(continued)

TABLE A.1   (Continued)

YEAR	AFFILIATES (FÖRBUND)	SECTIONS (AVDELNINGAR)	MEMBERS
1931	40	5,398	589,176
1932	41	5,783	638,593
1933	41	5,906	633,351
1934	41	6,043	653,331
1935	42	6,318	701,186
1936	41	6,622	757,376
1937	41	7,045	840,234
1938	42	7,407	897,947
1939	45	7,860	961,216
1940	46	7,602	971,103

Source: Johansson and Magnusson 1998, 343–44.

TABLE A.2   Number of study circles in the reformist organizations

YEAR	TOTAL NUMBER OF STUDY CIRCLES	LO	SAP	SSU	UNGA ÖRNAR
1922	1,387	224	190	100	-
1923	1,636	275	213	152	-
1924	1,783	331	208	215	-
1925	2,005	346	167	300	-
1926	2,251	403	174	408	-
1927	2,390	439	196	423	-
1928	2,737	459	182	539	-
1929	2,905	474	186	683	-
1930	3,060	496	213	800	-
1931	3,430	602	227	986	-
1932	4,306	670	262	1,172	-
1933	5,309	1,010	307	1,605	-
1934	5,826	1,015	341	1,855	-
1935	5,793	1,083	435	1,943	-
1936	5,886	1,302	445	1,718	-
1937	5,894	1,643	481	1,619	127
1938	6,136	1,875	681	1,344	122
1939	6,896	2,086	761	1,369	152
1940	6,138	1,674	590	1,120	160

Source: ABF annual reports, 1922–1940.

TABLE A.3 Number of study circles in the other organizations

YEAR	SAC	SUP	SKP	KUF	KF	NOV	OTHER	MIXED CIRCLES
1922	20	12	47	265	23	108	98	300
1923	42	11	54	284	29	114	52	410
1924	71	10	70	275	36	135	67	365
1925	81	4	72	265	40	116	62	552
1926	86	5	88	251	43	134	70	589
1927	92	3	92	234	46	120	56	689
1928	109	7	108	244	46	108	58	877
1929	120	4	-	-	55	97	58	1,228
1930	73	5	-	-	66	105	70	1,232
1931	75	5	-	-	89	105	65	1,276
1932	113	2	-	-	89	119	71	1,808
1933	170	2	-	-	89	124	31	1,971
1934	165	4	-	-	72	121	32	2,221
1935	96	0	-	-	75	123	21	2,017
1936	123	9	-	-	68	155	19	2,047
1937	75	-	-	-	80	136	35	1,698
1938	46	-	-	-	91	122	58	1,797
1939	59	-	29		100	106	22	2,212
1940	24	-	47		119	95	29	2,280

Source: ABF annual reports, 1922–1940.

TABLE A.4 Number of ABF libraries, books, and book loans

YEAR	NUMBER OF ABF LIBRARIES	NUMBER OF BOOKS	NUMBER OF BOOK LOANS
1922	620	119,481	386,896
1923	702	144,290	396,958
1924	723	167,524	409,847
1925	791	193,465	483,689
1926	881	212,918	475,537
1927	933	241,266	537,585
1928	974	265,794	558,977
1929	1,021	295,701	591,960
1930	1,053	296,497	480,552
1931	1,063	322,860	609,961
1932	1,097	350,209	813,460

(continued)

TABLE A.4   (Continued)

YEAR	NUMBER OF ABF LIBRARIES	NUMBER OF BOOKS	NUMBER OF BOOK LOANS
1933	1,131	389,966	1,016,768
1934	1,170	419,260	1,224,268
1935	1,338	457,866	1,160,164
1936	1,431	488,702	1,135,770
1937	1,469	517,475	1,101,260
1938	1,509	549,131	1,061,006
1939	1,539	575,072	1,097,082
1940	1,497	612,942	1,111,482

Source: ABF annual reports, 1922–1940.

Notes

1. THE REFORMIST CHOICE

1. Sweden had the highest number of strikes per hundred thousand workers among thirteen Western industrial countries as well as the highest number of work days lost per strike. After 1945, Sweden had the lowest strike rate among the same countries.

2. For thorough discussion of the concept, see Berg and Edquist 2017, 11–14; and Åberg 2008, 55–56.

3. Nikolaj Frederik Severin Grundtvig was a Danish pastor and the father of the folk high school.

2. PROBLEMS IDENTIFIED BY THE LO LEADERSHIP

1. People's high schools or folk high schools are independent adult education colleges common in the Nordic countries.

2. My translation here and throughout the book.

3. See the debate recorded in Landssekretariatet 1920b, in which the Metal Workers' Union criticized the Secretariat for meddling in their ongoing conflict, and the Secretariat replied that the methods used by the union (they had tried to persuade the Wood Industry Workers' Union to start a sympathy strike) contravened LO policy. The problem of the number of strikes has been recognized by other researchers, and research into "varieties of capitalism" states that the employers more or less forced the workers to centralize their organizations through the threat of "bloodletting" the unions' strike funds (Landsorganisationen 1917, 40–41; Swenson 1989; Swenson 1991).

4. Awareness of the consequences of a divided union movement are apparent, for example, in articles in *Fackföreningsrörelsen* in 1924, in which the split is cited as a reason for fighting SAC (J.-O. Johansson 1924a; J.-O. Johansson 1924b; Zetterling 1924).

5. In her book on the Swedish syndicalists in the mining industry, Eva Blomberg comes to similar conclusions (Blomberg 1995, 95–99).

6. A merger of the LO and the SAC was discussed seriously in 1928. The SAC, along with the communist organizations, had long advocated a merger, for obvious reasons. The SAC had invited the LO to join them in conflicts several times in the 1920s, but the LO Secretariat had always declined. The LO's change of heart was probably due to the de-radicalization of several of the syndicalist theorists (though not the grass-roots). These men, including Ragnar Casparsson and Frans Severin, were ideologically close to the reformists. They supported a merger. Of course, a merger could also have co-opted the radical forces. However, the negotiations broke down because the radical (i.e., anarchist) factions of the SAC under the leadership of Albert Jensen refused to accept the LO's conditions, arguing that the LO was trying to "absorb" its left-wing competition. One consequence of the failed merger was that several leading syndicalists left the SAC, and some of them (e.g., Casparsson and Severin) were recruited by the LO. Casparsson became the ombudsman at LO in 1933, responsible for press issues, and thus became a member of the Secretariat. The defecting syndicalists were also assigned the task of lecturing about the problems of syndicalism (Casparsson 1951, 155–78; Landssekretariatet 1935; Nilsson 1977, 199–217).

3. A PLAN FOR IDENTITY MANAGEMENT

1. See, for example, Landsorganisationen "LO-Tidningens korrespondens 1920–26," LO 2964/E/12/1, ARAB, Stockholm.

2. For example, Hansson 1918; Hansson 1919; Hansson 1920; Hansson 1922a; Hansson 1925b; Hansson 1931; Hansson 1936b.

3. See Sätterberg 1928a; Sätterberg 1928b; Sätterberg 1932a; Sätterberg 1932b.

4. CONSTRUCTING IDENTITY

1. In the county of Uppsala, catalogs have been preserved from only six libraries, five of which subscribed to either *Bokstugan* or *Studiekamraten* (ABF Bålsta 1926–; ABF Johannisfors 1925–; ABF Raklösen 1913; ABF Risingegård 1934; ABF Skutskär 1917a). The catalog from the sixth library, in Söderfors, is dated 1918, when *Studiekamraten* had not yet been founded and *Bokstugan* was only one year old and had not yet gained nationwide distribution (ABF Söderfors 1918).

2. Berg's syllabus was not mentioned once in the 1936–37 period in the study circle reports from the four counties of Gävleborg, Lund and Malmö, Norrbotten, and Uppsala (Studiecirkelrapporter för Norrbotten, Uppsala, Skåne o Gävleborg 1927–1928, 1936–1937).

3. The guild system was abolished in 1846.

4. In Hansson's book on shoemakers, he described the guild system thoroughly and noted that the masters and journeymen were unable to reconcile their differences, which in Hansson's account was problematic (Hansson 1919, 140).

5. This article was also part of the course literature for trade union studies.

6. Hansson and Wigforss went on a study trip to England to study guild socialism. The trip resulted in numerous articles on this particular form of socialism in *Fackföreningsrörelsen* (Hansson 1921b; Hansson 1921c; Hansson 1922f; Landsorganisationen 1921, 88; Wagner 1924).

7. A similar formulation was also used later by Hansson (Hansson 1927a, 109; Hansson 1934a, 113).

8. The same statement had earlier been used by the same author (Hansson 1934a, 275–76; Hansson 1927a, 267).

9. Ragnar Casparsson was a journalist at *Social-demokraten* who painted a very different picture of employers; he frequently used class rhetoric and described the relationship between the LO and the employers as a class struggle.

10. According to the annual report, approximately forty study circles had followed this lecture course as a complement to the reading (ABF 1931, 14).

5. IMPLEMENTING THE EDUCATION STRATEGY

1. For the history of the Skutskär LS see, for example, Eling 1989, 68. For the support of the Social Democratic Left Party's local organization in Skutskär, see, for example, Sågverksindustriarbetareförbundet avd 2 1923.

2. Local sections of the SDU were usually named the SDUK, Socialdemokratiska ungdomsklubben.

3. Local sections of SAP were usually named workers' communes, *arbetarkommuner*.

4. In 1917, the Paper Mill Workers' Union Section 2 was still called the Factory Workers' Union Section 60.

5. Karl Hammarström and August Lindberg founded the Left Party Commune. Lindberg left Skutskär in the early 1920s, but Hammarström stayed and occupied various positions in the Sawmill Workers' Union Sections 2 and 54 and the Paper Mill Workers' Union Section 2 (Vänsterkommunen Skutskär 1917b).

6. Ernst Wigforss was the minister of finance in the Social Democratic governments in the 1930–40s and was one of the designers of the Swedish welfare state.

7. The ABF's activities were financed mainly through government grants—for example, for the libraries. Again, the legislation required a nationwide organization that would organize the libraries (this was why Sandler founded the ABF). The grants from the state to the libraries increased in 1930. It also became possible for individual study circles to apply for funding from the state in 1930 (Andersson 1980, 260; Arvidson 1985, 117).

8. The People's Houses were buildings built and owned by the labor movement. Local labor movement organizations formed a People's House association, and that association became formally responsible for the house. The association could apply for funding from a specific "People's House trust" that the LO had, to finance the construction of the house. The temperance movement and the Free Church movement had similar systems. The houses were used for meetings and cultural events, and most villages had one.

9. Since it has not been reported anywhere how many participated in the study circles before 1923 or after 1939, calculations are based on these seventeen years. The trade unionists comprised members of the Saw Mill Workers' Union Cections 2 and 54, the Paper Mill Workers' Union Section 2, and the syndicalist organization LS.

10. Esperanto was part of labor movement culture for the purpose of uniting all workers worldwide and had been for some time (Sandelin 2013). At the LO congress of 1926, the Miners' Union and the Railroad Workers' Union suggested that the LO should intensify efforts to make Esperanto the world language. The workers could never unite without a common language, the proposers claimed. The LO leaders replied that since there was no consensus among the world's trade unions as to what language should be the workers' language, the LO should improve language studies in general but not Esperanto in particular (Landsorganisationen 1926b, 427–31).

11. Macroeconomics could have been placed in the ideological category since parts of the course contained ideological (socialist) messages regarding the economy.

12. Pelle Åberg has made a distinction between problem-based and supply-based circles (Åberg 2008, 64).

13. Hansson had not yet published his 1927 syllabus for trade union studies. However, he had arranged study circle leader courses at Brunnsvik each summer, and his syllabus for that course became the unofficial syllabus for trade union studies used by study circles around the country, including in Skutskär.

References

ABBREVIATIONS

ABF   Arbetarnas bildningsförbund
ARAB   Arbetarrörelsens arkiv och bibliotek
FAC   Folkrörelsearkivet för Uppsala län
FAJ   Föreningsarkivet i Jämtlands län
SAC   Sveriges arbetares centralorganisation
SCB   Statistiska centralbyrån
SDUK   Socialdemokratiska ungdomsklubben
SOU   Statens offentliga utredningar

Åberg, Pelle. 2008. *Translating Popular Education: Civil Society Cooperation between Sweden and Estonia*. Stockholm: Department of Political Science, Stockholm University.

ABF. 1912. *Verksamhetsberättelse*, Stockholm.

ABF. 1913. *Verksamhetsberättelse arbetsåret 1912–13*, Stockholm.

ABF. 1915. *Verksamhetsberättelse för arbetsåret 1914–15*, Stockholm.

ABF. 1916. *Verksamhetsberättelse arbetsåret 1915–16*, Stockholm.

ABF. 1919. *Verksamhetsberättelse för arbetsåret 1918–19*, Stockholm.

ABF. 1920a. "Studiecirkelrapport 1919/20." ABF, E/04/3, ARAB, Stockholm.

ABF. 1920b. *Verksamhetsberättelse arbetsåret 1919–20*, Stockholm.

ABF. 1921a. "Studiecirkelrapporter 1921/22." ABF, E/04/05, ARAB, Stockholm.

ABF. 1921b. *Verksamhetsberättelse arbetsåret 1920–21*, Stockholm.

ABF. 1924a. "Enkät angående 8-timmarsdagen." ABF, E/2/01, ARAB, Stockholm.

ABF. 1924b. *Verksamhetsberättelse arbetsåret 1923–24*, Stockholm.

ABF. 1926. "Studiecirkel rapport, cirkel 457 Skutskär 1925/26." ABF, 2831/E/04/09, ARAB, Stockholm.

ABF. 1927. "Studiecirkel rapport, cirkel 457 Skutskär 1926/27." ABF, 2831/E/04/10, ARAB, Stockholm.

ABF. 1928. "Prospekt över planlagda kurser och studiecirklar arbetsåret 1928–1929."

ABF. 1930. "Ett ord till arbetarna. Cirkulär från ABF till bildningsutskotten med broschyr angående bildning."

ABF. 1931. *Verksamhetsberättelse 1930–31*, Stockholm.

ABF. 1933a. "Cirkulär från ABF." ABF 2831/B/3/1, ARAB, Stockholm.

ABF. 1933b. "Studiecirkelrapporter 1933/34." ABF, E/04/21, ARAB, Stockholm.

ABF Bålsta. 1926–. "Inventarielista," ABF Bibliotek 780, Bålsta, fragment 108, Folkrörelsearkivet för Uppsala län, Uppsala.

ABF Föllinge. 1936. "Protokoll från studiecirkel annordnad av ABF Föllinge," ABF:s lokalavdelning nr 1402 Föllinge, Föreningsarkivet i Jämtlands län, Östersund.

ABF Johannisfors. 1925–. "Förvärvskatalog," ABF bibliotek 803, Johannisfors, fragment 77, FAC, Uppsala.

ABF Raklösen. 1913. "Förvärvskatalog 1913–34," ABF bibliotek nr 11, Raklösen, fragment 32, FAC, Uppsala.

178   REFERENCES

ABF Representantskap. 1913. "Protokoll fört vid sammanträde med representantskapet för arbetarnas bildningsförbund den 26 september," ABF, A/01/A/01, Arbetarrörelsens arkiv och bibliotek, Stockholm.

ABF Representantskap. 1915. "Protokoll fört vid sammanträde med ABF 17 september," ABF, A/01/A/01, ARAB, Stockholm.

ABF Representantskap. 1918a. "Protokoll fört vid ABFs representantskapsmöte den 8 augusti," ABF, A/01/A/01, ARAB, Stockholm.

ABF Representantskap. 1918b. "Protokoll fört vid sammanträde med ABFs representantskap den 10 maj," ABF, A/01/A/01, ARAB, Stockholm.

ABF Representantskap. 1919a. "Protokoll fört vid ABFs representantskaps ajournerade årsmöte i Stockholm den 9 oktober," ABF, A/01/A/01, ARAB, Stockholm.

ABF Representantskap. 1919b. "Protokoll fört vid ABFs representantskaps årsmöte den 13 juli," ABF, A/01/A/01, ARAB, Stockholm.

ABF Representantskap. 1919c. "Protokoll fört vid extra sammanträde med ABFs representantskap den 23 maj," ABF, A/01/A/01, ARAB, Stockholm.

ABF Representantskap. 1920a. "Protokoll fört vid ABF:s representantskaps möte den 23 september," ABF, A/01/A/01, ARAB, Stockholm.

ABF Representantskap. 1920b. "Protokoll fört vid ABFs representantskaps extra sammanträde den 21 mars," ABF, A/01/A/01, ARAB.

ABF Representantskap. 1926. "Protokoll fört vid ABF:s representantskaps årsmöte den 22 september," ABF, A/01/A/01, ARAB, Stockholm.

ABF Representantskap. 1930. "Protokoll fört vid ABFs representantskaps årsmöte 8 oktober," ABF, A/01/A/01, ARAB, Stockholm.

ABF Risingegård. 1934. "Förvärvskatalog 1934—," ABF Risingegård bibliotek nr 1395, 1852/D/1/1, FAC, Uppsala.

ABF Skutskär. 1914. "Kassabok studiecirkel nr 457." ABF avd. Skutskär, G/1/A/1, FAC, Uppsala.

ABF Skutskär. 1917a. "Förvärvskatalog ABFs bildningsutskott bibliotek nr 246, 1917–33." ABF avd. Skutskär, FAC, Uppsala.

ABF Skutskär. 1917b. "Skutskärs lokala bildningsutskott, möte den 17 februari." ABF avd. Skutskär, A1/1, FAC, Uppsala.

ABF Skutskär. 1920a. "Skutskärs lokala bildningsutskott, extra möte den 2 december," ABF avd. Skutskär, A/1, FAC, Uppsala.

ABF Skutskär. 1920b. "Skutskärs lokala bildningsutskott, möte den 14 november," ABF avd. Skutskär, A/1, FAC, Uppsala.

ABF Skutskär. 1920c. "Skutskärs lokala bildningsutskott, årsmöte 1 juni," ABF avd. Skutskär, A1/1, FAC, Uppsala.

ABF Skutskär. 1922. "Protokoll bildningsutskottet den 8 december," ABF avd. Skutskär, FAC, Uppsala.

ABF Skutskär. 1923a. "Rapport för ABFs lokalavdelning i Skutskär för verksamhetsåret 1922–1923," ABF avd. Skutskär, B1/1, FAC, Uppsala.

ABF Skutskär. 1923b. "Skutskärs lokala bildningsutskott, möte den 12 augusti." ABF avd. Skutskär, FAC, Uppsala.

ABF Skutskär. 1925. "Protokoll fört vid möte i Skutskärs lokala bildningsutskott 6 mars," ABF avd. Skutskär, A/1/1, FAC, Uppsala.

ABF Skutskär. 1926. "Protokoll fört vid möte i Skutskärs lokala bildningsutskott den 12 juni," ABF avd. Skutskär, A/1, FAC, Uppsala.

ABF Skutskär. 1928a. "Protokoll fört vid möte med bildningsutskottet maj," ABF avd. Skutskär, A/1, FAC, Uppsala.

ABF Skutskär. 1928b. "Verksamhetsrapport från ABF Skutskärs avdelning för verksamhetsåret 1927–1928," ABF avd. Skutskär, B1/1, FAC, Uppsala.

ABF Skutskär. 1928c. "Årsberättelse för ABFs lokalavdelning i Skutskär för verksamhetsåret 1 maj 1927–30 april 1928," ABF avd. Skutskär, B1/1, FAC, Uppsala.

ABF Skutskär. 1929. "Protokoll fört vid årsmöte i Skutskärs bildningsutskott 6 oktober," ABF avd. Skutskär, A/1, FAC, Uppsala.

ABF Skutskär. 1930. "Protokoll fört vid möte i bildningsutskottet 13 september," ABF avd. Skutskär, A/1, FAC, Uppsala.

ABF Skutskär. 1931. "Årsberättelse för ABFs lokalavdelning i Skutskär för verksamhetsåret 1 maj 1930–30 april 1931," ABF avd. Skutskär, B1/1, FAC, Uppsala.

ABF Skutskär. 1932. "Årsberättelse för ABFs lokalavdelning i Skutskär för tiden 1 maj 1931–30 april 1932," ABF avd. Skutskär, B1/1, FAC, Uppsala.

ABF Skutskär. 1933. "Årsberättelse för ABFs lokalavdelning i Skutskär för tiden 1 maj 1932–30 april 1933," ABF avd. Skutskär, B1/1, FAC, Uppsala.

ABF Skutskär. 1934. "Årsberättelse för ABFs lokalavdelning i Skutskär för tiden 1 maj 1933–30 april 1934," ABF avd. Skutskär, B1/1, FAC, Uppsala.

ABF Skutskär. 1937. "Årsberättelse från Skutskärs lokalavdelning av ABF för tiden 1/5 1936–30/4 1937," ABF avd. Skutskär, B1/1, FAC, Uppsala.

ABF Skutskär. 1940. "Årsberättelse från Skutskärs lokalavdelning av ABF för tiden 1/5 1939–30/4 1940," ABF avd. Skutskär, B1/1, FAC, Uppsala.

ABF Söderfors. 1918. "Katalog över böcker i ABFs studiecirkelbibliotek i Söderfors," ABF avd. Söderfors, fragment 24, FAC, Uppsala.

ABF Uppsala. 1927. "Protokoll från studiecirkel 1450 annordnad av statens sjukhuspersonalsförbund avd. 11," ABF avd. Uppsala, studiecirkel 1450, FAC, Uppsala.

Afonso, Alexandre. 2012. "Employer Strategies, Cross-Class Coalitions and the Free Movement of Labour in the Enlarged European Union." *Socio-Economic Review* 10, no. 4: 705–30.

Albert, Stuart, and David A. Whetten. 1985. "Organizational Identity." *Research in Organizational Behavior* 7: 263–95.

Allern, Elin Haugsgjerd, and Tim Bale. 2017. *Left-of-Centre Parties and Trade Unions in the Twenty-First Century*. Oxford: Oxford University Press.

Alvesson, Mats, and Hugh Willmott. 2002. "Identity Regulation as Organizational Control: Producing the Appropriate Individual." *Journal of Management Studies* 39, no. 5: 619–44.

Åmark, Klas. 1986. *Facklig makt och fackligt medlemskap: De svenska fackförbundens medlemsutveckling 1890–1940*. Lund: Arkiv.

Åmark, Klas. 1989. *Maktkamp i byggbransch: Avtalsrörelser och konflikter i byggbranschen 1914–1920*. Lund: Arkiv.

Åmark, Klas. 1994. *Vem styr marknaden? Facket, makten och marknaden 1850–1990*. Stockholm: Tiden.

Andersson, Bo. 1980. *Folkbildning i perspektiv: studieförbunden 1870–2000, organisering, etablering och profilering*. Stockholm: LTs förlag.

Andersson, E., A. M. Laginder, S. Larsson, and G. Sundgren. 1996. "Cirkelsamhället." *Studiecirklars betydelse för individ och lokalsamhälle*. SOU, 47.

Andersson, Emil. 1921. "Vad vill fackliga propagandaförbundet?" *Fackliga propagandaförbundets skriftserie* (4).

Andersson, Uno. 1935. "Företaget ur arbetaresynpunkt." LO, F/14/B/31, ARAB, Stockholm.

Arvidson, Lars. 1985. *Folkbildning i rörelse: pedagogisk syn i folkbildning inom svensk arbetarrörelse och frikyrkorörelse under 1900-talet: en jämförelse*. Malmö: LiberFörlag/Gleerup.

Ashforth, Blake E., and Fred Mael. 1989. "Social Identity Theory and the Organization." *Academy of Management Review* 14, no. 1: 20–39.

August, Andrew. 2011. "Narrative, Experience and Class: Nineteenth-Century Social History in Light of the Linguistic Turn." *History Compass* 9, no. 5: 384–96.

Bäckström, Knut. 1963a. *Arbetarrörelsen i Sverige. Bok 1, Den svenska arbetarrörelsens uppkomst och förening med socialismen.* Stockholm: Arbetarkultur.

Bäckström, Knut. 1963b. *Arbetarrörelsen i Sverige. Bok 2, Den politiska arbetarrörelsens sprängning och ett nytt revolutionärt arbetarpartis uppkomst.* Stockholm: Arbetarkultur.

Balibar, Étienne. 1979. "On Reproduction." In *Reading Capital,* edited by Louis Althusser and Étienne Balibar, translated by Ben Brewster and David Fernbach, 341–66. London: Verso.

Bartolini, Stefano. 2000. *The Political Mobilization of the European Left, 1860–1980: The Class Cleavage.* Cambridge: Cambridge University Press.

Beckholmen, Kuno. 1984. *Hundra år med Metall-ettan. Del 1, 1884–1928,* Stockholm: Liber Förlag.

Bell, Donald H. 1978. "Worker Culture and Worker Politics: The Experience of an Italian Town, 1880–1915." *Social History* 3, no. 1: 1–21.

Bell, Donald Howard. 1984. "Working-Class Culture and Fascism in an Italian Industrial Town, 1918–22." *Social History* 9, no. 1: 1–24.

Bengtsson, Bengt. 1931. "De lokala bildningsmöjligheterna." ABF avd. Skutskär, rapport till studiecirkeln i möteskultur, FAC, Uppsala.

Bengtsson, Berit. 2006. *Kampen mot § 23. Facklig makt vid anställning och avsked i Sverige före 1940.* Uppsala: Acta Universitatis Upsaliensis.

Berg, Anne, and Samuel Edquist. 2017. *The Capitalist State and the Construction of Civil Society: Public Funding and the Regulation of Popular Education in Sweden, 1870–1991.* Cham: Springer Palgrave Macmillan.

Berg, David. 1924. "Arbetsplan för studiecirklar i föreningskunskap." *Studiekamraten.*

Berger, Stefan. 2005. "A Return to the National Paradigm? National History Writing in Germany, Italy, France, and Britain from 1945 to the Present." *Journal of Modern History* 77, no. 3: 629–78.

Berger, Stefan, Mark Donovan, and Kevin Passmore. 2002. "Apologias for the Nation-State in Western Europe since 1800." In *Writing National Histories: Western Europe since 1800,* edited by S. Berger, M. Donovan, and K. Passmore, 3–14. London: Taylor and Francis.

Bergkvist, Karl, and Evert Arvidsson. 1960. *SAC 1910–1960. Jubileumsskrift.* Stockholm: Federativs förlag.

Bergman, Per. 1920. *Vår fackliga kamp 1914–1919.* Stockholm.

Bergman, Per. 1929a. "Rapport från föreläsningskurs i fackföreningskunskap i Eksjö och i Orrefors 22–29 mars." *Agitationsrapporter, bilagor till Landssekretariatets protokoll.*

Bergman, Per. 1929b. "Rapport över agitationsturné i Värmland 2–20 februari." *Agitationsrapporter, bilagor till Landssekretariatets protokoll.*

Berman, Sheri. 1998. *The Social Democratic Moment: Ideas and Politics in the Making of Interwar Europe.* Cambridge, Mass.: Harvard University Press.

Berman, Sheri. 2006. *The Primacy of Politics: Social Democracy and the Making of Europe's Twentieth Century.* Cambridge: Cambridge University Press.

Björlin, Lars. 2012. "Riksdagsmannen inför domstol." In . . . *faror för staten av svåraste slag: politiska fångar på Långholmen 1880–1950,* edited by K. Bosdotter, L. Ekdal, B. Isacson, P. Kindal, and B. Larsson, 154–67. Stockholm: Stockholmia Förlag.

Blomberg, Eva. 1995. *Män i mörker. Arbetsgivare, reformister och syndikalister.* Stockholm: Acta Universitatis Stockholmiensis.

Blomberg, Eva, and Ulla Blomberg. 1993. *Samhällets fiender: Stripakonflikten 1925–1927*. Stockholm: Federativ.

Blomqvist, Håkan. 2017. *Potatisrevolutionen och kvinnoupploppet på Södermalm 1917: ett historiskt reportage om hunger och demokrati*. Stockholm: Hjalmarson & Högberg.

Bolin, Jan. 2004. *Parti av ny typ? Skapandet av ett svenskt kommunistiskt parti 1917–1933*. Stockholm: Acta Universitatis Stockholmiensis.

Bosdotter, Kjersti, Lars Ekdahl, Anne-Marie Lindgren, and Lars Gogman. 2017. *Då var det 1917*. Huddinge: Arbetarnas Kulturhistoriska Sällskap.

Brunnsvik. 1930. "Brunnsviks folkhögskolas årsberättelse 1929–30." LO, 2964/F/14/B, ARAB, Stockholm.

Burawoy, Michael. 1982. *Manufacturing Consent: Changes in the Labor Process under Monopoly Capitalism*. Chicago: University of Chicago Press.

Cardador, M. Teresa, and Michael G. Pratt. 2006. "Identification Management and Its Bases: Bridging Management and Marketing Perspectives through a Focus on Affiliation Dimensions." *Journal of the Academy of Marketing Science* 34, no. 2: 174–84.

Casparsson, Ragnar. 1931. "Högerhetsen mot fackföreningarna." *Landsorganisationens skriftserie XXVI*.

Casparsson, Ragnar. 1947. *LO under fem årtionden 1898–1923, del I*. Stockholm: Tiden.

Casparsson, Ragnar. 1951. *LO under fem årtionden 1924–47, del II*. Stockholm: Tidens Förlag.

Casparsson, Ragnar. 1966. *LO: Bakgrund, utveckling, verksamhet*. Stockholm: Prisma.

Cronin, James E. 1980. "Labor Insurgency and Class Formation: Comparative Perspectives on the Crisis of 1917–1920 in Europe." *Social Science History* 4, no. 1: 125–52.

Dahl, Torsten. 1946. "Hansson, Sigfrid." In *Svenska män och kvinnor, G–H*. Stockholm: Albert Bonniers Förlag.

Dalin, Stefan. 2007. *Mellan massan och Marx: En studie av den politiska kampen inom fackföreningsrörelsen i Hofors 1917–1946*. Umeå: Institutionen för historiska studier, Umeå universitet.

de Geer, Gerhard. 1935. "Brev till Sigfrid Hansson 1 maj." Hansson personarkiv, 205/2/A/1/4, ARAB, Stockholm.

Dudley, Robert L., and Alan R. Gitelson 2002. "Political Literacy, Civic Education, and Civic Engagement: A Return to Political Socialization?" *Applied Developmental Science* 6, no. 4: 175–82.

Eling, Tommy. 1989. *Brytningstider: arbetarrörelsens framväxt i Skutskär åren 1869–1939*. Älvkarleby: Älvkarleby arbetarekommun.

Elsbach, Kimberly D., and C. B. Bhattacharya 2001. "Defining Who You Are by What You're Not: Organizational Disidentification and the National Rifle Association." *Organization Science* 12, no. 4: 393–413.

Eraut, Michael. 2004. "Informal Learning in the Workplace." *Studies in Continuing Education* 26, no. 2: 247–73.

Eriksson, Ulf. 1991. *Gruva och arbete: Kiirunavaara 1890–1990. Avsnitt 1, 1890–1920*. Uppsala: Uppsala universitet, Ekonomisk-historiska institutionen.

Eshach, Haim. 2007. "Bridging In-School and Out-of-School Learning: Formal, Non-Formal, and Informal Education." *Journal of Science Education and Technology* 16, no. 2: 171–90.

Fackföreningsrörelsen. 1930. "Öppningstal till Fackföreningsinternationalen i Stockholm 1930." *Fackföreningsrörelsen*, no. 27, 3 July.

Fackföreningsrörelsen. 1936a. "Veckans perspektiv nr 1." *Fackföreningsrörelsen*, no. 1, 3 January.
Fackföreningsrörelsen. 1936b. "Veckans perspektiv nr 9." *Fackföreningsrörelsen*, no. 9, 27 February.
Fackföreningsrörelsen. 1936c. "Veckans perspektiv nr 13." *Fackföreningsrörelsen*, no. 13, 26 March.
Fackföreningsrörelsen. 1938. "Per Bergman." *Fackföreningsrörelsen*, no. 27, 7 July.
Fernström, Karl. 1950. *Ungsocialismen: en krönika*. Stockholm: Federativs förlag.
Flink, Ingvar. 1978. *Strejkbryteriet och arbetets frihet: En studie av svensk arbetsmarknad fram till 1938*. Uppsala: Acta Universitatis Upsaliensis.
Flyckt, Tore. 1935. "Företaget ur arbetarens synpunkt. Uppsats skriven på LO:s skola, Brunnsvik." LO, F/14/B/31, ARAB, Stockholm.
Friedman, Jonathan. 1992. "The Past in the Future: History and the Politics of Identity." *American Anthropologist* 94, no. 4: 837–59.
Friesen, Gerald, and Lucy Taksa. 1996. "Workers' Education in Australia and Canada: A Comparative Approach to Labour's Cultural History." *Labour/Le Travail* 38: 170–97.
Furuland, Lars. 1968. "Folkhögskolan: en bildningsväg för svenska författare." In *Svensk folkhögskola 100 år. D. 4*, edited by A. Degerman, B. Pfannenstill, A. Helldén, and L. Furuland, 227–52. Stockholm: Liber.
Galston, William A. 2007. "Civic Knowledge, Civic Education, and Civic Engagement: A Summary of Recent Research." *International Journal of Public Administration* 30, nos. 6–7: 623–42.
Geijer, Arne. 1935. "Brev till Landsorganisationen 15 april." Arne Geijer/5150/10/ARAB/ Stockholm.
Gidlund, Gullan. 1992. "From Popular Movement to Political Party: Development of the Social Democratic Labor Party Organization." In *Creating Social Democracy: A Century of the Social Democratic Labor Party in Sweden*, edited by K. Misgeld, K. Molin, and K. Åmark, 97–130. University Park: Pennsylvania State University Press.
Goldman, Lawrence. 1999. "Education as Politics: University Adult Education in England since 1870." *Oxford Review of Education* 25, nos. 1–2: 89–101.
Gröning, Lotta. 1988. *Vägen till makten: SAP:s organisation och dess betydelse för den politiska verksamheten 1900–1933*. Uppsala: Acta Universitatis Upsaliensis.
Gumbrell-McCormick, Rebecca, and Richard Hyman. 2014. *Trade Unions in Western Europe: Hard Times, Hard Choices*. Oxford: Oxford University Press.
Gunnarson, Gunnar. 1965. *Arbetarrörelsens genombrottsår i dokument*. Stockholm: Prisma.
Gustavsson, Bernt. 1991. *Bildningens väg: Tre bildningsideal i svensk arbetarrörelse 1880–1930*. Stockholm: Wahlström & Widstrand.
Gustavsson, Bernt, and Matilda Wiklund. 2013. *Nyttan med folklig bildning: En studie av kapitalformer i folkbildande verk*. Lund: Nordic Academic Press.
Hadenius, Axel. 1976. *Facklig organisationsutveckling. En studie av Landsorganisationen i Sverige*. Stockholm: Rabén & Sjögren.
Håkansson, Einar. 1935. "Arbetaren och företaget." LO, F/14/B/31, ARAB, Stockholm.
Hansson, Per Albin. 1909. "Brev till Per Bergman daterat 5 november." Per Bergman personarkiv, 61/2, ARAB, Stockholm.
Hansson, Sigfrid. 1918. *Ett kvartssekel av Svenska bleck- och plåtslagareförbundets historia 1893–1918*. Stockholm: Svenska bleck- och plåtslagareförbundet.
Hansson, Sigfrid. 1919. *Ur skomakaryrkets historia: en studie över skråväsendet*. Stockholm: Tiden.

Hansson, Sigfrid. 1920. *Bidrag till den svenska: Svenska sko- och läderindustriar-betareförbundet*. Stockholm: Tiden.

Hansson, Sigfrid. 1921a. "Inför nya uppgifter. 1. Fackföreningsrörelsens utvecklingsskeden." *Fackföreningsrörelsen*, no. 32, 8 September.

Hansson, Sigfrid. 1921b. "Praktisk socialism I. Ett studiebesök hos engelska byggnadsgillen." *Fackföreningsrörelsen*, no. 43, 27 October.

Hansson, Sigfrid. 1921c. "Praktisk Socialism II. Ett studiebesök hos engelska byggnadsgillen." *Fackföreningsrörelsen*, no. 44, 3 November.

Hansson, Sigfrid. 1921, 10 October. "Dagbok den 10 oktober." Personarkiv Sigfrid Hansson, ARAB, Stockholm.

Hansson, Sigfrid. 1922a. *Bidrag till den svenska fackföreningsrörelsens historia: Stockholms bokbinderiarbetareförening, B.A.F., 1872–1922*. Göteborg: Nordiska boktryckeriet.

Hansson, Sigfrid. 1922b. "Kongressmotionerna. 3. Obstruktion, generalstrejk och register." *Fackföreningsrörelsen*, no. 31, 3 August.

Hansson, Sigfrid. 1922d. "Samhällets plikt." *Fackföreningsrörelsen*, no. 6, 9 February.

Hansson, Sigfrid. 1922e. "Vår kongress. Organisationsformerna." *Fackföreningsrörelsen*, no. 39, 28 September.

Hansson, Sigfrid. 1922f. "Våra byggnadsgillen." *Fackföreningsrörelsen*, no. 49, 7 December.

Hansson, Sigfrid. 1923. *Den svenska fackföreningsrörelsen*. Stockholm: Tidens Förlag.

Hansson, Sigfrid. 1923, 14 June. "Brev till Arbetarnas bildningsförbund, Brunnsvik." LO, 2964/E/12/1, ARAB, Stockholm.

Hansson, Sigfrid. 1924. "Fackföreningsrörelsens organisationsformer. Historiska och psykologiska förutsättningar." *Fackföreningsrörelsen*, no. 47, 20 November.

Hansson, Sigfrid. 1925a. "Solidaritetens rågångar." *Fackföreningsrörelsen*, no. 25, 18 June.

Hansson, Sigfrid. 1925b. *Svenska träarbetareförbundets historia 1889–1923*. Stockholm: Svenska träarbetareförbundet.

Hansson, Sigfrid. 1926a. *Solidaritet och monopolism. Fackföreningsrörelsens aktuella problem*. Stockholm: Tidens förlag.

Hansson, Sigfrid. 1926b. "Svensk fackföreningsrörelse och socialism på 1880-talet." *Tidskriften Tiden*.

Hansson, Sigfrid. 1926, 12 April. "Brev till John Johnsson, Ersta." LO, 2964/E/12/1, ARAB, Stockholm.

Hansson, Sigfrid. 1927a. *Den svenska fackföreningsrörelsen*. Stockholm: Tidens förlag.

Hansson, Sigfrid. 1927b. "I min gröna ungdom. Minnen från socialdemokratiska ungdomsförbundet." Sigfrid Hansson personarkiv, 205/B/7, ARAB, Stockholm.

Hansson, Sigfrid. 1927c. "Studieplan i fackföreningskunskap." *Landsorganisationens skriftserie* no. 15.

Hansson, Sigfrid. 1928a. "Arbetaren i fackföreningen och arbetsföretaget." 30 oktober 1928 intalat på grammofonskiva. Unpublished manuscript. Sigfrid Hansson personarkiv, B/13, ARAB, Stockholm.

Hansson, Sigfrid. 1928b. "Samförståndskonferensen." *Fackföreningsrörelsen*, no. 49, 6 December.

Hansson, Sigfrid. 1928c. "Till Landsorganisationen från fackföreningsskolans förvaltningsnämnd." LO, 2964/F/14/B/1, ARAB, Stockholm.

Hansson, Sigfrid. 1929. "Till deltagarna i studieledarkurserna i fackföreningskunskap, cirkulär, ABF." ABF, 2831/B/3/1, ARAB, Stockholm.

Hansson, Sigfrid. 1930a. *Arbetarrörelsen i Sverige: en historisk, organisationsteknisk och statistisk översikt*. Stockholm: Tiden.

Hansson, Sigfrid. 1930b. "Arvid Thorberg." *Fackföreningsrörelsen*, no. 16, 17 April.
Hansson, Sigfrid. 1930c. "Fackföreningsrörelsen som högerns valspöke." *Fackföreningsrörelsen*, no. 36, 4 September.
Hansson, Sigfrid. 1930d. "Till dagskrönikan 18 december." *Fackföreningsrörelsen*, no. 51, 18 December.
Hansson, Sigfrid. 1931. *Svenska murareförbundet 1890–1930: minnesskrift*. Stockholm: Svenska murareförbundet.
Hansson, Sigfrid. 1932. *Svenskt fackföreningsliv*. Stockholm: Tiden.
Hansson, Sigfrid. 1933a. "Veckans perspektiv." *Fackföreningsrörelsen*, no. 44, 2 November.
Hansson, Sigfrid. 1933b. "Veckans perspektiv." *Fackföreningsrörelsen*, no. 41, 12 October.
Hansson, Sigfrid. 1933c. "Veckans perspektiv." *Fackföreningsrörelsen*, no. 35, 31 August.
Hansson, Sigfrid. 1933d. "Veckans perspektiv." *Fackföreningsrörelsen*, no. 27, 6 July.
Hansson, Sigfrid. 1934a. *Den svenska fackföreningsrörelsen*. Stockholm: Tidens Förlag.
Hansson, Sigfrid. 1934b. "Veckans perspektiv." *Fackföreningsrörelsen*, no. 29, 20 July.
Hansson, Sigfrid. 1934c. "Veckans perspektiv." *Fackföreningsrörelsen*, no. 33, 17 August.
Hansson, Sigfrid. 1935a. "Arbetsgivarföreningen på Brunnsvik." *Fackföreningsrörelsen*, no. 29, 20 July.
Hansson, Sigfrid. 1935b. "A. B. C. Fragment av artiklar i tidskriften Fackföreningsrörelsen 1929–34." In *Arbetare, arbetsgivare, samhälle*, 23–39. Stockholm: Tidens Förlag.
Hansson, Sigfrid. 1935c. "Brev till disponent Gerhard de Geer 29 april." LO, 2964/F/14/B/1, ARAB, Stockholm.
Hansson, Sigfrid. 1935d. "En av grundvalarna. Ur ett tal vid terminsavslutningen i Stockholms stads skolor för yrkesundervisning den 14 juni 1929." In *Arbetare, arbetsgivare, samhälle*, 9–17. Stockholm: Tidens Förlag.
Hansson, Sigfrid. 1935e. "Näringsfrihet, arbetsfrihet och arbetsfred. Inledningsanförande vid en radiodiskussion i Uppsala den 13 november 1930." In *Arbetare, arbetsgivare, samhälle*, 55–68. Stockholm: Tidens Förlag.
Hansson, Sigfrid. 1935f. "Reformism och revolutionarism," in *Arbetare, arbetsgivare, samhälle*, 40–56. Stockholm: Tidens Förlag.
Hansson, Sigfrid. 1936a. "En fackföreningsrörelsens veckotidning utgiven av LO." LO, 2964/B/3/5, ARAB, Stockholm.
Hansson, Sigfrid. 1936b. *Svenska folkrörelser. 1, Nykterhetsrörelse. Politisk arbetarrörelse. Fackföreningsrörelse. Folkbildning. Kooperation*. Stockholm: Lindfors.
Hansson, Sigfrid. 1938a. "Arbetare och arbetsgivare i Sverige." Unpublished manuscript. Sigfrid Hanssons personarkiv, B/13, ARAB, Stockholm.
Hansson, Sigfrid. 1938b. *Den svenska fackföreningsrörelsen*. Stockholm: Tidens förlag.
Hansson, Sigfrid. 1942. *Den svenska fackföreningsrörelsen*. Stockholm: Tiden.
Hansson, Sven Ove. 1991. "Introduktion till Thomas Humphrey Marshall." In *Idéer om reformism*, edited by S. O. Hansson and J. Hermansson, 7–19. Stockholm: Tidens förlag.
Haslam, S. Alexander, and Stephen Reicher. 2007. "Identity Entrepreneurship and the Consequences of Identity Failure: The Dynamics of Leadership in the BBC Prison Study." *Social Psychology Quarterly* 70, no. 2: 125–47.
Haslam, S. Alexander, Stephen Reicher, and Michael Platow. 2010. *The New Psychology of Leadership: Identity, Influence, and Power*. New York: Psychology Press.
Hedström, Peter, Rickard Sandell, and Charlotta Stern. 2000. "Mesolevel Networks and the Diffusion of Social Movements: The Case of the Swedish Social Democratic Party." *American Journal of Sociology* 106, no. 1: 145–72.
Heffler, Hugo. 1962. *Arbetarnas bildningsförbund 1912–1962: Krönika vid halvsekelgränsen*. Stockholm: Arbetarnas bildningsförbund.

Hellblom, L. 1985. *Från primitiv till organiserad demokrati: en studie av några offentligheter inom den socialdemokratiska arbetarrörelsen med utgångspunkt i 1970-talets studiecirklar i Vikmanshyttan och Söderfors*. Lidingö: Salamander.

Hermansson, Jörgen. 1984. *Kommunism på svenska? SKP/VPK:s idéutveckling efter Komintern*. Uppsala: Acta Universitatis Upsaliensis.

Hirdman, Yvonne. 1990. *Vi bygger landet: Den svenska arbetarrörelsens historia från Per Götrek till Olof Palme*. Stockholm: Tiden.

Hogg, Michael A., Deborah J. Terry, and Katherine M. White. 1995. "A Tale of Two Theories: A Critical Comparison of Identity Theory with Social Identity Theory." *Social Psychology Quarterly* 58, no. 4: 255–69.

Höglund, Zeth. 1939. *Hjalmar Branting och hans livsgärning*. Stockholm: Tiden.

Holford, John. 1994. "Old Themes, New Variations: Politics, the State, and the Shaping of Labor Education in Singapore and Hong Kong." *Labor Studies Journal* 19, no. 1: 92–106.

Holme, Rud. 1924. "Studiecirkelplan för orienterande studier om fackföreningsrörelsen och syndikalismen." ABF, 2831/B/05/01, ARAB, Stockholm.

Holme, Rud. 1926. "Förslag till studieplan i allmän föreningskunskap." ABF, 2831/B/05/03, ARAB, Stockholm.

Holme, Rudolf. 1928. "Föreningskunskap. Förslag till studieplan." ABF, 2831/B/05/01, ARAB, Stockholm.

Horgby, Björn. 1997. *Med dynamit och argument: Gruvarbetarna och deras fackliga kamp under ett sekel*. Stockholm: Svenska metallindustriarbetareförbundet.

Horgby, Björn. 2012. *Kampen om facket*. Umeå: Boréa.

Huddy, Leonie. 2001. "From Social to Political Identity: A Critical Examination of Social Identity Theory." *Political Psychology* 22, no. 1: 127–56.

Jakobsson, Harry. 1935. "Företaget ur arbetarens synpunkt. Uppsats, LO skolan, Brunnsvik." LO, F/14/B/31, ARAB, Stockholm.

Jansson, Evert. 1935. "Företaget ur arbetarens synpunkt." LO, F/14/B/31, ARAB, Stockholm.

Jansson, Jenny. 2015. "Från individ till människa: bildning och arbetarrörelsen." *Arbetarhistoria: Meddelande från Arbetarrörelsens Arkiv och Bibliotek* 153–54: 6–13.

Jansson, Jenny. 2016. "Class Formation in Sweden and Britain: Educating Workers." *International Labor and Working-Class History* 90: 52–69.

Jansson, Jenny. 2017. "Two branches of the Same Tree? Party-Union Links in Sweden in the 21st Century." In *Left-of-Centre Parties and Trade Unions in the Twenty-First Century*, edited by Elin Haugsgjerd Allern and Tim Bale, 206–25. Oxford: Oxford University Press.

Jansson, Jenny. 2018. "Building Organizations? Content and Scope of Workers' Education in Sweden and Britain." European Social Science History Conference, 4–7 April, Belfast.

Jensen, Albert. 1910. *Den svenska fackföreningsrörelsen i blixtbelysning från generalsträjken 1909*. Norrköping: Lindstam.

Jensen, Albert. 1912. *Vad är sabotage? En undersökning*. Stockholm: Ungsoc. partiets förl.

Jensen, Albert. 1920. *Storstrejk? Ett ord till kamraterna i fackföreningarna*. Örebro: S.A.C.

Jerlström, Magnus. "Erfarenheter och förändringar under SACs genombrottsår." SAC. https://www.sac.se/Om-SAC/Historik/Arkiv/Tidningsarkiv/Tidningar-och-tidskrifter-utgivna-av-SAC-och-IAA/Syndikalisten-1995/Erfarenheter-och-f%C3%B6r%C3%A4ndringar-under-SACs-genombrotts%C3%A5r.

Johansson, Anders L. 1989. *Tillväxt och klassamarbete: En studie av den svenska modellens uppkomst*. Stockholm: Tidens Förlag.

Johansson, Anders L, and Lars Magnusson. 1998. *LO andra halvseklet: Fackföreningsrörelsen och samhället*. Stockholm: Atlas.

Johansson, Birgitta. 2015. "Skuggan av bröd." *Arbetarhistoria* 153–54: 14–21.

Johansson, Inge. 2002. *Bildning och klasskamp: om arbetarbildningens förhistoria, idéer och utveckling*. Stockholm: Arbetarnas bildningsförbund.

Johansson, Johan-Olov. 1924a. "Strömningar inom fackföreningsrörelsen." *Fackföreningsrörelsen*, no. 28, 10 July.

Johansson, Johan-Olov. 1924b. "Strömningar och riktningar inom fackföreningsrörelsen II." *Fackföreningsrörelsen*, no. 31, 31 July.

Jones, Gareth Stedman. 1984. *Languages of Class: Studies in English Working Class History, 1832–1982*. Cambridge: Cambridge University Press.

Jönsson, Lennart, and Ingemar Gens. 1993. *Östan och västan ån: Älvkarleby förr och nu*. Skutskär: Kulturnämnden, Älvkarleby kommun.

Karlbom, Torvald. 1968. *Skogens arbetare: Till minnet av Svenska skogsarbetarförbundets 50-åriga verksamhet 1918–1968*. Stockholm: Sv. skogsarbetareförb.

Karlsson, Maria, and Rikard Warlenius. 2012. "De tidiga åren (1910–1922)." In *Ett sekel av syndikalism: Sveriges Arbetares Centralorganisation 1910–2010*, edited by K. Boréus, A. Ighe, M. Karlsson, and R. Warlenius, 10–27. Stockholm: Federativs förlag.

Katznelson, Ira. 1986. "Working-Class Formation: Constructing Cases and Comparisons." In *Working-Class Formation*, edited by I. Katznelson and A. R. Zolberg, 3–41 Princeton: Princeton University Press.

Kelly, John E. 1998. *Rethinking Industrial Relations: Mobilization, Collectivism and Long Waves*. New York: Routledge.

Kelly, Thomas. 1952. "The Origin of Mechanics' Institutes." *British Journal of Educational Studies* 1, no. 1: 17–27.

Kennerström, Bernt. 1974. *Mellan två internationaler*. Lund: Arkiv avhandlingsserie.

Kihlberg, Leif. 1963. *Karl Staaff. D. 2, Regeringschef, oppositionsledare: 1905–1915*. Stockholm: Bonnier.

Knippenberg, Daan van, and Naomi Ellemers. 2003. "Social Identity and Group Performance. Identification as the Key to Group-Oriented Effort." In *Social Identity at Work: Developing Theory for Organizational Practice*, edited by S. Alexander Haslam, Daan van Knippenberg, Michael J. Platow, and Naomi Ellemers, 29–59. New York: Psychology Press.

Koch, Martin. 1912. "Brev till Per Bergman daterat 6 maj." Per Bergman personarkiv, 61/2, ARAB, Stockholm.

Korpi, Walter. 1980. *Arbetarklassen i välfärdskapitalismen*. Stockholm: Prisma.

Korpi, Walter. 2006. "Power Resources and Employer-Centered Approaches in Explanations of Welfare States and Varieties of Capitalism." *World Politics* 58, 167–206.

KPU. 1926. "Brev till ABFs representantskaps VU, den 25 augusti." ABF, E/2/01, ARAB, Stockholm.

KPU Skutskär. 1921. "Styrelseberättelse över Skutskärs kommunistiska ungdomsklubb 1921." Skutskärs kommunistiska ungdomsklubb, A/1/1, FAC, Uppsala.

Kuczynski, Jürgen, Maj-Siri Österling, and Ulf Österling. 1967. *Arbetarklassens uppkomst*. Stockholm: Aldus/Bonnier.

Landsorganisationen. 1909. "Protokoll förda vid landsorganisationens i Sverige 5:te ordinarie kongress i Stockholm 22–30 november." AB Arbetarnes Tryckeri: Stockholm.

Landsorganisationen. 1912. "Protokoll förda vid Landsorganisationens i Sverige sjätte ordinarie kongress i Stockholm 6–12 september." AB Arbetarnes Tryckeri: Stockholm.

Landsorganisationen. 1916. "Berättelse över Landsorganisationens i Sverige verksamhet." AB Arbetarnes Tryckeri: Stockholm.

Landsorganisationen. 1917. "Protokoll förda vid Landsorganisationens sjunde ordinarie kongress i Stockholm 20–25 aug." AB Arbetarnes Tryckeri: Stockholm.

Landsorganisationen. 1919. "Berättelse över Landsorganisationens i Sverige verksamhet." AB Arbetarnes Tryckeri: Stockholm.

Landsorganisationen. 1920. "Berättelse över Landsorganisationens i Sverige verksamhet." AB Arbetarnes Tryckeri: Stockholm.

Landsorganisationen. 1920–26. "LO-Tidningens korrespondens." LO, 2964/E/12/1, ARAB, Stockholm.

Landsorganisationen. 1921. "Berättelse över Landsorganisationens i Sverige verksamhet." AB Arbetarnes Tryckeri: Stockholm.

Landsorganisationen. 1922a. "Berättelse över Landsorganisationens i Sverige verksamhet 1922." AB Arbetarnes Tryckeri: Stockholm.

Landsorganisationen. 1922b. "Protokoll förda vid Landsorganisationens åttonde ordinarie kongress i Stockholm 28 aug-4 sept." AB Arbetarnes Tryckeri: Stockholm.

Landsorganisationen. 1923a. "Cirkulär 429, 11 oktober." LO, 2964/B/3/3, ARAB, Stockholm.

Landsorganisationen. 1923b. "Cirkulär nr 429, 11 oktober." LO, 2964/B/3/3, ARAB, Stockholm.

Landsorganisationen. 1924a. "Cirkulär 452, 22 juli." LO, 2964/B/3/3, ARAB, Stockholm.

Landsorganisationen. 1924b. "Cirkulär nr 441, den 17 mars 1924." LO, 2694 ARAB, Stockholm.

Landsorganisationen. 1924c. "Cirkulär nr 452, 22 juli." LO, 2964/B/3/3, ARAB, Stockholm.

Landsorganisationen. 1924d. "Cirkulär nr 457, 24 oktober." LO, 2964/B/3/3, ARAB, Stockholm.

Landsorganisationen. 1924e. "Rapport av Sigfrid Hansson från Internationella arbetarebildningskonferensen i Oxford samt studiebesök i London." LO, 2964/E/14/4, ARAB, Stockholm.

Landsorganisationen. 1925a. "Berättelse över Landsorganisationens i Sverige verksamhet 1925." AB Arbetarnes Tryckeri: Stockholm.

Landsorganisationen. 1925b. "Cirkulär 9 oktober." LO, 2964/B/3/5, ARAB, Stockholm.

Landsorganisationen. 1925c. "Cirkulär nr 468, januari." LO, 2964/B/3/3, ARAB, Stockholm.

Landsorganisationen. 1925d. "Cirkulär nr 482, 18 mars." LO, 2964/B/3/3, ARAB, Stockholm.

Landsorganisationen. 1926a. "Berättelse av Sigvard Cruse över studieresa i Tyskland och Österrike 1926." LO, E/14/5, ARAB, Stockholm.

Landsorganisationen. 1926b. "Protokoll förda vid Landsorganisationens i Sverige nionde ordinarie kongress i Stockholm 29 augusti-5 september." AB Arbetarnes Tryckeri: Stockholm.

Landsorganisationen. 1927a. "Cirkulär nr 570, 18 november." LO, 2964/B/3/4, ARAB, Stockholm.

Landsorganisationen. 1927b. "Cirkulär nr 573, 18 november." LO, 2964/B/3/4, ARAB, Stockholm.

Landsorganisationen. 1928a. "Cirkulär nr 614, 25 oktober." LO, 2964/B/3/4, ARAB, Stockholm.
Landsorganisationen. 1928b. "Preliminär undervisningsplan för fackföreningsskolan i Brunnsvik, bilaga till Landssekretariatets cirkulär 613." Brunnsvik (samling) vol. 1, ARAB, Stockholm.
Landsorganisationen. 1929. "Rapport av Axel Svensson över studieresa till Tyskland och Österrike." LO, 2964/E/14/5, ARAB, Stockholm.
Landsorganisationen. 1934. "Cirkulär nr 870, 29 oktober." LO, 2964/B/3/5, ARAB, Stockholm.
Landsorganisationen. 1935. "Berättelse över Landsorganisationens verksamhet." AB Arbetarnes Tryckeri: Stockholm.
Landsorganisationen. 1936. "Protokoll förda vid Landsorganisationens Kongress 1936." AB Arbetarnes Tryckeri: Stockholm.
Landsorganisationen. 1937. "Cirkulär nr 967, 18 januari." LO, 2964/B/3/4, ARAB, Stockholm.
Landssekretariatet. 1920a. "Protokoll fört vid Landssekretariatets möte 2 februari." LO:s arkiv, Stockholm.
Landssekretariatet. 1920b. "Protokoll fört vid möte i Landssekretariatet 28 januari." LO:s arkiv, Stockholm.
Landssekretariatet. 1920c. "Protokoll vid landssekretariatets möte 13 september." LO:s arkiv, Stockholm.
Landssekretariatet. 1921a. "Protokoll." LO:s arkiv, Stockholm.
Landssekretariatet. 1921b. "Protokoll förda vid möte i Landssekretariatet den 11 mars." LO:s arkiv, Stockholm.
Landssekretariatet. 1921c. "Protokoll fört vid möte den 23 februari." LOs arkiv, LO, Stockholm.
Landssekretariatet. 1934a. "Förteckning över agitations- och upplysningsverksamhet i landssekretariatets protokollbok." LO:s arkiv, Stockholm.
Landssekretariatet. 1934b. "Protokoll fört vid landssekretariatets möte 30 december." LO:s arkiv, Stockholm.
Landssekretariatet. 1935. "Protokoll fört vid möte den 7 januari." LO:s arkiv, Stockholm.
Lapuente, Victor, and Bo Rothstein. 2014. "Civil War Spain versus Swedish Harmony." Comparative Political Studies 47, no. 10: 1416–41.
Larsson, Bror. 1964. "SSU i Skutskär 40 år: en återblick när seklet var ungt." SSU-klubb Skutskär, B1:1, Folkrörelsearkivet Uppsala.
Lindbom, Tage. 1938. Den svenska fackföreningsrörelsens uppkomst och tidigare historia 1872–1900. Stockholm: Tiden.
Lindbom, Tage. 1945. Den socialdemokratiska ungdomsrörelsen i Sverige: en historik. Stockholm: Tiden/Frihet.
Linderborg, Åsa. 2001. Socialdemokraterna skriver historia. Stockholm: Atlas.
Lindgren, John. 1950. Per Albin Hansson i svensk demokrati. D. 1., 1892–1920. Stockholm: Tiden.
Lindström, Rickard. 1924. "Marx och fackföreningarna," Fackföreningsrörelsen.
Lindström, Rickard. 1960. "Per Albin Hansson, arbetets söner och Sverige." In Arbetets söner. 3, Segrarnas tid, edited by F. Ström, R. Casparsson, and S. Sjöberg, 157–80. Stockholm: Steinsviks Bokförlag AB.
Ljunggren, Jens. 2015. Den uppskjutna vreden: socialdemokratisk känslopolitik från 1880- till 1980-talet. Lund: Nordic Academic Press.
Lundh, Christer. 2009. Nya perspektiv på Saltsjöbadsavtalet. Stockholm: SNS förlag.
Lundkvist, Sven. 1977. Folkrörelserna i det svenska samhället 1850–1920. Stockholm: Sober.

March, James G., and Johan P. Olsen 2004. *The Logic of Appropriateness*. Working paper 2004:9. Oslo: ARENA.

Marx, Karl. 1981. *Filosofins elände: Svar på Proudhons "Eländets filosofi."* Göteborg: Proletärkultur AB.

McDonald, G. W., and Howard F. Gospel. 1973. "The Mond-Turner Talks, 1927–1933: A Study in Industrial Co-operation." *Historical Journal* 16, no. 4: 807–29.

Mills, C Wright. 1948. *The New Men of Power*. New York: Harcourt, Brace.

Möller, Gustav, and Per Albin Hansson. 1916. *Stormklockepolitiken under kritisk granskning*. Stockholm: Tiden.

Morris, Aldon D., and Susan Staggenborg. 2004. "Leadership in Social Movements." In *The Blackwell Companion to Social Movements*, edited by D. A. Snow, S. A. Soule, and H. Kriesi, 171–96. Malden: Blackwell.

Möteskultur, Studiecirkel. 1931a. "Protokoll fört vid möte den 6 februari." ABF avd. Skutskär, Studiecirkel, FAC, Uppsala.

Möteskultur, Studiecirkel. 1931b. "Protokoll fört vid möte den 13 februari." ABF avd. Skutskär, Studiecirkel, FAC, Uppsala.

Möteskultur, Studiecirkel. 1932a. "Protokoll fört vid möte den 2 december." ABF avd. Skutskär, Studiecirkel, FAC, Uppsala.

Möteskultur, Studiecirkel. 1932b. "Referat från möte den 9 december." ABF avd. Skutskär, Studiecirkel, FAC, Uppsala.

Möteskultur, Studiecirkel. 1932c. "Referat från möte den 25 november." ABF avd. Skutskär, Studiecirkel, FAC, Uppsala.

Möteskultur, Studiecirkel. 1933a. "Referat av möte den 17 februari." ABF avd. Skutskär, Studiecirkel, FAC, Uppsala.

Möteskultur, Studiecirkel. 1933b. "Referat från möte den 10 februari." ABF avd. Skutskär, Studiecirkel, FAC, Uppsala.

Mustel, Kerstin. 2018. "Den svenska folkhögskolan. De första hundra åren." In *Folkhögskolan 150 år*, edited by A.-M. Laginder, E. Önnesjö, I. Carlsson, and E. Nylander, 13–39. Stockholm: Föreningen för folkbildningsforskning.

Nepstad, Sharon, and Clifford Bob. 2006. "When Do Leaders Matter? Hypotheses on Leadership Dynamics in Social Movements." *Mobilization: An International Quarterly* 11, no. 1: 1–22.

Nerman, Ture. 1952. *Studiecirkeln: historik kring ett halvsekelminne*. Stockholm: Eklund.

Nilsson, Torsten. 1977. *Människor och händelser i Norden*. Stockholm: Tiden.

Nordin, Rune. 1981. *Brunnsvik och arbetarrörelsen*. Brunnsvik: Brunnsvikarnas förbund.

Nordisk Familjebok. 1932. "Skutskär." In *Nordisk Familjebok*, edited by V. Söderberg, 1246–48. Albert Bonniers Förlag: Stockholm.

Nycander, Svante. 2002. *Makten över arbetsmarknaden: Ett perspektiv på Sveriges 1900-tal*. Stockholm: SNS Förlag.

Ohlsson, Per T. 2010. *Rickard Sandler*. Stockholm: Bonnier.

Oljelund, Stefan. 1935. "Brev till Sigfrid Hansson daterat den 22 juli 1935." Sigfrid Hansson personarkiv, 205/2/A/1/4, ARAB, Stockholm.

Olsson, Tom. 1980. *Pappersmassestrejken 1932: En studie av facklig ledning och opposition*. Lund: Arkiv för studier i arbetarrörelsens historia.

Organisationskunskap, Studiecirkel. 1935a. "Protokoll fört vid konstituerande sammanträde med studiecirkeln i organisationskunskap den 23 oktober." ABF avd. Skutskär, Studiecirkel, FAC, Uppsala.

Organisationskunskap, Studiecirkel. 1935b. "Protokoll fört vid möte med studiecirkel i organisationskunskap den 21 november." ABF avd. Skutskär, Studiecirkel, FAC, Uppsala.

Organisationskunskap, Studiecirkel. 1935c. "Protokoll fört vid möte med studiecirkel i organisationskunskap den 31 oktober." ABF avd. Skutskär, Studiecirkel, FAC, Uppsala.

Pappersindustriarbetareförbundet. 1917–40. *Berättelse över svenska pappersindustriarbetareförbundets verksamhet år 1917–40*. Gävle: Arbetarbladets tryckeri.

Pappersindustriarbetareförbundet. 1928. *Berättelse över svenska pappersindustriarbetareförbundets verksamhet år 1927*. Gävle: Arbetarbladets tryckeri.

Pappersindustriarbetareförbundet avd. 2, Skutskär. 1923. "Protokoll fört vid möte den 6 februari," Pappersindustriarbetareförbundet avd. 2 Skutskär, A/1/1, FAC, Uppsala.

Pappersindustriarbetareförbundet avd. 2, Skutskär. 1925. "Protokoll fört den 10 maj." Pappersindustriarbetareförbundet avd. 2 Skutskär, A/1/1, FAC, Uppsala.

Pappersindustriarbetareförbundet avd. 2, Skutskär. 1931. "Protokoll fört vid möte den 20 december." Pappersindustriarbetareförbundet avd. 2 Skutskär, A/1/2, FAC, Uppsala.

Pappersindustriarbetareförbundet avd. 2, Skutskär. 1932. "Protokoll fört vid möte den 2 mars." Pappersindustriarbetareförbundet avd. 2 Skutskär, A/1/2, FAC, Uppsala.

Pappersindustriarbetareförbundet avd. 2, Skutskär. 1935. "Protokoll fört vid möte den 10 mars," Pappersindustriarbetareförbundet avd. 2 Skutskär, A/1/2, FAC, Uppsala.

Pappersindustriarbetareförbundet, Svenska. 1932. "Berättelse över svenska pappersindustriarbetareförbundets verksamhet år 1932." Gävle: Arbetarbladets tryckeri.

Persson, Bo. 1991. *Skogens skördemän: Skogs- och flottningsarbetareförbundets kamp för arbete och kollektivavtal 1918–1927*. Lund: Arkiv.

Persson, Lennart K. 1975. *Syndikalismen i Sverige 1903–1922*. Stockholm: Federativs förlag.

Peterson, Carl-Gunnar. 1970. *SSU 1917–1967: en organisationsstudie*. Stockholm: Frihet.

Pichardo, Nelson A. 1997. "New Social Movements: A Critical Review." *Annual Review of Sociology* 23, no. 1: 411–30.

Ravasi, Davide, and Majken Schultz. 2006. "Responding to Organizational Identity Threats: Exploring the Role of Organizational Culture." *Academy of Management Journal* 49, no. 3: 433–58.

Representantskapet. 1920, 29–31 January. "Protokoll fört vid Landsorganisationens representantskaps möte, 29–31 januari." LO:s arkiv, Stockholm.

Representantskapet. 1921. "Protokoll fört vid Landsorganisationens representantskaps möte 27–28 april." LO:s arkiv, Stockholm.

Representantskapet. 1921, 10–11 October. "Protokoll fört vid Landsorganisationens Representantskap den 10–11 oktober 1921." LO:s arkiv, Stockholm.

Rolén, Mats, and Lars Thomasson. 1990. *Jämtlands och Härjedalens historia. D. 5, 1880–1980*. Östersund: Jämtlands läns museum.

Rolfsson, Leonard, Torbjörn Åkerlind, Lennart Sahlberg, Gösta Carlsson, Sven Ljung, John Johansson, Sven G. Larsson, Sven Kolm, and Rolf Levin. 1989. *Skutskärsverken 1894–1988*. Skutskär: Skutskärsverken.

Rose, Jonathan. 2001. *The Intellectual Life of the British Working Classes*. New Haven: Yale University Press.

Rothstein, Bo. 1987. "Corporatism and Reformism: The Social Democratic Institutionalization of Class Conflict." *Acta Sociologica* 30, no. 3–4: 295–311.

Rothstein, Bo. 1998. "Political Institutions: An Overview." In *A New Handbook of Political Science*, edited by R. E. Goodin and H.-D. Klingemann, 133–66. Oxford: Oxford University Press.

Rydbeck, Kerstin. 1995. *Nykter läsning: Den svenska godtemplarrörelsen och litteraturen 1896–1925*. Uppsala: Avd. för litteratursociologi vid Litteraturvetenskapliga institutionen, Univ.

SAC. 1910a. *Redogörelse för Sveriges Arbetares centralorganisation från dess bildande till 31 december 1910*. Stockholm: Rob Hultgren.

SAC. 1910b. "Stadgar för Sveriges Arbetares Centralorganisation." Bilaga 1 till protokoll fört vid Sveriges Arbetares Centralorganisations konstituerande kongress 25–27 juni, ARAB, Stockholm.

SAC. 1913. *Redogörelse för Sveriges Arbetares Centralorganisations verksamhet 1912*. Malmö: Accidens- & Reklamtryckeriet.

SAC. 1914. *Redogörelse över Sveriges arbetares centralorganisations verksamhet 1914*. Malmö: Accidens & Reklamtryckeriet.

SAC. 1915. *Redogörelse över Sveriges arbetares centralorganisations verksamhet 1915*. Malmö: Accidens & Reklamtryckeriet.

SAC. 1917. *Redogörelse för Sveriges Arbetares centralorganisation verksamhet 1917*. Örebro: Nya tryckeriet.

SAC. 1920. *Redogörelse över Sveriges Arbetares centralorganisation 1920*. Örebro: Tryckerif Solid.

SAC. 1922. *Redogörelse över Sveriges Arbetares Centralorganisation år 1922*. Stockholm: Federativ.

Sågverksindustriarbetareförbundet. 1910–40. *Berättelse över verksamheten år 1910–40*. Gävle: Arbetarbladets tryckeri.

Sågverksindustriarbetareförbundet. 1917–40. *Berättelse över verksamheten år 1917–40*. Gävle: Arbetarbladets tryckeri.

Sågverksindustriarbetareförbundet. 1926. "Berättelse över verksamheten år." Gävle: Arbetarbladets tryckeri.

Sågverksindustriarbetareförbundet avd. 2, Skutskär. 1923. "Styrelseberättelse för år 1923." Träindustriarbetareförbundet avd. 27, sektion Skutskär, B/1/1, FAC, Uppsala.

Sågverksindustriarbetareförbundet avd. 54, Skutskär. 1935. "Protokoll fört vid möte den 2 november." Protokollbok för Sågverksindustriarbetareförbundet avdelning 54, A/1/2 FAC, Uppsala.

Sågverksindustriarbetareförbundet avd. 2, Skutskär. 1916. "Protokoll fört vid möte den 22 augusti." Träindustriarbetareförbundet avd. 27 sektion Skutskär, A/1/1, FAC, Uppsala.

Sågverksindustriarbetareförbundet avd. 2, Skutskär. 1917a. "Protokoll fört vid möte den 18 februari." Träindustriarbetareförbundet avd. 27 sektion Skutskär, A/1/1, FAC, Uppsala.

Sågverksindustriarbetareförbundet avd. 2, Skutskär. 1917b. "Protokoll fört vid möte den 18 mars." Träindustriarbetareförbundet avd. 27, sektion Skutskär, A/1/1, FAC, Uppsala.

Sågverksindustriarbetareförbundet avd. 2, Skutskär. 1917c. "Protokoll fört vid årsmöte den 28 januari." Träindustriarbetareförbundet avd. 27 sektion Skutskär, A/1/1, FAC, Uppsala.

Sågverksindustriarbetareförbundet avd. 2, Skutskär. 1922. "Styrelseberättelse för år 1922." Träindustriarbetareförbundet avd. 27, sektion Skutskär, B/1/1, FAC, Uppsala.

Sågverksindustriarbetareförbundet avd. 2, Skutskär. 1925. "Styrelseberättelse för år 1925." Träindustriarbetareförbundet avd. 27, sektion Skutskär, B/1/1, FAC, Uppsala.

Sågverksindustriarbetareförbundet avd. 2, Skutskär. 1926. "Styrelseberättelse för år 1926." Träindustriarbetareförbundet avd. 27, sektion Skutskär, B/1/1, FAC, Uppsala.

Sågverksindustriarbetareförbundet avd. 2, Skutskär. 1928. "Styrelseberättelse för år 1928." Träindustriarbetareförbundet avd. 27, sektion Skutskär, B/1/1, FAC, Uppsala.

Sågverksindustriarbetareförbundet avd. 54, Skutskär. 1922. "Protokoll fört vid möte 17 december." Sågverksindustriarbetareförbundet avd. 54, A/1/2, FAC, Uppsala.

Sågverksindustriarbetareförbundet avd. 54, Skutskär. 1925. "Protokoll fört vid möte 20 mars." Sågverksindustriarbetareförbundet avd. 54, A/1/2, FAC, Uppsala.

Sågverksindustriarbetareförbundet avd. 54, Skutskär. 1927. "Styrelseberättelse för år 1927." Sågverksindustriarbetareförbundet avd. 54, Skutskär, A/4/1, FAC, Uppsala.

Sågverksindustriarbetareförbundet avd. 54, Skutskär. 1930. "Styrelseberättelse för år 1930." Sågverksindustriarbetareförbundet avd. 54, Skutskär, A/4/1, FAC, Uppsala.

Sågverksindustriarbetareförbundet avd. 54, Skutskär. 1931. "Styrelseberättelse för år 1931." Sågverksindustriarbetareförbundet avd. 54, Skutskär, A/4/1, FAC, Uppsala.

Sågverksindustriarbetareförbundet avd. 54, Skutskär. 1934. "Protokoll fört vid möte 14 november." Sågverksindustriarbetareförbundet avd. 54 Skutskär, A/1/3, FAC, Uppsala.

Sågverksindustriarbetareförbundet avd. 54, Skutskär. 1935. "Protokoll fört vid möte 15 september." Sågverksindustriarbetareförbundet avd. 54 Skutskär, A/1/3, FAC, Uppsala.

Sågverksindustriarbetareförbundet avd. 54, Skutskär. 1938. "Berättelse över avdelning 54 i Skutskär av Sv. Sågverksindustriarbetareförbundet verksamhet angiven vid avd. 40 års jubileum den 24/9." Sågverksindustriarbetareförbundet avd. 54 Skutskär, F/1/1 FAC, Uppsala.

Sandelin, Bo. 2013. *Esperanto: Drömmen om ett världsspråk*. Stockholm: Dialogos.

Sandler, Rickard. 1908. *Arbetarhögskolan och andra socialistiska kulturfrågor*. Fram: Malmö.

Sätterberg, Ernst. 1928a. "Rapport från agitation mars månad." LO, 2964/E/14/4, ARAB, Stockholm.

Sätterberg, Ernst. 1928b. "Rapport för januari månad." LO, 2964/E/14/4, ARAB, Stockholm.

Sätterberg, Ernst. 1932a. "Rapport till Landssekretariatet 12 juni 1932." LO, 2964/E/14/4, ARAB, Stockholm.

Sätterberg, Ernst. 1932b. "Rapport till Landssekretariatet 20 juni 1932." LO, 2964/E/14/4, ARAB, Stockholm.

SCB. 1921. *Statistisk årsbok för Sverige*. Stockholm: Statistiska centralbyrån.

SCB. 1925. *Statistisk årsbok för Sverige*. Stockholm: Statistiska centralbyrån.

SCB. 1928. *Statistisk årsbok för Sverige*. Stockholm: Statistiska centralbyrån.

SCB. 1933. *Statistisk årsbok för Sverige*. Stockholm: Statistiska centralbyrån.

SCB. 1940. *Statistisk årsbok för Sverige*. Stockholm: Statistiska centralbyrån.

SCB. 1942a. *Folkmängden inom administrativa områden den 31 december*. Stockholm: Statistiska centralbyrån.

SCB. 1942b. *Statistisk årsbok för Sverige*. Stockholm: Statistiska centralbyrån.

Schiller, Bernt. 1967. *Storstrejken 1909: förhistoria och orsaker*. Göteborg: Elander.

Schön, Lennart. 2007. *En modern svensk ekonomisk historia: Tillväxt och omvandling under två sekel*. Stockholm: SNS Förlag.

Schüllerqvist, Bengt. 1992. *Från kosackval till kohandel: SAP:s väg till makten.* Stockholm: Tiden.

SDUK Skutskär. 1928. "Studierådets berättelse för andra halvåret." Skutskärs SSU-klubb, B/1/1, FAC Uppsala.

SDUK Skutskär. 1930. "Verksamhetsberättelse." Skutskärs SSU-klubb, B/1/1, FAC, Uppsala.

SDUK Skutskär. 1932. "Verksamhetsberättelse." Skutskärs SSU-klubb, B/1/1, FAC, Uppsala.

SDUK Skutskär. 1933a. "Verksamhetsberättelse." Skutskärs SSU-klubb, B/1/1, FAC, Uppsala.

SDUK Skutskär. 1933b. "Verksamhetsberättelse för S.D.U.K.:s studieverksamhet 1932–33." Skutskärs SSU-klubb, B/1/1, FAC, Uppsala.

SDUK Skutskär. 1935a. "Referat från möte i studiecirkel nr 457 den 16 december." Skutskärs SSU-klubb, A/2/1, FAC, Uppsala.

SDUK Skutskär. 1935b. "Referat över cirkelmöten i organisationskunskap." Skutskärs SSU-klubb, A/2/1, FAC, Uppsala.

SDUK Skutskär. 1935c. "Verksamhetsberättelse för Skutskärs SDUK." Skutskärs SSU-klubb, B/1/1, FAC, Uppsala.

SDUK Skutskär. 1936. "Referat från möte i studiecirkel nr 457 den 12 januari." Skutskärs SSU-klubb, A/2/1, FAC, Uppsala.

Shapin, Steven, and Barry Barnes. 1977. "Science, Nature and Control: Interpreting Mechanics' Institutes." *Social Studies of Science* 7, no. 1: 31–74.

Shorter, Edward, and Charles Tilly. 1974. *Strikes in France, 1830–1968.* London: Cambridge University Press.

Socialdemokraterna. 2002. *Den socialdemokratiska arbetarrörelsen i Skutskär-Älvkarleby under 100 år: 1901–2001; från "Norra Upplands Arbetarekommun" till "Skutskär-Älvkarleby Socialdemokratiska Arbetarekommun."* Skutskär: S-tryck.

Socialdemokratiska Ungdomsförbundets studieråd. 1930. "Studieplan i organisationskunskap." *Bokstugan*, no. 9, 224–300.

Socialstyrelsen. 1921. "Sociala meddelanden, häften 7–12." Statistiska centralbyrån. www.scb.se.

Socialstyrelsen. 1940. "Sociala meddelanden, nr 1–6." Statistiska centralbyrån. www.scb.se.

Söderlund, Gustaf. 1935a. "Brev till Sigfrid Hansson daterat 25 juli 1935." Sigfrid Hansson personarkiv, 205/2/A/1/4, ARAB, Stockholm.

Söderlund, Gustaf. 1935b. "Brev till Sigfrid Hansson daterat 25 juni 1935." Sigfrid Hansson personarkiv, 205/2/A/1/4, ARAB, Stockholm.

Söderlund, Gustaf. 1935c. *Motsättningen mellan kapital och arbete: Föredrag vid landsorganisationens skola i Brunsvik den 25 juni 1935.* Stockholm: Svenska Arbetsgivarföreningen.

Söderlund, Gustaf. 1936. "Brev till Sigfrid Hansson daterat den 24 augusti 1936." Sigfrid Hansson personarkiv, 205/2/A/1/4, ARAB, Stockholm.

Söderqvist, Jonas. 2019. "Social rörlighet i en socialt rörig tid." PhD diss., Department of Economic History, Uppsala University, forthcoming.

Somers, Margaret R. 1992. "Narrativity, Narrative Identity, and Social Action: Rethinking English Working-Class Formation." *Social Science History* 16, no. 4: 591–630.

Somers, Margaret R., and Gloria D. Gibson. 1994. "Reclaiming the Epistemological 'Other': Narrative and the Social Construction of Identity." In *Social Theory and the Politics of Identity*, edited by Craig Calhoun, 37–99. Oxford: Blackwell.

SOU. 1927: 4. *Arbetsfredsfrågan.* Stockholm: Kungl. Boktryckeriet.

Standing, Guy. 2011. *The Precariat: The New Dangerous Class.* London: Bloomsbury.

Statskalendern. 1926. *Sveriges statskalender.* Uppsala: Almqvist & Wiksells.

Statskalendern. 1928. *Sveriges statskalender*. Uppsala: Almqvist & Wiksells.

Statskalendern. 1931. *Sveriges statskalender*. Uppsala: Almqvist & Wiksells.

Steele, Tom. 2007. *Knowledge Is Power! The Rise and Fall of European Popular Educational Movements, 1848–1939*. Bern: Peter Lang.

Steinberg, Marc W. 1999. *Fighting Words: Working-Class Formation, Collective Action, and Discourse in Early Nineteenth-Century England*. Ithaca: Cornell University Press.

Steinmetz, George. 1992. "Reflections on the Role of Social Narratives in Working-Class Formation: Narrative Theory in the Social Sciences." *Social Science History* 16, no. 3: 489–516.

Stryker, Sheldon. 2000. "Identity Competition: Key to Differential Social Movement Participation?," in S. Stryker, T. J. Owens, and R. W. White (eds.), *Self, Identity and Social Movements*. Minneapolis: University of Minnesota Press.

Studiecirkel 1450. 1927. "Protokoll fört vid möte 21 oktober 1927." ABF avd. Uppsala, studiecirkel 1450, FAC, Uppsala.

Studiecirkel 1450. 1930. "Protokoll fört vid möte 7 november 1930." ABF avd. Uppsala, studiecirkel 1450, FAC, Uppsala.

Stutje, Jan Willem. 2012. Introduction to *Charismatic Leadership and Social Movements: The Revolutionary Power of Ordinary Men and Women*, edited by J. W. Stutje. New York: Berghahn Books.

Stuveriarbetarefackförbund, Skutskär-Harnäs. 1920. "Protokoll fört vid möte den 28 november." Transportarbetareförbundet sektion Skutskär avd. 11, A/1/1, FAC Uppsala.

Swenson, Peter. 1989. *Fair Shares: Unions, Pay and Politics in Sweden and West Germany*. London: Adamantine Press Limited.

Swenson, Peter. 1991. "Bringing Capital Back In, or Social Democracy Reconsidered: Employer Power, Cross-Class Alliances, and Centralization of Industrial Relations in Denmark and Sweden." *World Politics* 43, no. 4: 513–44.

Swenson, Peter. 2002. *Capitalists against Markets*. Oxford: Oxford University Press.

Svensson, Torsten. 1935. "Företaget ur arbetarens synpunkt." LO, F/14/B/31, ARAB, Stockholm.

Tajfel, Henri. 1981. *Human Groups and Social Categories: Studies in Social Psychology*. Cambridge: Cambridge University Press.

Tajfel, Henri, and John Turner. 2004. "An Intergrative Theory of Intergroup Conflict." In *Organizational Identity: A Reader*, edited by Mary Jo Hatch and Majken Schultz, 56–65. Oxford: Oxford University Press.

Tegle, Stig. 2000. *Har den svenska modellen överlevt krisen?* Stockholm: Arbetslivsinstitutet.

Thompson, E.P. 1979. *The Making of the English Working Class*. Harmondsworth: Penguin Books.

Thorberg, Arvid. 1924. "Brev till David Berg daterat den 19 augusti 1924." Brev från Landssekretariatet, David Berg Personarkiv, ARAB, Stockholm.

Thorberg, Arvid. 1925. "Brev till David Berg daterat den 2 februari 1925." Brev från landssekretariatet, David Berg Personarkiv, ARAB, Stockholm.

Törnqvist, Ingvar. 1996. *Oscar Olsson folkbildaren: I synnerhet hans tankar om universitetens roll i folkbildningsarbetet*. Stockholm: Sober.

Tyler, Tom R., and Steven L. Blader. 2001. "Identity and Cooperative Behavior in Groups." *Group Processes and Intergroup Relations* 4, no. 3: 207–26.

Unga, Nils. 1976. *Socialdemokratin och arbetslöshetsfrågan 1912–34: framväxten av den "nya" arbetslöshetspolitiken*. Stockholm: Arkiv för studier i arbetarrörelsens historia.

Vänsterkommunen Skutskär, Socialdemokratiska. 1917a. "Kassabok 1917–23." Skutskärs socialdemokratiska vänsterkommun, A/1/1, FAC, Uppsala.

Vänsterkommunen Skutskär, Socialdemokratiska. 1917b. "Protokoll fört vid möte den 11 november." Skutskärs socialdemokratiska vänsterkommun, A/1/1, FAC, Uppsala.

Waddington, Jeremy. 2014. "Trade Union Membership Retention in Europe: The Challenge of Difficult Times." *European Journal of Industrial Relations* 21, no. 3: 205–21.

Wagner, Martin. 1924, 7 February. "Internationella gillesverksamheten." *Fackföreningsrörelsen*, 7 February.

Wallander, Kristina. 1982. *Metallarbetaren och litteraturen: Det litterära stoffet i en svensk fackförbundstidning 1890–1978*. Lund: Press & litteratur.

Wasserman, Janek. 2014. *Black Vienna*, Ithaca: Cornell University Press.

Westerståhl, Jörgen. 1945. *Svensk Fackföreningsrörelse*. Stockholm: Tidens Förlag.

Whetten, David A., and Alison Mackey. 2002. "A Social Actor Conception of Organizational Identity and Its Implications for the Study of Organizational Reputation." *Business Society* 41, no. 4: 393–414.

Wigforss, Ernst. 1921. "Industriell demokrati." *Fackföreningsrörelsen*.

Zald, Mayer N., and Roberta Ash. 1966. "Social Movement Organizations: Growth, Decay and Change." *Social Forces* 44, no. 3: 327–41.

Zetterling, Anton. 1924. "Särorganisationer inom fackföreningsrörelsen." *Fackföreningsrörelsen*, 27.

Index

Lightning Source UK Ltd.
Milton Keynes UK
UKHW012044050123
414892UK00004B/263